ELEMENTARY
SCHOOL
SCIENCE

ELEMENTARY

SCHOOL

SCIENCE

A Perspective for Teachers

William R. Zeitler
University of Georgia

James P. Barufaldi
University of Texas

Longman
New York & London

ELEMENTARY SCHOOL SCIENCE: A Perspective for Teachers

Longman Inc., 95 Church Street, White Plains, N. Y. 10601

Associated companies:
Longman Group Ltd., London
Longman Cheshire Pty., Melbourne
Longman Paul Pty., Auckland
Copp Clark Pitman, Toronto
Pitman Publishing Inc., New York

Senior Editor: Naomi Silverman
Production editor: Elsa van Bergen
Text design: Joseph DePinho
Cover design: Charlene Felker
Cover photo: Dr. William J. Dederick
Production supervisor: Pamela Teisler

Library of Congress Cataloging-in-Publication Data

Zeitler, William R.
  Elementary school science.

  Includes bibliographies and index.
  1. Science—Study and teaching (Elementary)—
United States.   I. Barufaldi, James P.   II. Title.
LB1585.3.Z45   1988   372.3′5044   87–29897
ISBN 0–582–28612–3

Compositor: Pine Tree Composition, Inc.
Printer: The Alpine Press, Inc.

88 89 90 91 92 93 9 8 7 6 5 4 3 2 1

To Mary Lou and Dorothy

Contents

Chapter 3: Teaching and Learning

Chapter 4: Integrating Science Content, Inquiry Skills, and Attitudes

Preface

Teaching elementary school science can be fun and exciting—yet challenging. This book will enable you to build upon the innate curiosity of children as you prepare to teach science in an educationally and scientifically sound way.

The focus of the book is on *you*, the instructor. You are the most important element in providing children with appropriate experiences. Once your concerns are alleviated, you can enjoy teaching science. We are aware of your concerns, and are prepared to help you address them so that you can feel confident in teaching science.

The book will provide you with the skills and competencies you need to gain that confidence. The combined comments, suggestions and tested ideas from many preservice and inservice elementary teachers form the very fabric of which this book is made. We appreciatively acknowledge the valuable contributions of those teachers.

As you read the book and complete the activities, never underestimate the vital role you play in this important learning process. Through your efforts, children can experience the mysteries of science far beyond the classroom.

W.R.Z. and J.P.B.

June, 1987

Acknowledgments

p. 6: Lesson: What Happens During Convection, from *Heath Science,* Level 5, Teacher's Edition, by James P. Barufaldi, George Ladd, and Alice Moses. D.C. Heath, 1981. Reprinted by permission.

p. 6: Lesson: Conducting Water In Stems, from *Heath Science,* Level 4, Teacher's Edition, by James P. Barufaldi, George Ladd, and Alice Moses. D.C. Heath, 1985. Reprinted by permission.

p. 7: Demonstration: Fog in a Bottle, from *Heath Science,* Level 5, Teacher's Edition, by James P. Barufaldi, George Ladd, and Alice Moses. D.C. Heath, 1985. Reprinted by permission.

pp. 8-9: Scenario: Water Exploration, from *Heath Science,* Level 3, Pupil's Edition, by James P. Barufaldi, George Ladd, and Alice Moses. D.C. Heath, 1985. Reprinted by permission.

p. 13: Lesson: Water Cycle, from *Heath Science,* Level 5, Teacher's Edition, by James P. Barufaldi, George Ladd, and Alice Moses. D.C. Heath, 1985. Reprinted by permission.

pp. 13-14: Lesson: Eyes as Organs for Sight, from *Heath Science,* Level K, by James P. Barufaldi, George Ladd, and Alice Moses. D.C. Heath, 1985. Reprinted by permission.

pp. 15-16: Isaac Isopod Narration, from *Elementary Science Program,* Level B, Teacher's Edition, by Biological Science Curriculum Study. Lippincott & Co., 1977.

p. 41: Elementary Science Study Units in "A Pilot Science Curriculum for Educable Mentally Handicapped Children Emphasizing Child-Centered Activities," by D. E. Brotski. Presented at the National Science Teachers Association Convention in Detroit, April, 1973.

p. 72: Lesson: Making Things Look Bigger, from *Heath Science,* Level 5, Teacher's Edition, by James P. Barufaldi, George Ladd, and Alice Moses. D.C. Heath, 1985. Reprinted by permission.

p. 118: Lesson: Soil-Makers, from *Heath Science,* Level 3, Pupil's Edition, by James P. Barufaldi, George Ladd, and Alice Moses. D.C. Heath, 1985. Reprinted by permission.

p. 119: "Teacher Section: Soil-Makers," from *Heath Science,* Level 3, Teacher's Edition, by James P. Barufaldi, George Ladd, and Alice Moses. D.C. Heath, 1985. Reprinted by permission.

pp. 137–141: Module on Comparing Lengths, by Ruby Stapleton. Reprinted by permission.

pp. 151–152: Reprinted from *Properties,* Delta Science Module, copyright 1987. Delta Education, Nashua, NH.

p. 159: From *Developing Attitudes Toward Learning,* by Robert Mager. Fearon Publishers, 1984.

pp. 260–261: Science Computer Software: A Handbook on Selection and Classroom Use, by SAMS Lab at Florida State University. Florida State University, July 1986. Reprinted by permission.

p. 264: Material from "Let's Use Microcomputers with Children," by Betty Ruth Baker. *Dimensions,* Vol. 14, No. 4, July 1986. Reprinted by permission.

ELEMENTARY
SCHOOL
SCIENCE

Setting the Stage for Teaching Elementary School Science

Objectives

1. To list characteristics of contemporary elementary school science.
2. To identify basic goals of science education.
3. To identify the inquiry skills and content of elementary school science.
4. To describe historical developments of elementary school science.
5. To describe the characteristics of a scientifically literate person.

_____ _LOOKING FORWARD_ _____

This chapter introduces you to contemporary elementary school science. The introduction treats two aspects of science for the elementary school: first, the nature of contemporary science and its influence upon the education of children; and second, a general approach to teaching children science. In addition, the chapter briefly covers the basic goals of the book.

In the first part of the chapter, you will discover that the basic goals of elementary school science are determined by the way "science" is defined. The text will also help you implement a basic goal of elementary school instruction: namely, the enhancement of scientific literacy. Scientific literacy can be defined as the melding of expanding science knowledge, inquiry skills, investigative experiences, and positive scientific attitudes. Through this chapter, you will become familiar with the characteristics of science lessons that encourage scientific literacy. The chapter includes activities, scenarios illustrating the teacher's role, and a list of tasks necessary in teaching science effectively.

You will be asked to recall your own past experiences in elementary school science and to ask how significant a part they played in your educational experience. You will also be asked to take a brief look at some resources—particularly textbooks—and practices, including inquiry skills, as they relate to the development of expertise in teaching children science.

In the latter part of the chapter, elementary school science is discussed from a historical perspective. The chapter culminates with a discussion of scientific literacy.

In this chapter and those following, we do not purport to show you "_the_ right way" to teach children. Rather, we assist you in developing your abilities by introducing you to many exciting components of effective teaching.

Scenario

The fourth-grade classroom appeared very excited. Numerous displays of children's work were attractively arranged throughout the room. Various bones, shells, and fossils covered one half of a table, intermixed with books about ancient and present-day animals. On the other half were levers, pulleys, string, and weights. A shelf near the equipment held a collection of books about simple machines. Across the room were a 20-gallon aquarium containing Elodea, fan tail guppies, and land snails; a collection of iridescent insects atop a bookcase; and a terrarium containing a brightly colored anole lizard. Several children stared as the lizard inched toward an unsuspecting brown cave cricket trapped within the terrarium. On the outside of a "science laboratory" constructed from a refrigerator box, a child placed a sign saying "Scientist Is In: Do Not Disturb." Uninterrupted, the "scientist" focused his efforts on a new software program dealing with plant growth.

The children were studying plants' reactions to stimuli. In several laboratory stations, children could read about factors affecting plant growth, construct a terrarium, mix fertilizer solutions of varying concentrations, or place plants under differing colors of light.

Just after the science lesson began, a girl bounced up to the teacher. "Do you want to see my marigold plant?" she asked. Before the teacher could respond, the girl ran to the plant storage area, picked up a container holding a tall, sturdy-looking plant, and brought it to the teacher. "Look at the flowers," she said, pointing to the opening buds. She was obviously very proud that her marigold was the first to bloom.

"Why do you think your marigold is growing so well?" the teacher asked.

"I took very good care of it," the girl replied. "I watered it when the soil began to get dry, I put it near the plant light, and I put liquid fertilizer on it."

"Did you do anything else to the plant?" the teacher asked.

The girl grinned, lowered her head and responded apprehensively, "Well, every time I went near it, I talked to it."

"Oh," the teacher said, "you talked to it?"

"I sure did!"

The marigold grower then mentioned several newspaper articles she had read concerning the effects of sound on plant growth.

"Anything else?" the teacher asked.

"Well," she said, "I also patted the leaves and stems." She then demonstrated, gently stroking the plant, but taking care not to touch the opening buds.

Sensing that this young student was eager to share "her secrets," the teacher finally asked, "Is there anything else you can tell me about your beautiful plant?"

The girl responded proudly, "I also gave it a name—Mary Marigold" (Barufaldi, 1975).

PERSPECTIVES ON TEACHING ELEMENTARY SCHOOL SCIENCE

Good things occurred in this fourth-grade classroom. The teacher engaged the children by asking clear, inquiry-oriented questions and by motivating children through colorful displays and materials that invited investigation. The teacher also helped children apply newly discovered concepts to experiences within their environment. Numerous extended activities provided enrichment or remediation, as needed. Finally, the teacher evaluated learning outcomes both formally and informally. And all investigations, displays, and activities were coordinated to promote students' interests, skills, and positive attitudes. The scenario illustrates one major goal of the book: *to help you engage children in learning, through practical application, extended activities, and relevant evaluation.*

This fourth-grade teacher understood the nature of the learner and the need for appropriate and diverse science activities. The teacher also realized that firsthand, manipulative experiences in science come naturally to children, whose intense curiosity and imagination leads them to explore their environment, in search of the *how, why, what,* and *where* of everything around them.

What scientists are taught to do deliberately, children do by instinct, exploring their surroundings to see "how things work." Their example suggests another major goal of the book: *To increase your skills as a science instructor by exploring the nature of learners.*

Elementary science teaching means different things to different people. Some educators believe that science should help children become familiar with inquiry skills. Others believe that science is basically a collection of concepts, principles, and information with which children should become familiar. Most science educators support the notion that science is more than content and inquiry skills; science is a way of thinking, an attitude, and a way of understanding the world by linking the concepts that have evolved through exploration and discovery. This perspective brings us to another major goal of this book: *to provide you with appropriate classroom methods for integrating science concepts, attitudes, principles, and information with inquiry skills.*

THE NATURE OF SCIENCE

The basic goals of elementary school science are often determined by how people define the term *science*. When asked for their definition, a group of fifth graders used such words as "listening," "hearing," and "finding out." Oliver Wendell Holmes suggested that "science [was] a first-rate piece of furniture for a man's upper chamber, if he had some common sense on the ground floor" (National Science Teachers Association, 1982). Herbert Spencer noted that science is organized knowledge (DeVito, 1983, p. 122). Clearly, science is viewed differently through the eyes of children, scientists, philosophers, and educators. So, in setting goals, we must ask, "What's really important? What do we want students—many of whom will become our future scientists—to gain from their instruction?" Surely something more than memorization of facts. A more worthy goal is to help them construct the building blocks, the concepts, that lead to further learning.

Science as Basic Knowledge: Content

Acquiring basic knowledge about science means learning about such concepts as variation, space, time, behavior, patterns, and change. This is equally true whether we're talking about physical science, life science, or earth science.

Physical science is the study of nonliving phenomena such as matter and energy. Topics include phases of matter, atoms, work, energy, electricity, magnetism, heat, sound, light, and machines. Life science, the study of living things, comprises zoology, botany, ecology, and the environment. Life science topics may include life cycles, classifications of animals and plants, seeds, pond life, forests, and human body structures. Earth science includes the study of astronomy, geology, and meteorology, and may include such topics as weather, rocks and minerals, stars, black holes, planets, clouds, and seasons.

Following are sample lessons illustrating each of these three major divisions.

PHYSICAL SCIENCE LESSON: WHAT HAPPENS DURING CONVECTION

Here is a way to see that convection is taking place. You will need a piece of white paper, a pencil, some foil, a pattern, and a pen. You will also need a pair of scissors, a piece of thread, a flat stick, some books, a pie pan, a candle, and a match.

With your pattern, make a drawing of a spiral on the white paper. Then put the paper on top of the foil and trace over the lines with the pen. Be sure to push hard as you trace. Now cut along the lines that you made on the foil. You should have a spiral.

Hang the piece of thread from the end of the stick between some books on your desk. Tape the other end of the thread to the center of the spiral. Stand a candle in the pie pan and put it under the foil.

What will happen when you light the candle? Try it and see. What made the spiral move? Caution: Because an open flame is used, you should wear safety goggles (Barufaldi, Ladd, & Moses, Level 5, 1985).

LIFE SCIENCE LESSON: CONDUCTING WATER IN STEMS

Here is a way to see how materials flow through a stem. You will need the stems and leaves of some celery, some water, three glasses, food coloring, a dropper, and a knife.

Add a few drops of food coloring to each glass of water. With your teacher's help, make a fresh cut at the bottom of three ribs of celery. Put each rib in one of the three glasses and let stand undisturbed overnight.

The next day, look at the celery ribs and leaves. Describe what you see.

Carefully cut the stems in half crosswise. Look at the cut ends. Which places have more color from the food coloring?

Now cut the stems lengthwise. Look at the stringy parts of the end of the stem. Do some of the strings have more color than others? The stringy parts of the stem are tubes. In what direction does the color in the tubes move? Water and minerals move up from the roots through these tubes (Barufaldi et al., Level 4, 1985).

EARTH SCIENCE LESSON DEMONSTRATION: FOG IN A BOTTLE

Obtain a clear, narrow-mouthed jar. Fill it with hot water. Then empty out about three-fourths of the water. Rest an ice cube on the mouth of the bottle. Hold the bottle up to light. You should see thin streams of fog move down into the bottle. The ice cube is cooling the hot, moist air, causing the molecules of water vapor to condense as fog (Barufaldi et al., Level 5, 1985).

One must remember that science content is subject to change as our knowledge grows. For example, in the weeks and months to come, we can expect to learn more about the planet Uranus; the creation of new organisms through genetic engineering; the "string theory," which holds that everything in the universe is unified; and magnetic resonance imagery, reflecting the interior of the human body. As long as scientific research continues, our knowledge will evolve. Adding new knowledge to the science program sometimes means deleting existing information. For instance, textbooks generally describe the process of vision this way: Light strikes the nerve endings in the retina of the eye, eventually forming two images superimposed on each other to produce a three-dimensional image. Research now suggests that only one stimulus at a time is transmitted to the brain, but that the eyes alternate several thousand times a second, transmitting stimuli to the brain that result in a three-dimensional image. If these new ideas or hypotheses are supported by further experiments, then textbook descriptions of vision will need to be revised.

The tentative nature of science underlies another major goal of the book: *to provide you with resources for obtaining up-to-date science content.*

Science as Basic Knowledge: Inquiry Skills

Inquiry skills, frequently referred to as the processes of science, include observing, classifying, measuring, hypothesizing, communicating, and inferring. (Inquiry skills are discussed in detail in Chapter 4.)

Inquiry skills are as old as man. When some ancient human touched a tree set afire by lightning, he made an observation that has held true throughout time: Fire burns. We don't have to repeat his experience (thankfully) to benefit from his conclusions. Observations can be communicated in many ways. We continue to use inquiry skills in our daily lives, and will do so as long as humanity exists.

Inquiry skills are essentially *thinking skills*. The major goal of any science education is to teach students to think. Thinking skills, which are basic to all future learning, serve as the tools of scientific investigation. Thus, an additional goal of the book becomes evident: *To assist you in learning and teaching inquiry skills.*

Science as Basic Knowledge: Attitudes

Positive attitudes are characterized by patience, willingness to share, openness, confidence, initiative, perseverance, and respect for another's ideas. Positive attitudes result when children feel successful in completing a task. Developing their "need" to seek reasonable responses and provide appropriate explanations enhances feelings of success, and is therefore crucial in changing attitudes toward the learning of science. Successful teachers initiate change as they build on the child's natural curiosity, helping each child to experience the satisfaction that comes with successful experience and the joy of discovery. This brings us to another major goal of the book: *To suggest ways you can assist children in developing scientific attitudes.*

The Rest of the Story

Content, inquiry skills, and attitudes do not tell the whole story about teaching science. Teachers must use their knowledge of these three in providing stimulating investigative experiences and developing good science lessons.

Teaching science through investigative experiences implies giving children ample opportunity to manipulate materials, make observations, explore the environment, and solve problems. Investigative experiences enhance inquiry skills. And sharpened inquiry skills promote new discoveries. Note the behavior of five-year-olds with water and a collection of objects in the scene that follows.

Scenario

Children in a kindergarten class are given small tubs of water and a collection of objects.

Happily and randomly, they explore the properties of water as they feel the weight of a cup decrease as water trickles into the basin. The children feel the water's wetness and observe its transparency. They describe their experience using words like *wet, cool, pour,* and *splash!* The sensory experience of feeling water, coupled with a functional vocabulary, initiates their understanding of some basic concepts. The interaction between highly manipulative materials (the water and cups) and language is vital. Their vocabulary is functional and accurate, linking the sensory image and its corresponding word in the child's mind. Similarly, new knowledge is "linked" to prior knowledge. This linkage is a major factor in learning.

As the children continue to interact with water and cups they develop inquiry skills. During this free exploration, random activities may become more guided, specific, and organized. Perhaps a child places a wooden toy boat in the water and reports that it floats.

The teacher may then ask a child why the boat floats. The response might be, "Because it's a boat." This response helps that teacher understand the child's inference that flotation is related to a boat's shape or design.

Then the child may place a metal toy boat in the water and watch it quickly sink. The apparent inconsistency may initiate a sense of surprise or frustration. It may also stimulate the child to ask why the boat sank. The child is confronted with a problem: Why does one boat float and the other sink? The child begins to inquire by asking "what if" questions. The child may hypothesize "what would happen if" I placed a ball, pencil, or marble in the water (Barufaldi et al., *Kindergarten Science,* 1985).

Investigative experiences promote scientific literacy among children. These experiences form the framework for designing good science lessons. The following list includes some characteristics of effective science lessons:

- Numerous opportunities to freely explore objects.
- Opportunity to share findings and discoveries.
- A learning environment that helps children solve problems by thinking critically and creatively.
- A chance for each child to grow according to his or her needs, interests, attitudes, and abilities.
- An integrated approach that builds skills in mathematics, social studies, and language arts.

The process of translating science instruction into effective experiences for children underscores another goal of the book: *To give you the skills and knowledge needed to design good science lessons.*

SCIENTIFIC LITERACY

We live in an age that has frequently been characterized as the "electronic era." But while science and technology may play an integral role in our lives, this does not necessarily imply that we think scientifically, nor that we are all scientifically or technologically literate.

An important goal of science education is the development of a scientifically literate citizenry. A contemporary elementary school science program will help children realize this goal.

The National Science Teachers Association has defined a scientifically literate person as one who

- uses science concepts, process skills, and values in making responsible everyday decisions;
- understands how society influences science and technology as well as how science and technology influence society;
- understands that society controls science and technology through the allocation of resources;
- recognizes the limitations as well as the usefulness of science and is able to use them;
- knows the major concepts, hypotheses, and theories of science and is able to use them;
- appreciates science and technology for the intellectual stimulus they provide;
- understands that the generation of science knowledge depends on the inquiry process and upon conceptual theories;
- distinguishes between scientific evidence and personal opinion;
- recognizes the origin of science and understands that science knowledge is tentative and subject to change as evidence accumulates;
- understands the applications of technology and the decisions entailed in the use of technology;
- has sufficient knowledge and experience to appreciate the worthiness of research and technology development;
- has a richer and more exciting view of the world as the result of science education;
- knows reliable sources of scientific and technology information and uses these sources in the process of decision making. (National Science Teachers Association, 1982)

The concept of scientific literacy is difficult to describe; yet, three attributes seem to emerge. One may define scientific literacy as the melding of investigative experiences, attitudes, and basic knowledge (see Figure 1.1). Evidence of scientific literacy may also be illustrated in the second-grade classroom visited in the next scenario.

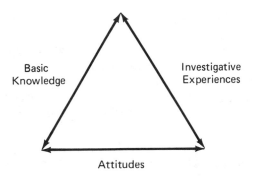

Figure 1.1. Scientific Literacy

Scenario

The children were observing isopods (pill bugs) in the classroom. After numerous discoveries the children decided to find out what kinds of food isopods prefer to eat. They decided to place four different kinds of food—a crust of bread, dry cereal, a piece of apple, and a piece of potato—one in each corner of a large plastic box. Then the children placed twenty isopods on the bottom of the container and waited patiently for fifteen minutes. After this time, the children counted the number of animals found eating the food. Eighteen isopods appeared to be eating the apple slice and two were approaching the potato. No isopods were found on the cereal or on the bread. The children enthusiastically concluded, "The isopods like apples more than anything else!"

All the children agreed with this general observation except for one boy, who said, "I don't think the isopods like the apple more than the other food. I think they needed the water from the apple more than anything else."

The skillful teacher capitalized on this situation in an exemplary manner, encouraging the children to discuss their observations and to ask additional questions. In fact, the children asked an unending stream of questions: "Do isopods need water? . . . Will they eat dry food? . . . How much food does one isopod eat? . . . What do they eat outdoors?"

The teacher used their own questions to engage the children and to help them discover reasonable explanations. Often, answers led to even more questions. This investigative experience resulted in a cycle of inquiry—sensing the problem, hypothesizing, gathering data, drawing conclusions, testing those conclusions, and finally, posing new questions or problems.

At length the teacher asked the boy who had initially questioned the results to further discuss his perceptions of the investigation.

His response: "We didn't do the experiment right. We didn't keep everything the same!"

The boy suggested repeating the investigation, and recommended that a few drops of water be added to the dry cereal and bread since the apple and potato were moist.

The children followed the boy's suggestions and fifteen minutes later made a surprising new discovery: The isopods were randomly distributed among the four different kinds of food. The boy who had objected felt great satisfaction with the results of this second experiment. "I told you that isopods need water more than anything else!" he exclaimed.

This highly inquiry-oriented activity demonstrates that when children are allowed to make mistakes, rethink their answers, and revise their methods, they eventually realize that science is a very tentative enterprise, and that what is supported today may be refuted tomorrow. Investigative experiences are crucial to the teaching of science at the elementary level. Scientific literacy, however, can take years to develop. At the elementary level we can provide a solid foundation. But achieving this goal fully can be a lifetime endeavor.

A HISTORICAL PERSPECTIVE ON ELEMENTARY SCHOOL SCIENCE

Science was not always taught as an organized discipline. Until the 1870s, the science "curriculum" was dependent on the (sometimes limited) knowledge, interests, and abilities of the teachers. Yet, one dominant theme permeated early science education: to use scientific fact in revealing the presence of God. This goal is reflected in a lesson from an 1827 school manual that directed students to place black and white pieces of cloth on snow in the sunlight. After observing the relationship between the heat absorbed and the melting that occurred under each piece of cloth, students were presented with this moralistic lesson:

> Knowledge and virtue are like the rays of light, and should act upon the heart in a very similar manner. The heart, like the piece of black cloth, should receive and retain every good and useful impression, and like the white reflect them upon all around us. Then we shall be esteemed and beloved by others and be happy in ourselves. (Bartlett, 1827)

During the lesson, of course, children had numerous opportunities to conduct investigations. Yet, the outcome of the lesson had very little to do with those investigations.

Now compare the following culminating lesson from a recent elementary science textbook:

> Summarize the chapter by reviewing the water cycle. As the earth is warmed by the sun, millions of tons of water evaporate into the air daily. Water vapor rises into the air from lakes, streams, oceans, moist land and even plants and animals.
>
> As warm, moist air rises, it is cooled; water vapor in it condenses to form clouds, and under certain conditions, rain, snow, hail or sleet falls. Evaporation, condensation, and precipitation go on constantly. This process is the water cycle. (Barufaldi et al., *Science,* Teachers Edition, 1985, p. 160)

1850s

Science was first taught as an organized discipline in elementary schools in the mid-nineteenth century. At that time, schooling prepared students to enter universities or pursue professional careers. Science teaching, therefore, focused on those university-bound students and included a method called *object teaching*. Object teaching derived its roots from faculty psychology, which promoted a hierarchical view of mental faculties—from simple observation up through higher level faculties like problem solving and reasoning. Therefore, children in science were presented with lessons that emphasized proper discipline of the mind.

A typical lesson from this period called for the teacher to select an object and present it to the child. The child was then asked to describe the properties of the object—its shape, size, color, texture, and composition—in great detail, using as many descriptors as possible. Then these terms and lists were memorized. The basic purpose of the lesson was to discipline the child's mind to acquire knowledge. Application of this stored knowledge was viewed as irrelevant, as the following excerpt clearly reveals:

> The mental faculties grow and are strengthened by exercise and we pursue certain studies not because we think we shall be called upon to apply them, but because we know that they make the mind fitter for the performance of whatever operation it may be required to understand. (Salmon, 1894, p. 3)

Now compare this object teaching technique with the approach in the following lesson from a contemporary elementary science textbook:

> Have the children look carefully at their eyes in a mirror. Have them describe their eyes. Call attention to the pupils.
>
> Have them observe a friend's eye and draw a picture of it. Help them label the eyelids, eyeball, and pupils. Now have the children

discuss what happens to the pupils of the eyes as one moves from a dark room into bright light. Group the children in pairs. Blindfold one child and take him or her to one area of the room. Have the child guess where he or she is by touching objects in the area. Stress the idea that the eyes are the organs for sight. (Barufaldi et al., *Kindergarten Science,* 1985, p. 6)

1890s

The industrial revolution of the 1890s was characterized by unprecedented mechanization, expansion of the textile industry, increasing demands for oil and its byproducts, growing production of electric power, and greater utilization of the internal combustion engine. Thanks to mass production of automobiles, industrial productivity peaked during World War I, and for a time there were more jobs than people to fill them. More than one million people immigrated to the United States. The country also witnessed a 30 percent increase in urbanization. In an effort to check this mass exodus from the rural areas to the urban, industrialized regions, the federal government supported the nature study movement that was prevalent in science teaching at the time.

The primary aim of this movement was to instill in children a love of nature by encouraging them to know their environment through observation. The underlying intent, of course, was to make children more satisfied with rural life. Terms such as *appreciate, love, poetry, beauty,* and *value* permeated nature study lessons. These terms, consistent with the romanticism that prevailed at the time, led to a degree of emotionalism in science. This emotionalism, in turn, promoted the practice of attributing living characteristics to nonliving objects, and ascribing human characteristics to nonhuman beings.

Anthropomorphism—the practice of ascribing human characteristics to nonhuman things—dominated nature study materials. Fable and fancy were usually interspersed with science, as the following account illustrates:

THE PROCESS OF EVAPORATION
We put some water in a cup Friday.
We put the cup in the window.
Monday there was not so much water in the cup.
The water went into the air.
Who took the water?
The air fairies took the water.
The water evaporated.
Friday we put a cup of water on the window and on the radiator.
The air fairies took the water from both cups.
Which cup had the least water in it on Monday?
The cup in the warm place had the least water in it on Monday.

Why did the cup on the warm place have the least water in it?
The heat fairies helped the air fairies to take the water from the cup
in the warm place.
If the heat fairies help the air fairies, the water goes away quicker.
(Scott, 1900, p. 470)

The preceding excerpt was used as an example of a good science
lesson. Notice how "good science" (evaporation) alternates with romantic metaphor (air and heat fairies).

The nature study movement appealed to many people, but had
little basis in philosophy or psychology. Thus, by 1920, much of the
movement died out. Nonetheless, traces of the movement are yet found
in elementary school science programs as illustrated in the following
excerpt, "Isaac Isopod," from Biological Sciences Curriculum Study
(1977, p. 63).

Isaac Isopod tugs on a twig he was dragging along to give his friend,
Irma. Irma wanted another piece of furniture for her home. Isaac
thought the twig would be just right. He dragged it a little way and
then stopped in a shady damp spot. Then he tugged some more. Finally he decided to stop for a rest and eat his lunch.

What does an Isopod have for lunch? We-e-ll-ll, Isaac had a lettuce
sandwich, and while Isaac was eating his lunch, some of his friends
came out from under a rock. "Hello there, Isaac," they said. "What
are you doing here anyway?"

"Oh," said Isaac, "I just stopped to rest for a while and eat some
lunch. I'm going to take this twig to Irma's house. Do you think she
will like it?" While he sat there, his coat began to change. It began
getting drier and lighter in color. Isaac worried that Irma wouldn't
like what was happening to his coat, and so he sat there for days and
days. His friends came to talk with him. They noticed his coat was
getting drier and drier every day. One day his friend said, "Your old
coat is dropping off."

"Oh, no!" said Isaac. "What am I going to wear?"

"Don't you see?" asked Ira, Inez, and Irene. "You've got a new
coat. It's right there."

And sure enough, Isaac had shed his old coat. The new one had
been underneath it all the time. This made Isaac feel really good.
"It's true! I've got a new coat!" he said. "And I've got good friends,
too—all of you." So, they all set out for Irma's house, with Isaac
leading the way.

When they arrived at her house on Bug Lane, Isaac knocked on
the door. As Irma opened the door, the first thing she saw was
Isaac's new coat. "Oh, what a beautiful new coat!" she exclaimed.
(Of course, this made Isaac feel very happy.) "Come in, Isaac. Come
on in, all of you. This is a wonderful surprise!"

Everyone went inside. Irma's house was damp and dark with
shades at the windows to keep out the strong sunlight. Ira, Inez,

and Irene sat on the new twig while Irma served them a potato salad. Guess who was the happiest isopod of all?

1920s

The prevalent economic and social crises of the 1920s and 1930s prompted a great period of questioning, a lapse of faith in an inherently benign nature, and a further decline of earlier romantic inclinations. Science education shifted its focus to the individual child's social, economic, and personal welfare. To meet immediate needs, "science" in the 1920s often consisted of instruction in health and hygiene.

In the 1920s, John Dewey, a prominent progressive educator, suggested that the method of science—or science as inquiry—was at least as important for children to learn as the actual knowledge accumulated. In the late 1920s Gerald Craig developed a science curriculum based on what successful citizens thought should be included. Craig suggested that science was important to a citizen's general education and that the affective parts of science—attitude, appreciation, and interest—should be taught through investigation rather than rote exercise. Health, safety, and economics were directly related to science in Craig's curriculum. The influence of Dewey and Craig on science materials and curricula has been long lasting.

1930s

In 1932, *A Program for Teaching Science*, a report sponsored by the National Society for the Study of Education (NSSE), advocated basing the selection of science content on personal and social criteria—in keeping with the educational thinking of the time. The report urged development of a comprehensive science program for grades one through twelve, based on selected scientific principles instead of broad objectives, and emphasizing a functional, concept-based approach (Powers, 1932).

The following selected recommendations from a report sponsored by the Progressive Education Association of 1932 typifies much of the general philosophy about science instruction that characterized this period:

- The democratic way of life constitutes the goals of education.
- The concept of science teaching exists within the context of general education rather than contributing to it.
- Courses should be organized around large units of human experiences, rather than the logic of the subject.
- The personal-social needs of students should be the point of departure in curriculum construction.
- Functional or operative science instruction is sought rather than the memorization of masses of facts. (Hurd, 1961)

1940s

Following World War II and the birth of the atomic age, science curricula and education in general underwent a new round of critical review. The 1947 edition of the NSSE Yearbook recognized the impact science was having on society, and reaffirmed its recommendations for a continuous K–12 science program stressing the fundamental understanding of concepts and functional application of scientific skills, attitudes, interest, and appreciation.

The Dawn of Contemporary Elementary School Science

The 1950s might be characterized as the dawn of the space age and the dawn of contemporary science education. During this period, it became apparent that the scientific revolution, resulting from the accelerated growth of science and technology following World War II, made science education imperative for all people (Barufaldi, 1977, p. 7).

The launching of Sputnik I by the USSR in the fall of 1957 augmented national concern about the place of science in education. That year, the U.S. Office of Education released a two-year study of the Soviet educational system, revealing vast strides in science education. That report, coupled with the growing belief that America was losing the space race, encouraged acceptance of greater federal intervention in financing public education.

The 59th Yearbook of NSSE, published in 1960, reflected continually changing attitudes toward science. The yearbook stressed problem solving and critical thinking, and emphasized the importance of inquiry and a process approach to science instruction.

The 1960s witnessed unprecedented growth in federal support for education. And with that support came the first major reform in science curricula—a reform unique in American education. Dede and Hardin summarize it this way:

> First, it attempted to replace the present curriculum rather than revise it. Second, it employed leadership from professional scientists. Third, it used money from foundations and federal grants rather than the usual state and local sources of funding. (Dede & Hardin, 1973, p. 486)

With the new flow of federal funds, many science curriculum projects were initiated for improving the teaching and learning of science. Initially, programs were developed primarily for high school, then for middle school/junior high, and finally for elementary school.

Among the projects developed for the elementary school level, three became particularly popular throughout the United States.

These were the Science Curriculum Improvement Study, Science: A Process Approach, and the Elementary Science Study. You will learn more about these programs as you read this book.

In general, all three programs focused on two basic goals: scientific literacy for all citizens and greater competence among persons pursuing careers in science and science-related areas. In addition, they attempted to define contemporary science by organizing it around a basic conceptual scheme such as one of the following:

- All matter is composed of units called fundamental particles.
- Matter consists of units that can be classified in hierarchical fashion.
- Units of matter interact.
- Living things are affected by their environment.
- The most advanced and complex activity of an organism within its environment constitutes behavior.

As you may gather from reviewing this excerpt of a list from the National Science Teachers Association (1961), a conceptual scheme comprises a set of underlying concepts. By studying these schemes, a child comes to understand that science is more than a body of facts—that it is a way of organizing information into some model that furthers our understanding.

All three programs focused on scientific inquiry. They supported a discovery approach, emphasizing hands-on, activity-centered experience that would provide children with numerous opportunities to manipulate materials. Reading materials were limited. Generally, the program promoted extensive involvement with materials by children, direct participation by teachers in planning and developing curriculum, extensive field testing of materials by teachers and children, greater attention to the recommendations of learning theorists and scientists, and more guidance and encouragement for classroom teachers.

1980s and Beyond

Today, the ideas, lessons, materials, and strategies from the 1960s are being refined to reflect current goals for elementary school science:

- Enhancing literacy in science and technology among children.
- Helping children to think critically and creatively.
- Encouraging children to develop problem-solving skills.
- Helping children understand the interrelationships among science, technology, and society.
- Having children become aware of their environment and the need to protect it.
- Helping children understand the process of change and its effects on people and other living things.

- Nurturing children in ways that can help them to reach their full potential.

The final major goal of the book is this: *to help you gain the necessary competencies to plan and implement lessons that encourage attainment of these basic goals of contemporary elementary school science.*

You are now ready to embark on an adventure: preparing to teach children science. You have some information about how contemporary science came into existence. You know that all of your teaching efforts should be directed toward developing a scientifically literate person; but since this is a life-long task, it's one you must share with other teachers. You have also been given a brief glimpse of the basic knowledge areas of science, and the ways they interact. Thus, your course throughout the book has been charted. It's time now to bring all the aspects of effective planning together in dynamic, interesting, and valuable learning experiences. We hope you'll learn a lot before you reach the end of this book. But remember: that's only the beginning. Each day brings its own challenge. And the ultimate scope of your own science education will be bound only by the limits of your curiosity.

―――――― *LOOKING BACK* ――――――――――――――――――――

1. What is your philosophy for teaching science in the elementary school?
2. What are some characteristics of a scientifically literate person?
3. Describe various approaches used in teaching science from the mid-1850s to the present.

ACTIVITIES

1. Write recollections of your science experiences in elementary school. How do they compare with the experiences in the fourth-grade classroom described earlier? What do you think "the teaching of science" meant to your elementary school teachers?
2. Draw a picture of what the term *science* means to you. Compare it with your description of the impressions you have of your elementary school teachers' conceptions of science. Can you find any common elements? Keep your picture and comment on it with your ideas after completing this book.
3. Examine a few elementary school science textbooks. Try to define how the authors define science. Do they seem to agree? Would their definitions support your meaning of science as illustrated by your drawing? What similarities and differences do you note?
4. Examine a teacher's edition of an elementary school science textbook series. Identify three lessons, one from each science content area. How did you determine whether they were physical, life, or earth science? What criteria did you use to identify the area of science each topic represented?

REFERENCES

Bartlett, Montgomery R. (1827). *Common school manual.* Utica, NY: Northway and Bennett.

Barufaldi, James P. (November 1975). The bean plant. In *BSCS Newsletter No. 61.* Colorado Springs, Colorado. Biological Sciences Curriculum Study.

Barufaldi, James P. (January 1977). Realities of the times in science teacher education. In G.E. Hall (Ed.), *AETS Yearbook, Science Teacher Education: Vantage Point 1976.* Association for the Education of Teachers in Science.

Barufaldi, James P., Ladd, George, and Moses, Alice (1985). *Kindergarten science.* Lexington, MA: D.C. Heath & Co.

Barufaldi, James P., Ladd, George, and Moses, Alice (1985). *Science* (Teacher's edition, Level 1). Lexington, MA: D.C. Heath & Co.

Barufaldi, James P., Ladd, George, and Moses, Alice (1985). *Science* (Teacher's edition, Level 4). Lexington, MA: D.C. Heath & Co.

Barufaldi, James P., Ladd, George, and Moses, Alice (1985). *Science* (Teacher's edition, Level 5). Lexington, MA: D.C. Heath & Co.

Biological Sciences Curriculum Study (1977). *Elementary school sciences program* (Level B). Philadelphia: Lippincott & Co.

Dede, Christopher, and Hardin, Joy (October–December 1973). Reforms, revisions, reexaminations: Secondary science education since World War II. *Science Education 57 (4)*.

DeVito, Alfred (1983). *Teaching with quotes*. West Lafayette, IN: Creative Ventures, Inc.

Hurd, Paul (1961). *Biological education in American schools 1890–1960*. Washington, D.C.: American Institute of Biological Sciences.

National Science Teachers Association (1961). *Theory into action*. Washington, D.C.

National Science Teachers Association (1982). *Science-technology-society: Science education for the 1980s*. Washington, D.C.

Powers, Samuel R., Chairman (1932). *A program for teaching science*, Part I. (The 31st Yearbook of the National Society for the Study of Education, NSSE.) Bloomington, IL: Public School Publishing Company.

Salmon David (1894). *Longman's object lesson*. New York: Longman.

Scott, Charles B. (1900). *Nature study and the child*. Boston: D.C. Heath & Co.

The Nature of the Learner

2

Objectives

1. To identify the influences of children's developmental characteristics and skills upon the teaching of science.
2. To identify science experiences that are appropriate for children as they mature.
3. To identify the special learning needs of children with physical or mental impairments.
4. To describe adaptations in science instruction and equipment for children with impairments.

LOOKING FORWARD

This chapter looks at the most important person in any instructional model: the learner. Descriptions of the learner have frequently focused solely on cognitive development as described by Piaget. The view discussed in this chapter differs in two important respects: First, our view of cognitive development does not strictly adhere to the levels described by Piaget. We tend to see cognitive development as continuous rather than occurring in definite stages. Second, we believe that development within three important domains—cognitive, affective, and psychomotor—occurs simultaneously.

The chapter does not attempt a comprehensive treatment of the many cognitive characteristics that appear as a learner matures. We prefer instead to focus on selected characteristics of the maturing learner that enhance science instruction.

The first part of the chapter deals with the maturing learner, and for convenience, the discussion is organized by grade level. To illustrate some of the characteristics discussed, actual science lessons observed by the authors are included. Appropriate science experiences are also discussed.

The latter part of the chapter deals with the physical or mental impairments of some children, and adaptations in science instruction that can help accommodate the needs of those children. The chapter includes sample activities illustrating some adaptations.

If asked to name their greatest concerns about teaching children science, most preservice or inservice teachers would likely mention a lack of knowledge about science or uncertainty about the best teaching methods. Both content knowledge and effective strategies for presenting that knowledge are vital to good instruction. However, a third factor is equally important: the factor of understanding the nature of the learner.

The following scenarios illustrate some characteristics associated with learners at very different levels of maturation.

Scenario

In a kindergarten classroom, children were sitting on the floor around the teacher. They watched intently as the teacher placed a tablespoon of sugar in a glass of water, then stirred the sugar and water until the sugar dissolved completely. The teacher asked the children if they saw the sugar being put in the water. They responded "Yes." The teacher then asked where the sugar was. After looking at the glass containing the sugar water, the children told the teacher that the sugar was gone. Each child was given a spoon and asked to taste some of the water from the glass. After this was done, the teacher again asked where the sugar was. Again the children responded that the sugar was gone. The teacher got a second glass of water and asked the children to taste the water from both glasses, the one containing sugar water and the one containing water only. Following the tasting, all of the children agreed again that the sugar was gone.

Scenario

A sixth-grade class had been studying a unit on planets and constellations. Bill had learned the names of the planets, as well as many of the stars in various constellations. After class one day, Bill told the teacher that he had read several articles from the school library about binary stars, and that he was interested in further reading. He posed several questions that the teacher was unable to answer; however, the teacher suggested that they both try to get additional information.

In the kindergarten classroom, the children were unable to draw accurate conclusions from their observations; they concluded that the sugar was gone since they could no longer see it. Although the children tasted both the sugar water and the water without sugar, they continued to use sight rather than taste as the basis for their observations. The fact that some water tasted sweet while the other did not was ignored.

In the sixth-grade classroom, Bill was able to quickly grasp the information presented, and wanted to explore the topic in greater depth. The lesson was of little difficulty for him; he was a motivated learner who enjoyed digging deeper into topics than most of his classmates.

These scenarios illustrate the challenge teachers face in attempting to cope with the wide range of children's developing cognitive and physical skills.

Characteristics of learners may be grouped into three categories: cognitive skills, affective skills, and psychomotor skills. Each category should be considered when planning science instruction. Cognitive skills relate essentially to the accumulation of knowledge. Affective skills include development of attitudes, interests, values, and beliefs. And psychomotor skills include the development of motor skills and muscular coordination. All three types of skills are necessary in science instruction.

For effective science teaching, teachers must also be aware that the child's ability to reason and think logically is governed by mental maturity and prior knowledge. Teachers must be aware that cognition of adults is based upon extensive prior knowledge and experience that children do not have. Consequently, adults are able to think abstractly while children are not.

THE MATURING LEARNER

Carefully planned lessons can provide experiences that will help a maturing learner develop and expand skills—and ultimately increase his or her understanding and appreciation of science.

Kindergarten: Observing Explorers

Young learners are bound by sensory perceptions; they are constantly looking at objects, listening to them, smelling and, at times, tasting them. These activities require both cognitive and psychomotor skills. Usually, kindergarten children concentrate on one attribute at a time. Further, they believe that everyone perceives objects and events as they do. Their explorations take a trial-and-error approach. Following a series of changes or putting objects or events in a series is a challenge for many kindergarten children. In addition, many of their explanations may be based upon fantasy rather than logic—especially when fantasizing seems more appropriate. Young children tend to judge situations based on appearance and develop the ability to think using language. Contradictory observations are of little concern to them.

Cognitive development in kindergarten children results essentially from their interactions with their environment. Frequent interactions stimulate intellectual growth. In an experienced adult's view of things, the information children select for solving a problem may seem grossly insufficient; however, it may be adequate for *their* purpose.

The following one-day lesson illustrates some of the characteristics of kindergarten children.

Scenario

A class of kindergarten children was beginning a lesson on three parts of a plant: the root, stem, and leaf. The children were asked to bring a weed from home. They were instructed to carefully loosen the soil from around the weed so that the total plant—roots and all—could be brought to school. It was suggested that they ask a parent or other adult to help them.

The teacher had several potted plants for children who were unable to bring a weed. As the children arrived at school, their weeds were labeled and placed in water.

The science lesson began with the children seated at tables. Plants were distributed to their owners. Children without plants were given small pots containing a plant; the teacher assisted them, removing the entire plant from the potting soil. The plants were laid on paper towels; children were asked to look at their plants carefully. They were asked to find the part of the plant that was normally under the ground. The teacher observed the children as they pointed to the part. Then the children watched the teacher remove a plant from a pot and point to several parts of the plant. The children were asked to tell her when she was pointing to the part that was normally under the soil. When that activity was completed, the children were asked to exchange plants and to point to the part of the plant that was normally underground; again, the teacher observed the part identified by each child. The plants were then returned to the original owners.

The teacher asked the children if anyone knew the name of the part of the plant that grows under the ground; no one responded. The teacher said that the part that grows under the ground is called a "root." Children were asked to repeat the word "root." Children then were asked to point to the root of their plants and to name the part. The teacher held her plant by the root; she asked children to name the part that she was holding. They responded "Root." Children were then asked to show the roots of their plants to others sitting at their table. They were asked if all the roots looked the same; the response was "No." The teacher asked them to tell others at their table how the roots looked. Various roots were evident on the weeds. Next, children were asked to draw the root of their plant; the drawings would be used later in the lesson. When the drawings were completed, the plants were returned to the water for the next lesson.

The children were asked if they thought that they could point to the root of a plant the next day when they arrived at school. They shouted "Yes." The teacher said she felt sure that no one would remember to point to a root of a plant when they arrived at school. The children responded that they would, that they would surprise the teacher.

The lesson for the next day dealt with the identification of roots of potted plants and exposed roots of trees on the school campus. The drawings of roots that the children made were placed on a bulletin board for use in a later evaluation of the lesson. The next part of the plant that children studied was the leaf.

Several techniques were used to increase the effectiveness of this lesson. One technique was *engagement,* in which children worked with the actual roots they collected. Their attention was directed to one part of the plant at a time, an expansion of the engagement technique. *Application* was also used as children had direct experiences in identifying differences among the roots. The *extension* technique was used as children identified the roots of a variety of plants; this included roots that were exposed as well as those beneath the ground. An *evaluation* technique was used as children were asked to identify roots, to indicate where roots grew, and to identify which part of a given plant was the root. To initiate *engagement* within the lesson the next day, a challenge was given to the children: namely, that they would be unable to identify the root of a plant when they arrived at school.

Grades 1 and 2: Beginning Investigators

Children in grades 1 and 2 continue to be avid explorers. They are beginning to refine their inquiry skills, and to understand relationships among objects and events. However, fantasy continues to be an important facet of their life. For example, a stick may at one moment become a laser gun to vaporize an enemy, and the next moment turn into a boat. At this age, children begin constructing a variety of objects with materials. There seems little limitation to their creativity.

This is also a time when children can begin understanding abstractions if they are properly illustrated. The following lesson illustrates effective presentation of an abstract concept.

Scenario

Children in a first-grade classroom are beginning to study gravity. They are seated at tables and given crayons. Mr. Jones directs the children's attention to a pencil he is holding. They are asked to observe the pencil as he releases it. As he pulls his fingers away, the pencil falls to the floor. Mr. Jones asks the children what happened to the pencil. They reply that it fell to the floor. The children look puzzled but intently watch the pencil as he releases it a second time. Many of the children say that they knew the pencil would fall. The children are asked if they think that a crayon would fall like the pencil if held above the table and released. All the children respond that the crayon would fall.

Mr. Jones instructs them to try it and observe the crayon. The action is repeated a second time. Now the children are instructed to hold the crayon above the table as if ready to release it. They are asked to look on top of the crayon, at each end of the crayon, and below the crayon to see if they can observe anything that might make the crayon fall. They reply that they can see nothing. The children are instructed to observe the crayon carefully as it falls. Can anything be *seen* that causes the crayon to fall? The children drop the crayon twice, and after each drop state that they could see nothing that caused the crayon to fall. Mr. Jones asks them if they are sure; they answer that yes, they are. He states that something caused his pencil to fall and the children's crayons to fall but no one could see anything that caused the objects to fall. The children are asked whether anyone knows the name for the "something" that causes objects to fall when they are not being held. The children remain silent. Mr. Jones tells the children that the thing causing his pencil and their crayons to fall is called *gravity.* Gravity cannot be seen, smelled, heard, tasted or touched—but it is real. Children can see the effect of gravity on the pencil and crayon as well as other objects they may test.

Children in grades 1 and 2 continue to be perceptually oriented. They become increasingly aware of details and their ability to compare and categorize objects develops. In addition to categorizing, children begin to order objects in a series, but their ability to insert additional objects into an ordered set is limited. The ability to identify some changes in observed events begins to develop.

Grades 3 and 4: Manipulating Investigators

At this age, children are able to make mental comparisons and explore similarities and differences. For example, rocks may be classified on the basis of their physical properties (hardness, streak, and/or colors); an extra mental operation is necessary to classify rocks into the two categories simultaneously. Children tend to think logically when provided with concrete objects to manipulate, but this logic does not yet extend to symbols or abstractions.

While children in grades 3 and 4 continue to base judgments on perceptions, they also begin to interpret evidence from their investigations, and to identify relationships among events. The inquiry skill of measuring develops as their observations become refined.

In addition, two significant concepts begin to emerge: reversibility and conservation. With reversibility, children can mentally reverse conditions and anticipate the future; they understand that ice is frozen water or that salt does not disappear as it dissolves in water. Children who conserve realize that objects are the same although some change has occurred in their appearance. For instance, changing the shape of an object does not change the amount of substance in that object.

Children also learn to differentiate between observations and inferences, thus permitting them to explain events and make predictions based on past experiences or observations. The beginnings of true logical thinking appear, as children increasingly ask "why." Children at this age are capable of a purposeful investigation in which variables are identified, manipulated, and controlled. However, these inquiry skills tend to be limited by their need for manipulation and interactions with concrete objects. Children are not yet able to study science through abstract thinking alone.

The following classroom scene illustrates some of the characteristics of these children. The purpose of the lesson is to develop children's ability to investigate using a variety of manipulative experiences and inquiry skills.

Scenario

Ms. Smith, a fourth-grade science teacher, is conducting a science lesson using several investigative learning centers. The children keep Ms. Smith very busy answering questions, giving suggestions, evaluating progress in the investigations, and providing resource materials. Small groups are working on selected projects of interest in several of the centers. One group is investigating the effects of heat on matter. They have observed the effects of removing heat from water, heat being applied to ice, and the rate of change in a thermometer when differing amounts of heat are applied. They also observed the expansion of metals when heated, and the expansion of air in a balloon placed over a soft drink bottle in a pan of heated water. Another group is working with the problem of reclaiming substances, such as salt and sugar, from water in which they were dissolved and observing recovered substances after the water has evaporated.

One group is using various solids and liquids in investigating the effects of heat on matter, making appropriate measurements with their equipment.

Note that the emphasis in all centers is on using a variety of investigative skills to explore the main topic: the interaction of heat with objects. What characteristics do we see among these learners? Reversibility of thinking, for one thing. The students are able to "think back" to a previous condition or starting point and compare it with present conditions. (For example, the children comparing water in the liquid phase with the same water in the solid phase were dealing with reversible operations.)

The children also demonstrate the concept of conservation. That is, they are developing an awareness that objects remain the same although some changes have occurred in their appearance. For example, in the group reclaiming dissolved substances, students were able to identify the dissolved substance although it could not be seen.

Grades 5 and 6: Thinking Investigators

Most people continue to develop thinking skills throughout their lives. However, at these grades the learner begins to cope mentally with events and problems—to engage in what is frequently called "formal thinking."

Children capable of formal thinking can deal with several aspects of a problem simultaneously. They can also apply prior knowledge and experience in solving a problem. And, with the assistance of a teacher, they can use inquiry skills to state and test a hypothesis. Thinking investigators feel comfortable with models, representations, and vicarious experiences if the actual object or event cannot be observed. They think about the ideas illustrated—not just about objects themselves.

The next scenario illustrates some characteristics of the formal thinker.

Scenario

Mr. Nix, a sixth-grade science teacher, found that he had an unusual student in one of his science classes. Joe seemed to grasp quickly all information that Mr. Nix presented.

He was constantly asking Mr. Nix questions: "Since most seeds are planted in the ground, does light influence the rate of germination?" "Will plants grow as tall if given a fertilizer which is 10 percent nitrate and 5 percent phosphate as they would if the ratio of nitrate to phosphate were reversed?" "Will heating the leaves of the coleus plant in alcohol remove all pigments or just chlorophyll?"

On one occasion Joe conducted an experiment at a nearby stream to determine the rate of erosion during periods of high water and low water.

Let's look at some characteristics of the beginning formal thinker. He or she can identify problems and mentally construct tentative solutions. Joe wondered about a technique for removing pigmentation from a multicolored leaf; he knew that heating a green leaf in alcohol removed some of the pigmentation.

The formal thinker can also mentally identify the tentative effects of variables in an investigation. Remember Joe's questions about the amount of light required for seed germination, and the effects of varying amounts of nitrates and phosphates on the tallness of a plant? Both illustrate this characteristic.

Formal thinkers can also identify and analyze the processes used in deriving answers to questions. Joe demonstrated this characteristic when he determined which processes to use in the erosion experiment. He identified logical procedures for conducting the experiment *before* the experiment was initiated.

SCIENCE FOR MATURING LEARNERS

Effective instruction should be coordinated with the cognitive, affective, and psychomotor development of learners. Therefore, selecting an appropriate instructional strategy is just as important as finding an intriguing topic.

Kindergarten: Exploratory Science

The young child needs and wants to interact with the natural and physical world. Opportunities should be provided for these students to observe, compare, measure, and classify. Asking these children to deal with an event in abstract terms—"What would happen if . . . "—is of little value. They must interact with objects and events that may be directly perceived. For example, they can learn to classify concrete objects like rocks, books, leaves, and people. Identifying the basis for classification is a vital inquiry task. Extensive explanations about objects and events, however, appear to be of limited value. Experiences with the "here and now" seem most appropriate at this level.

Grades 1 and 2: Beginning Investigations

Appropriate science topics for first and second graders can be similar to those for the kindergartener; however, older children are generally more discriminating in their ability to observe. For example, they are able to construct two groups of objects, one with a selected attribute and a second without that attribute. They can use several senses in combination to make an observation. And they can also begin to distinguish degrees—such as the *degree* of hardness or color or size or temperature.

In order to take advantage of these emerging skills, we must make the science content for grades 1 and 2 a little different from that for kindergarten—in two ways. First, it should require more discriminating observation. Students need the challenge of dealing with more subtle observations, such as discovering two-dimensional shapes within three-dimensional shapes, or identifying parts of a whole, such as parts of the human body.

The range of objects or events to be observed may be expanded. Students may be asked to arrange objects to include such things as plants, weather, insects, and simple machines in a series according to the degree of the attribute they represent; this requires close observation.

During these grades science should become more purposeful, less a series of fragmented experiences. Children should begin to follow defined rules to achieve intended ends. But remember: Children can focus on specified goals only when presented with organized activities planned by the teacher.

Grades 3 and 4: Beginning Problem Solving

Science experiences selected for children in grades 3 and 4 should still involve manipulation of concrete objects. To increase their understanding, children need numerous experiences involving reversibility of thinking and conservation. They also need extensive opportunity to answer questions through direct investigation. For instance, they might use investigation to answer this question: "How many ceramic tiles can be placed in a boat made from 50 grams of clay before the boat will sink?"

Science instruction for children in grades 3 and 4 can be very exciting. These children ask many questions. They are curious about stories they've seen on television, the operations of computers, current events they've heard about on the news, and questions that arise from their own thinking. They feel the thrill of discovery. They are learning to apply past knowledge and experience in solving new problems. Because of their developing inquiry skills—particularly conservation and reversibility—they want to both plan and participate in problem-solving experiences. However, children in the third and fourth grades continue to be perceptually oriented, and have a far easier time manipulating concrete objects than struggling with abstractions.

Grades 5 and 6: Beginning of Formal Thought

Science for the formal thinker should be varied and challenging. However, these *beginning* formal thinkers still need to manipulate concrete objects to verify procedures for formulating or testing hypotheses. Since these learners are able to solve some problems by thinking, they can be introduced to such abstract topics as atomic particles, conditions in outer space, and transmission of genetic traits. Keep in mind, however, that their ability to use abstract inquiry skills is just developing. Interaction with concrete objects and events remains vital for clarifying problems, testing hypotheses, and drawing conclusions.

The role of the teacher continues to be that of a guide, planning science lessons that will enable children to use emerging cognitive and physical capabilities.

As formal thinkers become more skillful at using inquiry strategies, they want to have more information. Under proper guidance, they continue to enjoy science and learn to be tolerant of those who may disagree with them. Increasingly, their ideas or inferences are based on observation and evidence rather than on opinion. This is the stage where understanding about contemporary science could begin. These learners are beginning to feel comfortable with many technological developments that will become part of their lives. Unlike many adults, young learners rarely feel intimidated by computers, word processors, laser disks, and holograms.

FURTHER COGNITIVE DEVELOPMENT IN CHILDREN

Cognitive development in the maturing learner involves reaching and maintaining a conceptual balance between new observations and experiences on the one hand and prior knowledge on the other. When this balance, or equilibrium, is upset by some unexpected event or observation, children make an effort to restore it.

Two mechanisms—assimilation and accommodation—are important in restoring equilibrium. Assimilation occurs each time data from a new experience are incorporated into a child's existing conceptual framework. These data expand and enrich the learner's understanding, possibly enabling him or her to conceptually relate objects and events in ways not considered before. For example, a child of age five or six may observe a helium-filled balloon rise from the earth. The child continues to observe the balloon until it disappears from sight. This observation is incorporated into the child's conceptual framework. The question is: When the balloon disappears, does it cease to exist? Telling the child that the balloon rises to a certain level above the earth where the densities of air outside the balloon and helium within are the same has little effect in helping the child wrestle with this question. The child may *say* that the balloon still exists, but act in a way that shows he or she believes otherwise. Repeated explanations from the teacher are not especially helpful. In the child's mind, the balloon is gone. The child's observations have been assimilated into a conceptual framework that explains what happens when a helium-filled balloon is released. With maturation children are able to accept that even when the balloon floats out of sight, it continues to exist. At this point, the child is ready to begin understanding density.

Accommodation is another mechanism through which conceptual frameworks are modified. If an observation, event, or experience is inconsistent with a concept the child has developed, the child can regain equilibrium in any of three ways: (1) by ignoring the observation (this may be the alternative selected by younger children); (2) by isolating the observation from other concepts (this alternative tends to treat the observation as trivial or irrelevant); and (3) by changing the existing framework to accommodate the new observation.

For instance, everyone knows from experience that ice cubes float in liquids. If an experiment is performed in which ice cubes are placed in a transparent liquid and sink, the concept that ice floats in water-like liquids is upset. The learner must process this observation in some manner. The young learner ignores the situation by stating that ice sometimes floats in water and sometimes sinks in water. Contradictions of this nature rarely concern a young child. An older child may isolate this observation, stating that while ice normally floats in water, this was a "once in a lifetime" event. The learner who accommodates observes the liquid closely and finds that it is not water at all, but alcohol. The concept that ice floats in liquids must be accommodated to accept this new observation. The new conceptual framework is based on the understanding that ice floats in some liquids and sinks in others.

Conceptual frameworks constantly undergo change through assimilation and accommodation. As learners strive for equilibrium, they alter their concepts to incorporate new information, constantly expanding and enriching their understanding.

As young children mature, new cognitive, affective, and psychological developments become evident. Cognitive development occurs as children gain new information through various means: problem solving, directed laboratory experiences, or free exploration of the natural environment. Psychomotor development is encouraged through the use of scientific equipment and the need to make refined observations. Many viable science programs encourage the concurrent development of cognitive and psychomotor skills. Although affective development is critical in successful science instruction, it seems frequently overshadowed by emphasis on the cognitive domain.

THE EXCEPTIONAL LEARNER

Contemporary education seeks ways to enhance learning of *all* children, including the gifted and talented, the disadvantaged, those with auditory and visual impairments, those with learning disabilities, and the orthopedically impaired. Among these categories, perhaps the one to receive the least attention in elementary education has been the gifted and talented learner. More about this group in a moment. Conversely, a great deal of attention has been focused on children with learning difficulties. It has been estimated that there are approximately 8 million learners in the United States with some form of impairment—emotional, mental, physical, or social (Bennett, 1979, pp. 12–14). Few of these impairments interfere with the child's ability to participate in so-called "normal" classroom procedures. Thus, impaired children in grade school can expect to enjoy success in science (Thompson, 1979, p. 16).

Attention on the education of children with impairments and handicaps has been directed by legislation at both federal and state levels. The Education for All Handicapped Children Act of 1975 seeks to guarantee the availability of a free, appropriate, public education for all handicapped children. The group of children for whom the act was intended includes those three to twenty-one years of age who are mentally retarded, hard of hearing, deaf, speech impaired, visually handicapped, seriously emotionally disturbed, orthopedically impaired, or otherwise health impaired, or children with specific learning disabilities who by reason thereof require special education and related services (Education for a Handicapped Child Act, 1976, pp. 94–142).

It is beyond the scope of this book to describe all types of special learners in detail. However, the following sections offer suggestions for dealing with children in some categories.

Creative/Gifted Learners

Although gifted and creative children do not display identical characteristics, they can benefit from similar science experiences. Thus the two groups are discussed together.

Osburn describes creative persons this way: " . . . from [within] their constructive imagination arise poems, paintings, sonatas, and symphonies that have never before been perceived. It is they who can see 'angles in a block of marble,' 'sermons in stones' and 'theories in deep sea ooze'" (Osburn, 1931, p. 27). Gifted children have been described as those with the ability to grasp concepts and facts more quickly than other children (Awkerman & Teller, 1979, p. 10). Although creativity implies production of something new, children's creativity frequently involves identifying or producing something new to *them*, rather than something new to human knowledge as a whole.

Creative learners are characterized by curiosity, self-assurance, extensive experiential and informational background, and keen enjoyment of a challenge. They are persistent investigators and seek hidden meanings in problems. Creative people seek to solve problems in their own way. They are continuously searching for ways to modify problems, manipulate variables, and to work independently on projects. These children like to be with other creative children, although they tend to get along well with children from many groups.

Research on creative people shows that persons who have received recognition for their unique accomplishments and creative contributions possess three relatively well-defined clusters of traits: one is above average, although not necessarily superior, general ability; the second is task commitment; and the third, creativity. Creativity is not necessarily a function of measured intelligence. The most productive persons are not necessarily those who scored in the ninety-fifth percentile on standardized tests. However, the gifted learner seems to become totally absorbed in solving specific problems (Renzulli, 1979, p. 15).

Occasionally a gifted student may also be impaired. And too often, such a student may be stereotyped because of restrictions imposed by his or her impairment. Provided with the educational opportunity, the gifted/creative scientist may find a way to overcome the impairment. Some examples include Herbert Hoffman, a meteorologist afflicted with cerebral palsy; Robert Menchel, a deaf physicist; and Robert Rehwoldt, a chemist who is also a paraplegic (Stefanich & Schunu, 1979, p. 18).

Creativity can be encouraged when a teacher views it as the learner's way of becoming aware of new relationships and hidden meanings. For example, a teacher may encourage creativity by permitting children to discuss "What happens if. . . . " Children may manipulate equipment to help them answer a question or to find what happens under a certain set of circumstances. Young children frequently do this through trial and error. Providing riddles or puzzles, or asking students to write captions for cartoons or complete a partially written story are additional ways of encouraging creativity. Creative exploration isn't a hurry-up process. Children need sufficient time to investigate. They need a wide range of resources to explore, and equipment to support their explorations. They need a chance to solve many kinds of problems and to discuss their findings with their peers and with the teacher.

The Disadvantaged Learner

Disadvantaged learners are characterized by negative self-concept, lack of an experiential background, lack of interest in learning, and limited success in learning. Many also lack family roots in the community. Many are from low socioeconomic backgrounds.

Of those characteristics mentioned, the two that most directly affect learning in science are negative self–concept and lack of an experiential background. For instance, disadvantaged children in the second grade may not be at the reading readiness level, may not know how to hold a book, or may be unable to follow a line of print from left to right. If questioned about objects or events outside their experience, they may be unable to respond constructively and may even withdraw from class participation. The following transcript illustrates this.

Scenario

A classroom of second graders is holding a discussion on common animals.

Teacher: Sally, do you know what a cow looks like?
   Sally: Yes.
Teacher: Pick out a picture of a cow from this group of pictures.
   Sally: That one [pointing to a picture of a cow].
Teacher: That's fine, Sally. How big is a cow?
   Sally: About the size of a rat.
Teacher: Are you sure?
   Sally: Yes, I seen a picture of a cow and a rat in the book over there and they look the same size.

Children who come from homes where magazines, books, and newspapers are uncommon have limited opportunities to gain information through reading or through hearing someone read to them. They may watch television, but frequently the programs are selected for adult entertainment rather than educational value. Visits to libraries, museums, and educational exhibits are rare. Overall, these children have few opportunities to develop language skills, to develop interests beyond the confines of the immediate neighborhood, or to learn in a structured setting. Many of them enter school with few basic skills and little background knowledge that would facilitate learning in a school setting. In addition, their desire to learn may be minimal.

Disadvantaged learners tend to feel that they are unable to participate in usual classroom activities. These children enter the classroom convinced that they are of little value as people, and this attitude tends to be reinforced by many educational failures. They face the dilemma of being isolated from other children in compensatory classes or being placed in regular classes where they are unable to progress with the other children. Either alternative tends to reinforce feelings of academic and social failure.

Occasionally disadvantaged learners are considered mentally retarded. But in reality, lack of background experience, rather than mental ability, is responsible for hindering their progress. The problem may be compounded by lack of interest or lack of encouragement. Typical learning situations may present expectations far beyond the comprehension of the disadvantaged learner. The child may appear *unwilling* to respond in a learning activity when in truth he or she may be *unable* to respond appropriately. Perhaps the teaching method is confusing, the content is confusing, or the teacher's expectations are confusing. Too often, unresponsive learners are classified as deficient in mental ability. The intelligence is there. It needs only to be developed.

Disadvantaged children *can* learn, given the opportunity and understanding. Teachers can help by not assuming that all children necessarily come to school wanting to learn or seeing the need for education. Many children desire authority and close direction rather than self-direction. They prefer to be active rather than passive. And they prefer structured learning activities accompanied by concrete, demonstrable explanations. For example, many children need to feel the attraction between north and south poles of a magnet, or the repulsion between two north poles.

Disadvantaged children are capable of abstract thinking, though at a slower rate than more able children. There is some lag in their concept development. Still, these children are able to benefit from the elementary school science program if minor adjustments are made. For example, it may help to segment a lesson into small parts, present appropriate content at a slower rate, and provide additional learning experiences or extra background information. Constant reinforcement is vital. A great deal of support, encouragement, and understanding are required of the teacher. The chance to feel some measure of success in every learning activity helps the disadvantaged learner develop a sense of self-worth.

Educable Mentally Handicapped (EMH) Learners

The term *educable mentally handicapped* (EMH) is used to designate children who formally were called educable mentally retarded (EMR) and trainable mentally retarded (TMR). The term *handicapped* implies that these children experience difficulties with learning; however, with appropriate adjustments to accommodate their learning styles, they are able to learn from the study of science.

In general, EMH children are somewhat slow to mature, both mentally and socially. They also tend to have difficulty with visual-motor coordination, and tend to learn more slowly than other children of the same chronological age (Holzberg, 1976, p. 19). They have limited ability to understand abstractions and relationships. In addition, most have short attention spans, deflated self-concepts, limited language skills, and a history of low academic achievement (Lambardi & Belch, 1976, p. 20). In comparison with other children of the same chronological age, EMH children exhibit difficulty in recall, transfer skills, and conceptualization (Holzberg, 1976, p. 19).

In a study conducted by Midgott and Esler, it was found that science activities improved many communication skills of mildly retarded children (Midgott & Esler, 1981, p. 31). Comprehension skills improved as children learned to use sensory information in recounting the steps of an activity or when explaining auditory and graphic symbols. The children realized they must remember science terminology, locate materials, and follow directions to participate in the activities. Small-group instruction promoted skills in observing, recording, and communicating data. The children's obvious enthusiasm and their demonstrated ability to learn vocabulary words, to read and follow directions, suggested that their study of science had real educational value.

All EMH children are not alike. Each child displays individual characteristics, and when matched with children of the same mental age, their patterns of cognitive abilities, strengths, and weaknesses are as varied as those of any group of children (Lambardi & Belch, 1976, p. 20).

One of the fundamental goals of education is to help *all* children grow to the limits of their capabilities. Although the mentally handicapped experience learning challenges, they share many characteristics and behaviors common among children everywhere. As Lambardi and Belch (1976, p. 20) point out, they care for pets, get cavities, reach puberty, travel on airplanes, fall in love, seek employment, and become parents.

At the same time, however, they display some characteristics that merit special attention in designing science lessons and experiences. For one thing, they tend to be rigid in their thinking; thus, their repertoire of learning styles is small. Unfamiliar teaching techniques may upset or confuse them. Teaching procedures must begin with the familiar, moving very gradually to what is new. EMH children with a history of academic failure may have a negative self-image—that manifests itself in an uncaring attitude. This attitude can be overcome only when the child experiences success. Each success must be reinforced with teacher praise directed toward the completed task, rather than toward the learner.

Lessons designed for EMH students should be individualized as much as possible, and the concepts around which lessons are designed should incorporate prior knowledge as well as the child's natural curiosity. Instruction should occur in small sequential steps that proceed quickly. Repetition is essential. Lessons dealing with abstractions must be revised to incorporate concrete illustrations. In addition, the concepts taught should have immediate application in the daily life of the child.

Some science programs have been developed and adapted for the EMH child. Units from the Elementary Science Study, listed in Table 2.1, may be used with the EMH child (Brotski, 1973). Adaptations tend to focus on teaching strategies rather than content. Within these units, children are encouraged to explore with equipment, to learn in-

TABLE 2.1. ELEMENTARY SCIENCE STUDY UNITS

Units	Age Level			
	Lower Primary (ages 5-8)	Upper Primary (ages 9-11)	Intermediate (ages 12-13)	Junior High (ages 14-)
Geo Blocks	X		X	
Peas and Particles				X
Match and Measure		X		X
Primary Balancing	X			
Structures			X	X
Tangrams	X	X	X	X
Rocks and Charts				X
Sand			X	
Eggs and Tadpoles		X		
Small Things			X	
Crayfish	X	X		
Earthworms			X	
Pond Water			X	
Tracks			X	
Batteries and Bulbs				X
Clay Boats			X	
Colored Solutions		X		
Mystery Powders			X	

vestigative skills, and to approach their immediate environment with both curiosity and confidence.

A program developed for middle school children ages thirteen to fourteen is directed toward development of strong self-concept and feelings of self-worth. The curriculum consists of three parts: *Me Now, Me and My Environment* (BSCS, 1972) and *Me in the Future* (developed by BSCS in 1975 but never published). This program is further described in Chapter 9.

Science lessons for mentally handicapped children at the primary level were observed for five years by one of the authors. The lessons were planned by the teacher but actually taught by the children. Following is a short presentation of a sample lesson on the care of pets.

Scenario

One class member, Mary, had a pet rabbit. At home Mary was able to feed the rabbit, give it water, and clean the cage.

Because the teacher was presenting a lesson on the care of pets, she asked Mary to bring her rabbit to school and teach the other children about caring for it. Mary was happy to do this.

On the appointed day, the eight children sat on the floor around the cage. Mary began the lesson.

> **Mary:** This is Bobby [taking the rabbit from the cage and holding it]. I feed him this stuff [holding up some rabbit pellets, which Bobby began to sniff]. I feed Bobby every day. He eats this stuff and lettuce. Do you want to feed him?
>
> **Children:** Yes!
>
> **Mary:** Take one of these [indicating the pellets] and give it to Bobby.

The children laid their pellets on the floor as Mary put Bobby down. As Bobby ate, many children touched his fur, ears, and tail. Following this, Bobby was put in his cage and the children returned to their tables.

One boy asked if he could bring his puppy to class for others to feed and pet the next day. Permission was granted.

Later in the day the teacher asked several children how Mary cared for Bobby. They responded that Bobby was given food. Those who had pets at home stated that they were eager to get home and feed their pets.

The children returned to touch the rabbit many times during the day. They were eager to pet the animal regardless of the number of times they had touched it previously. They seemed to enjoy repeating the same action all day.

The attention span of mentally handicapped learners is extremely short. But, as the preceding scenario illustrates, they can focus on the activity of the moment if it involves some manipulation. The children in Mary's class were interested in the rabbit when they could touch it and feed it. However, they did not mention any observations about the rabbit except that it ate.

The Orthopedically Handicapped Learners

Teaching the orthopedically handicapped child necessitates special planning. Orthopedically handicapped children frequently have impairments with arms or legs, or have other muscular control difficulties. Seldom do these children require adaptations in lesson content. They may, however, require alterations in equipment and facilities. Children confined to a wheelchair need a barrier-free environment. Doorways should be wide enough to accommodate the wheelchair. Tables or other learning sites should be at a proper height to let them work comfortably from their chairs. Equipment should be within easy reach. Similarly, children on crutches need equipment that's readily accessible, and they need sufficient space in which to move. It may help to provide these children with a seat inside the work area.

Children with muscular problems may require special attention when handling equipment. Safety is the primary concern. Sometimes a peer can help out if an activity does not demand the learner's direct involvement.

The Visually Impaired Learners

Visually impaired learners may totally lack sight, may be able to see only light and shadows, or may have limited ability to distinguish objects. Some children have normal vision in a very limited field, but lack peripheral vision. Others may be able to see large objects like chairs and tables, but not smaller objects like pins or the print in books.

Since their field of vision may be restricted, the space in which visually impaired children can conduct an activity may be limited. Furniture and equipment should always be kept in exactly the same place since these children often depend upon memory to locate objects. Activities that emphasize tactile and auditory experiences are especially well suited to the sensory learning skills of these children.

Visually impaired children enjoy two advantages not available to sighted children. First, they are not affected by visual distractions. And second, they *must* experience most activities firsthand since often they cannot learn through demonstrations or illustrated lectures. In effect, the nature of their impairment forces them to become active learners.

Of course, there are also rather severe disadvantages for visually impaired children. A sighted child is able to scan an entire area, to see where equipment is placed, and to note how various items relate to each other. The blind child can explore only a small area at a time, using the sense of touch to determine how each object relates to all others around it. A sighted child may take in an entire electric circuit with a glance; the visually impaired child must explore that same circuit an inch at a time, reconstructing the circuit mentally on the basis of memory alone. Descriptions of color changes are meaningless to a child who has never seen color. Imagine a visually impaired child learning about the parts of a cell from a relief sketch. Each area within the sketch must have a different texture to distinguish it from other areas. Otherwise, the student cannot perceive the structure of the cell or the relationships among various parts.

Most science programs stress visual experiences. These must be adapted for the visually impaired learner, or alternate activities provided. Similarly, equipment designed for the sighted student may need to be adapted, or students may need to be given special assistance. And finally, special care must be taken in arranging the classroom for the visually impaired student.

Several projects are underway to produce programs for the visually handicapped. The American Printing House for the Blind has developed educational aids compatible with several curricula and textbooks. Kits of materials are available for such topics as measurement, simple machines, biological models, and insect identification. These kits include equipment that can be used essentially with the sense of touch.

Another project, *Adapting Science Materials for the Blind*, is directed toward adaptation of the Science Curriculum Improvement Study to provide hands-on, concrete experiences for visually impaired children. This program, developed at and published in 1977 by the Lawrence Hall of Science, University of California at Berkeley, permits children to participate in science lessons along with their sighted peers. For example, sighted children may deal with color while visually impaired children may deal with texture. Some activities require more extensive adaptations. Sighted children study the paths of rolling spheres by having the spheres roll on carbon paper so the path is recorded on white paper underneath. Visually impaired students roll spheres across a rubber sheet covered with aluminum foil placed on coarse sandpaper. They can feel the same path that the sighted child can see.

The Adapting Science program consists of a series of modules on the physical and biological sciences. Each activity introduces a fundamental concept or process related to a specified topic. Sample modules include the *Structure of Life* and *Relative Position, Crayfish, Mapping and Matching,* and *Motion.* Students can explore each module through hands-on activities designed for the visually impaired.

The Aurally Impaired Learner

Two immediate problems are evident relating to aurally impaired learners. Unless these children are aware that a teacher wishes to communicate with them, they may miss instructions altogether. They may be unable to participate fully in discussions, particularly when scientific terminology is used. Both problems can be overcome, however, given enough time and patience.

Pronunciation of scientific terms can be taught by placing a child's hands on the teacher's throat as a term is pronounced, then placing the child's hands on his or her own throat, and asking the child to try reproducing the vibration pattern. In addition, children may try to imitate lip, mouth, and tongue movements of the teacher. Once the term is pronounced, it must be defined in some manner meaningful to the child.

It may also be difficult for aurally impaired children to comprehend abstractions. Although the child may read about an abstraction, concrete examples may be needed for clarification. Films and filmstrips may be of limited value to deaf children unless they are captioned.

Seldom do students with hearing problems require substantial alterations in lesson content. Some adaptations may be necessary, however. For example, concepts and words describing those concepts should be repeated and illustrated in a variety of contexts. Problems should be presented through direct demonstration whenever possible, not simply through oral instruction. Students should have many direct experiences before words are used, and there should be adequate opportunity for laboratory work. Finally, the pace of lessons should be slowed.

In addition, teachers can do some simple things to make learning easier for aurally impaired children. They can face children as they are talking to them. They can remain in one place, remembering that an aurally impaired child may not call aloud for help. And they can keep discussion brief.

Other Impairments

Some children experience learning obstacles that fit none of the categories mentioned previously. One of these is learning disability (LD). LD children are not retarded, but they do experience difficulties in communications. For example, the LD child may have difficulty comprehending the spoken word. The child hears what is said but does not understand its meaning. Speaking slowly and using illustrations may help. Some LD children are unable to say words although they do understand their meaning. Such children should be encouraged to use alternative communication methods—gestures, sketches, or writing. However, they should also be given opportunities to retest their speaking skills. Some LD children are unable to associate visual symbols with sounds in reading. This problem may be simplest to overcome by reading to children or using tapes.

Nonverbal learning disabilities include inability to place shoes on the proper foot, tell time, find a classroom or measure distances, or conceptualize mathematically. Children with these disabilities may become impulsive, destructive, frustrated, stubborn, disruptive, and extremely disorganized.

Interestingly, science activities may provide an outlet. A great number of activities in a variety of settings may assist the LD child in learning. Frequent interactions between teacher and child, coupled with much positive reinforcement, are also helpful. But while the instruction must be adjusted to accommodate the LD learner's needs, it must progress without disrupting the learning of other children.

In one classroom of seventeen children, ages eleven to thirteen, with reading abilities from first grade through high third grade levels, the following strategy proved effective. Each child was asked to complete a project for display at the school's science fair. Once the children began to work on the project, their interest was aroused and they became motivated. They became less frustrated and argumentative; there were fewer displays of anger. They were able to control their behavior and to cooperate in solving difficult problems. As work on their project progressed, their self-concept became more positive. The project provided the children with an opportunity to become actively involved in their learning without struggling through a textbook too difficult for them to read. When their project was completed and displayed at the science fair, many children who had never felt successful experienced the joy of success for the first time (Rice, 1983, p. 16).

MAINSTREAMING

Mainstreaming is the conscientious effort to place children with various handicaps in the regular classroom for selected educational experiences (Monaco, 1976, p. 11). Mainstreaming attempts to place handicapped children in the least restrictive setting appropriate for their needs; the ultimate goal is for the child to become a self-reliant adult. In assessing children for placement, the emphasis is on their abilities rather than their disabilities.

Sometimes children with impairments are already in a regular classroom. Teachers may have identified children with some hearing or sight problems, those with delayed muscular development, or those with limited muscular control. Other regular classroom children may display perceptual problems or difficulties forming concepts. Some learners are aurally oriented while others are visually oriented. One learner may display a haptic or kinesthetic preference; another may use a combination of sensory approaches. Children with mild mental retardation may also be assigned to the regular classroom. Thus, working with children who display a variety of physical and mental abilities, as well as a variety of learning styles, may be a usual practice for a teacher.

Mainstreaming seems to have two purposes. One is to include children previously assigned to special classes in the regular classroom program along with nonhandicapped children—at least for certain learning activities. The second is to utilize an educational program that meets the learning requirements of children in a classroom as fully as possible.

Teachers in schools where mainstreaming is the practice must prepare for it in many ways. Here are some general suggestions: Sensory experiences can provide *all* children with effective learning opportunities. Important information in a textbook can be simplified and summarized for slower students. Audiovisual aids should be carefully scrutinized to ensure that they are not confusing. Many texts, films, filmstrips, and tapes used by the regular class are too complicated and fast-paced for some learners. Short, simple lessons tend to be most successful. The discussion on personalizing instruction, in Chapter 3, may also suggest ways that a teacher can help the handicapped learner feel more secure in the classroom.

_____ *LOOKING BACK* _____

1. What relationships can you identify among the developmental characteristics of different groups of children?
2. How should the content of science lessons change as children mature?
3. What kinds of lesson adaptations facilitate learning for children with
   various kinds of impairments?
4. It has been noted that equipment adapted for children *with* impairments
   is often used effectively by children *without* impairments. Can you suggest some reasons this might be so?

ACTIVITIES

1. Read the following and identify some characteristics of children.

   Scenario

   Miss Ross is sitting on the floor with her kindergarten class. A
   plant has been placed on the floor for the children to see. The science lesson is about plant growth. Miss Ross asks the children if
   they are going to have fun with their science lesson; a chorus of
   yes's fills the room. Johnny hits Mary who is sitting next to him;
   she apparently bumped him as she moved. Miss Ross separates
   Mary and Johnny and begins the lesson.

   Miss Ross describes the appearance of the plant the last time
   the children saw it. She asks the children if they remember and
   they respond that, yes, they do. Susie is asked to describe the
   plant today. Susie says it is green, small, and, after some hesita-
   tion, that it feels fuzzy. Fred says he sees clouds through the window and they are big. Miss Ross redirects Fred's attention to the
   plant under study.

   Sarah stands up and begins to leave the group. Quickly Miss
   Ross asks her to describe the plant. Sarah looks at the plant from
   where she is standing. She says it is bigger than the container in
   which it is growing. Miss Ross reminds the group that Susie described the plant as small. Sarah disagrees and says she can see
   parts of the leaves extending over the sides of the container. Miss
   Ross tells Sarah to sit down.

   Robert is given a stick to measure the height of the plant. He
   holds the stick next to the plant and tells the group that the stick
   is bigger than the plant. He is directed to make a mark on the
   stick where the top of the plant is. The marked stick, indicating
   the height of the plant, is compared with a chart of heights from
   the past week. Several children state that the mark on the stick is

bigger than the mark on the chart. Miss Ross asks about a change in the height of the plant; the children say nothing.

Billy is piling blocks on top of each other to equal the height of the plant. The stack of blocks falls. Several children scramble for the blocks. The blocks are removed and Miss Ross begins to describe changes in the plant and the conditions necessary for plants to grow. Tammy and Terry are pushing each other; Phillip asks when he can eat his lunch and Jack says he saw Linda hide some blocks in her pocket.

Miss Ross concludes the lesson by stating that today the group measured the plant, compared its height with past measurements, and learned that the plant grew taller. Johnny quickly asks why the plant grows up. Miss Ross tells Johnny that she will answer that question later. The children are instructed to get in line and go to the playground.

What kinds of observations did the children make?

a. Observations of the plant from the day before.
b. Observations of the actual plant on the day the lesson was taught.
c. Observations about the increase in the plant's height.

Note that Miss Ross, not the children, describes the previous appearance of the plant. The children concentrate on characteristics of the plant that they can observe immediately. Therefore, response **a** is inappropriate.

As we've noted already, children are perceptually oriented; they judge events and objects on their appearance. Note the responses of Susie, Fred, and Robert. Their comments are based upon visual observation.

Children tend to concentrate on one attribute of an object at a time. Robert observes height, Susie color, then texture.

Children are egocentric; they are unable to imagine the appearance of an object from another's point of view. Sarah is unable to coordinate her observations with those of Susie.

Children frequently investigate through trial and error. Billy stacks blocks in a random manner rather than planning procedures for stacking.

Children tend to focus on the present; they are often unable to follow a series of changes in an object such as the changes in plant height described previously. The children observe that the mark on the stick is higher up than the marks on the chart, but they are unable to relate this information to the height of the plant. Response **b** best describes the observations that children made.

Since children may have difficulty in placing events or objects in a sequence and using symbols to represent the sequence, they are

unable to interpret the chart. Thus, when asked about it, they simply remain silent.
2. Read the following lesson and answer the questions.

SCIENCE LESSON: GROUPING LEAVES

Given a collection of at least five leaves, first-grade children are asked to
place them into two groups, based on one attribute and the lack of that
attribute. The attribute must be one that can be seen. After the leaves are
grouped, the children are asked to tell the group what attribute they selected, and the group is asked to determine whether the leaves are accurately categorized.

Then the children are blindfolded and asked to group the leaves according to an attribute that can be felt. After the leaves are grouped and
blindfolds are removed, the bases for classification are given and the accuracy determined.

Next, the children are asked to arrange the leaves according to size.
They are asked to select a size-related criterion (e.g., width) for arranging
the leaves. After the leaves are arranged, children reveal their criterion for
arranging the leaves. The accuracy of arranging is determined.

Finally, small samples of several fresh or dried herbs are given to the
children. The samples contain parsley, sage, oregano, basil, thyme, and
rosemary. Children are asked to group the herbs according to odor. The
groupings are shown to the class and their accuracy determined.

In what way do these activities require refined observational
abilities?

    a. Children are given the opportunity to observe actual objects.

    b. Children are able to apply their observational ability to iden-
tify and group objects according to attributes specified by
the teacher.

    c. Children are encouraged to use a variety of senses in group-
ing objects.

If you selected response a, you are thinking about the observational abilities of kindergarten children. The activity as described
requires children to observe much more critically and to use multi-
sensory actions to group the leaves.

If you selected response b, you are still thinking of kindergarten children. Children in the first grade are able to use higher levels
of observation than would be required to group objects according
to specified attributes. Again, the cognition of the children is not
challenged.

If you selected response c, you recognize the abilities of children who can perceive more critically than kindergarten children. The lesson requires the children to use several senses in addition to sight. Another cognitively expansive feature of the activity is that the children must select the criterion used in grouping.

3. If possible, try the following activities with children in grades 3 and 4. It may also be interesting to try the activities with adults.

   a. Conservation of volume: Give children 1 cup of water in a transparent container. Mark the water level with a wax pencil or tape. Place the water in a freezer overnight. Remove the container with the ice in it. Observe the level of the ice and compare the level of the ice with that of the water. Tell children that no water has been added to the container. If the ice were melted, would there be more water in the container than there was before the container was placed in the freezer? Ask the children to explain their comments. Permit children to test their guesses by letting the ice melt. Do this AFTER the children have finished discussing their observations.

   b. Conservation of matter (substance): Give children 2–3 grams of sugar and a container of water. Ask them to place the sugar in the water and to stir the water with their fingers. Where is the sugar? Ask children to explain their comments. If no child suggests it, ask what would happen if the water evaporated. Permit the children to evaporate the water and observe the results.

   c. Conceptualization of liquid levels: Look at a bottle half full of colored water. Wrap a paper towel or sheet of paper around the bottle and tip the bottle at a 45° angle. Ask the children to show or draw on the paper where the level of water is now that the bottle is tipped. Note the difference between the sketches of children at the two grade levels. Ask for an explanation of their responses.

   d. Ordering events: Using photos or drawings of a plant maturing from the time of seed germination to the adult plant stage, ask children to place the photos or drawings in sequence from seed to mature plant. The same procedure may be used with the life cycle of an insect (egg, larva, pupa, and adult), phases of the moon, or position of the earth relative to the sun during the seasons of the year.

   e. Conservation of length: Cut two lengths of garden hose approximately 25 feet long. Tell the children that these represent part of the food tube or digestive system (small intestines) of a person. It may be helpful to show the children a picture of the human digestive system and point to the small intestines. Tell children that digested food passes through the part of the digestive system shown. Place the one length of hose in a manner similar to that of the small intestine; let the other hose remain uncoiled. Ask children if food were to pass through the hose, as it does in the human body, through which length of hose would it travel the greatest distance? Ask for an explanation or illustration of their responses.

4. Suppose you had a child in your class who was at the formal thinking stage. Which of the following problems would you select for study?

   a. Through how many sheets of paper will a magnet attract a paperclip?
   b. What changes on earth may be attributed to the earth's passing through the tail of a comet?
   c. What effect does varying the amount of liquid fertilizer have on the length of a plant stem in three weeks?

   Problem **a** would present little challenge for the formal thinker. Using a magnet and paper the question could be answered quickly and would require little cognition.

   Problem **b** has no solution. There is limited evidence of changes on earth resulting from the earth's passing through or close to the tail of a comet. Responses to the problem may range from superstitions to scientific opinion.

   Problem **c** would provide a challenge for the formal thinker because a hypothesis could be formulated and then tested. This problem provides opportunities for abstract thinking, problem organization, and hypothesis formation.

5. Which of the questions below might challenge a gifted or creative learner?

   a. Can you construct an electromagnet with a steel nail, insulated wire, and a dry cell? Wrap the wire around the nail and attach the end of the wire to a D-cell.
   b. What objects can you find in the classroom that can be placed in an electric circuit to complete the circuit?
   c. What do you see happening to the needle of a magnet as it is brought near a wire through which electricity is flowing?

   Question **a** presents very little challenge to the learner. Specific instructions for conducting the activity are given for the learner to follow.

   Question **b** encourages the learner to test objects in the room. There is no indication which objects are to be used, or how they are to be incorporated into the circuit. The activity encourages the learner to test hypothesis to answer the question. This question would offer a challenge.

In question c specific instructions are given for conducting the activity. The opportunity to hypothesize and to test the hypothesis is very limited. If the question were expanded to include wires transmitting electricity of various voltages, the learner would be challenged more.

6. Which of the following science activities would be most appropriate for the EMH learners?
    a. Select all the red shapes from the set of shapes you have.
    b. Name all the red objects seen on the way to school this morning.
    c. Look at the color wheel and name the colors that can be mixed with red to make purple and orange. Then select those colors from a set of colored shapes that you were given.

In activity a learners can select all the red objects from a set of objects within their perceptual field. One task is requested and it deals with objects the learners have before them.

The accuracy of activity b is questionable. Perhaps the child did not see a red object; perhaps the child did not even notice whether there were red objects on the way to school. Further, verifying the accuracy of the learner's response could be a difficult task for the teacher.

Activity c requires the child to do two tasks, both dealing with recall. Some children would be able to recall which colors could be mixed to make purple and orange; others would not. This lesson would have greater value if it offered children the opportunity to mix colors, not just name and select them.

REFERENCES

Awkerman, G., and Teller, P. (1979). Mass management for gifted students. *Science and Children 16(6).*

Bennett, L. M. (January 1979). Science and special students. *Science and Children, 15(4).*

Biological Sciences Curriculum Study. (1972). *Me Now* and *Me and My Environment.* (Developed under a grant from the U.S. Office of Education.) Northbrook, IL: Hubbard.

Brotski, D. E. (1973). A pilot science program for educable mentally handicapped children emphasizing child-centered activities. Paper presented at the National Science Teachers Association Convention, Detroit.

The Education for Handicapped Child Act (1976). Prepared by The Council for Exceptional Children for the Bureau of Education for the Handicapped, U.S. Office of Education. Washington, D. C.

Holzberg, R. (1976). The educable retarded. *Science and Children 13(6).*

Lambardi, T. P., and Belch, P. E. (1976). Science experiences and the mentally retarded. *Science and Children 13(6).*

Midgott, J., and Esler, W. K. (1981). Science activities as an alternative reading program for EMR students. *Science and Children 18(7).*

Monaco, T. M. (1976). Mainstreaming, who? *Science and Children, 13(6).*

Osburn, J. W. (1931). *Enriching the curriculum for gifted children.* New York: The Macmillan Company.

Renzulli, J. J. (1979). What makes giftedness: A reexamination for the definition. *Science and Children 16(6).*

Rice, J. R. (1983). A special science fair: LD children learn what they can do. *Science and Children 20(4).*

Schatz, Dennis, Franks, Frank, Thien, Herbert D., and Linn, Marcia C. (1976). Hands-on science for the blind. *Science and Children 13(6).*

Stefanich, G., and Schunu, J. O. (1979). Identifying the handicapped-gifted child. *Science and Children 17(3).*

Thompson, B. (1979). Myths and science for the handicapped. *Science and Children, 17(3).*

3

Teaching and Learning

Objectives

1. To analyze teaching as an art and a science.
2. To identify relationships among the teacher, student, and curriculum content.
3. To analyze the interactions between teacher and student, and student and content, as they affect teaching and learning.
4. To analyze effective instructional techniques that can meet teachers' and students' needs.

_____ *LOOKING FORWARD* _____

In this chapter, we present techniques designed to enhance your teaching effectiveness—and your students' learning. We begin with a discussion of teaching as an art and science, and later in the chapter address the needs of teachers and learners.

Special attention is given to the interactions between the teacher and learner and between the learner and content. Methods for enhancing these interactions are discussed.

By the end of the chapter, you should have identified many of your needs as an instructor, and gained some insight regarding ways you can meet the needs of your students through appropriate science content and effective teaching strategies.

If asked to describe teaching, most teachers would likely mention such things as planning, questioning, gathering resources, managing children, and evaluating learning. Similarly, children might describe learning as talking, listening, reading, answering questions, and taking tests. These descriptions seem reasonable enough. Yet they're not really comprehensive. For there is a great deal more to both teaching and learning than we can summarize in a few key steps.

In order to really understand teaching and learning, we must look at the interactions among teacher, learner, and content. We must consider teaching both as an art and as a science, and we must carefully analyze the needs of both learner and teacher.

Teaching science to children requires special methodology unique to science, as well as traditional, proven instructional techniques. Because science learning deals with a special body of information, as well as the potential discovery of new information, successful science instruction and learning depend heavily on the skillful use of inquiry skills. Developing inquiring minds is not an overnight task, however. It requires dynamic give and take between instructor and student. That's what this chapter is all about.

TEACHING AS AN ART AND A SCIENCE

Teaching has been described as both an art and a science, the implication being that teaching may be an intuitive process as well as one that can be analyzed.

Teaching is an art to the extent that some aspects of teaching can be individualized, or personalized, based on a teacher's experiences as a student and instructor, and on his or her values, needs, and concept of teaching. For instance, one teacher may successfully introduce a new science topic through a bulletin board display, then use the bulletin board to organize and summarize concepts presented in a science lesson. Another teacher may prefer to introduce a new topic through an interesting narrative. At the climax of the narrative, when students are clamoring for more information, the teacher refers them to the pages in the textbook where additional information can be found. Each teacher uses whatever technique seems most satisfying and effective to introduce a given lesson. Thus, a teacher's instruction becomes a repertoire of methods and techniques with which that teacher feels most comfortable and successful.

Viewing teaching as a science implies that some components are common among teachers, and that these components can be identified and studied. For example, the effectiveness of various instructional strategies may be measured—through tests, classroom observations, peer evaluation, and other means.

Some components of teaching as an art and science are presented in Table 3.1. Note that what "the teacher is" combines with what "the teacher uses" to determine what "the teacher does." Developing expertise with the science of teaching may consequently enhance skills in the art of teaching. For instance, a teacher who learns to use microscopes and slides proficiently may gain enough confidence to begin planning additional activities he or she would otherwise have avoided. Losing the fear of working with unfamiliar equipment changes and broadens his or her personal approach to instruction. Notice that as teachers gain skills in the art and science of teaching, they tend to demonstrate increased concern for the learning of children.

Teachers cannot separate themselves from their attitudes. These attitudes become very evident to and are frequently adopted by children. If teachers display a positive attitude toward science, that it can be enjoyable and rewarding to teach, children become excited about learning. They do not expect teachers to know all the answers; in fact, they may appreciate the openmindedness of a teacher who is willing to learn along with them. Relax, think positively, focus on your strengths rather than worrying over weaknesses, and both you and the children will enjoy science.

THE TRIADIC NATURE OF TEACHING

Teaching is by nature triadic. That is, it involves interrelationships among three key elements: student, instructor, and content. Hyman (1974) summarizes the implications of the triadic view of teaching quite well:

> . . . it is quite clear that teaching must be viewed both as triadic and dynamic. We cannot understand the nature of teaching by looking at only one or two elements of the teaching relationship or by thinking of teaching as static. We must consider all three elements

TABLE 3.1. THE ART AND SCIENCE OF TEACHING

The Teacher Has/Feels ... (Personal Qualities)	The Teacher Uses ... (Knowledge)	The Teacher Does ... (Art and Science Teaching)
Values	Variety of instructional tools	Identifies the needs of the learners
Positive self-concept	Variety of elementary science experiences	Develops flexible teaching plans
Security as a teacher	Variety of scientific equipment	Conducts preassessment of learner's knowledge
A strong science content background	Variety of assessment and evaluative techniques	Defines content and objectives consistent with the needs of the learner
Interest in the development of the elementary school curriculum	Variety of instructional techniques	Provides instruction consistent with the needs of the learner
High regard for science in the elementary school curriculum	Many resources for teaching children science	Selects content consistent with the needs of learners
Effective experience with a variety of instructional techniques	Alternatives for science equipment	Assesses and evaluates learning
	Plans for effective teaching	Secures and utilizes learning resources
Willingness to become a learner with children	Relationship between science and other areas of the elementary school curriculum	Adjusts instruction to the individual needs of the learner
High regard for all children as individuals	Variety of strategies and techniques	Manages a learning situation
Willingness to accept and try new teaching strategies	Variety of methods and rehearses them before implementation	Constructs an appropriate learning setting

(teacher, content, learner) together in order to understand the interaction that occurs during teaching. We must see that the relationships are always changing. Furthermore, *we must note that the interaction between any two elements influences how each of the two will react to the third and, in turn, how all the elements react together.*

Each element influences and is influenced by the relationship between the other two elements. Further, the removal of any one ele-

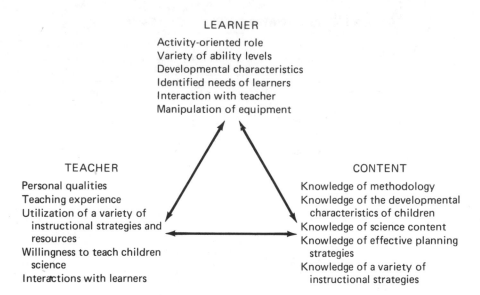

LEARNER

Activity-oriented role
Variety of ability levels
Developmental characteristics
Identified needs of learners
Interaction with teacher
Manipulation of equipment

TEACHER

Personal qualities
Teaching experience
Utilization of a variety of
  instructional strategies and
  resources
Willingness to teach children
  science
Interactions with learners

CONTENT

Knowledge of methodology
Knowledge of the developmental
  characteristics of children
Knowledge of science content
Knowledge of effective planning
  strategies
Knowledge of a variety of
  instructional strategies

Figure 3.1. Teaching Triad

---

*Emphases added.

ment *or the breakdown of any relationship between two elements
destroys the entire teaching triad.**

The recognition of the triadic and dynamic qualities of the teaching act is essential to an understanding of teaching. The points suggested here go beyond the definition of teaching . . . . The points also
go beyond the common but incorrect notion that the teacher must
merely diagnose the student's behavior and action. The teacher
must also analyze his own relationship with the subject matter as
well as his student's relations with him and with the subject matter.

Teacher, Content, Learner

Figure 3.1 illustrates the triadic view of teaching.

In all classrooms, the teacher is responsible for managing classroom activities. Usually, the teacher is a person. However, with the
utilization of modern educational technology, the teacher's role may
sometimes be assumed temporarily by a video monitor, computer terminal, learning center or learning module. Regardless, this element of
the triad provides the central structure for each learning activity.

The content consists of what the teacher knows about teaching
methodology, about children, and about science. Although content
may appear to be well defined, it is really tentative in nature. For one
thing, scientific knowledge is expanding at a dramatic rate; as discov-

eries are made, previously accepted ideas become obsolete. Learning theory is also under constant revision. As research findings show certain theories to be inadequate, teachers must renew and refresh their perspectives on learning theory.

Learners are usually children. They may be children assigned to the classroom on a regular basis, or some combination of groups assigned to the classroom for a specific purpose. Teachers are also learners in the classroom. They may, in fact, be among the most productive learners, constantly extending their knowledge of content and teaching methodology as they interact with the other components of the teaching triad. A key factor in promoting effective learning is positive interaction among the elements of the teaching triad. Let's see why.

INTERACTIONS BETWEEN TEACHER AND LEARNER

Interactions between teacher and learner may be verbal or nonverbal. Verbal interactions tend to receive greater attention from teachers. However, nonverbal interactions are equally important.

Nonverbal interactions tend to communicate personal responses: approval vs. disapproval; interest vs. indifference; friendliness vs. intolerance. These interactions also reflect the individual nature of the teacher; they are one expression of the art of teaching. A teacher circulating among members of a class, for example, shows interest in the work of the children. A teacher standing behind the desk, or at the front of the room—at a distance—may communicate disapproval, criticism, or indifference. The teacher who participates in an activity along with the children, or who observes each child's work, offers positive nonverbal communication.

Clear, concise verbal communications between children and teacher are vital to positive interactions. Verbal communications are necessary for transmitting information, giving directions, providing reinforcement, asking questions, discussing topics, reinforcing performance, identifying obstacles to learning, and assessing learning. An effective communication system facilitates interactions from teacher to child, child to teacher, and child to child.

Here are some suggestions for promoting clear communications in the classroom:

- Use words and illustrations that the learner can understand.
- Be certain the learner is listening.
- Illustrate using examples, pictures, or actions.
- Be as brief as possible, yet complete.

- Ask questions to ascertain that the communications are understood.
- When communications are complex, write or audiotape them.
- Pace communication according to the learner's ability to absorb
  and retain information.

Giving Directions

Many teachers commonly give oral, rather than written, directions.
This saves time, but it does have some definite disadvantages. For instance, once given, oral directions are no longer available for reference.
If a child did not hear or understand the directions, he or she may not
be able to carry out the instructions correctly. Or, he or she may need
to have the instructions repeated. Either way, the initial time saved
has now been lost.

To give clear directions, a teacher must understand fully what is
desired of the children and what directions are necessary to help them
perform the tasks. One way to test the clarity and completeness of
your directions is to try following them precisely yourself. If the directions are clear, you won't need to make inferences, mentally insert
steps, or change the order.

Making an audiotape of directions allows children to listen to directions several times. This tends to minimize questions. The tape
might contain not only initial instructions about performing an activity, but also information about checking the appropriateness or completeness of the work done. Although the audiotape has several advantages, it also has one important disadvantage: it may not be complete.
In making the tape, a teacher may assume that children are quite familiar with the directions and may omit some vital steps. Or a teacher
may be so familiar with the necessary steps in performing an activity
that it is easy to skip over some in making the tape. Teachers who
use audiotapes should play them back and try following the directions
themselves to be sure all steps are included before giving the tapes to
students.

Questioning

Asking and answering questions is an integral part of any learning
experience. Most of the verbal interactions in a classroom utilize some
form of questioning. A publication of the National Science Teachers
Association has identified four types of questions (Blosser, 1975).
These are shown in Table 3.2.

Managerial questions provide information about learning progress, completion of activities, management of resources, or logistics.
Examples include "Has everyone completed the activity?" or "Did all
of you return the equipment to the box?" Responses to such questions

TABLE 3.2. FOUR TYPES OF QUESTIONS

Question Type	Question Function
Managerial	To keep the classroom operations moving
Rhetorical	To emphasize a point, to reinforce an idea or statement
Closed	To check the retention of previously learned information, to focus thinking on a particular point or commonly held set of ideas
Open	To promote discussion or student interaction; to stimulate student thinking; to allow freedom to hypothesize, speculate, share ideas about possible activities, etc.

enable a teacher to assess progress, identify problems, and pace a lesson appropriately.

Rhetorical questions are used to induce thinking. They are not meant to be answered directly. An example might be "Have you ever thought what it would be like on earth if one day the sun ceased to exist?" The question is simply intended to get children thinking about the importance of sunlight for life on earth.

The closed question deals with specific information or interpretation of that information: "What happened to the plant which was not watered?" or "What is the purpose of a switch in the electric circuit?" Closed questions provide a teacher with a means for assessing recall and determining whether children are making the intended observations. Responses to closed questions frequently are well specified and may be identified as correct or incorrect.

Open questions may have a range of acceptable responses. Examples include "How do you account for your getting different temperature readings for the boiling point of water each time you tried?" or "What factors may have affected the height of the plant kept in the dark when compared with the plant kept in the light?" Open questions tend to encourage thinking while they test recall. They also give the child an opportunity to express ideas, guesses, predictions that other types of questions do not invite.

Classroom questions serve a variety of purposes:

- To arouse interest.
- To evaluate a student's preparation.
- To review and summarize.
- To develop insights.
- To stimulate critical thinking.
- To stimulate further investigation.
- To evaluate achievement.

Questioning is one of the most useful communication strategies that teachers use. However, the way a question is phrased can be as important as the question itself. One way of phrasing questions may provide clues to the answer the teacher is seeking. For instance, "We observed refraction of light, didn't we?" implies that the teacher expects a "Yes." "What is the most important organ in the digestive system?" doesn't reveal the response directly, but does provide an important clue about the nature of the desired response. "Did you find that two like poles of a magnet repel each other?" probably indicates that the teacher anticipates a "Yes"—depending somewhat on how the question is expressed.

Another way of phrasing questions encourages children to express ideas. "What did you observe when . . . ?" "What are some factors which may explain . . . ?" "Did you notice any differences when . . . ?" These questions do not have one right answer; they call for children to synthesize information gained through their observations. Children usually respond to this type of question in full sentences, rather than with one or two words. Although such questions require a higher level of thought than recall questions, children may well see them as less threatening because they do not involve precise right or wrong answers.

Aschner (1961) suggests that teachers are professional question askers; they may ask 2,000 questions or more per week. In an analysis of question asking by teachers during science lessons, Rowe (1978) found that the number of questions asked varied from 3 to 5 questions per minute. The children had little or no time to ask questions. Asking too many questions places a teacher in the role of inquisitor, which can inhibit students' learning. Responding to rapid-fire questions allows students little time to concentrate on the task at hand. Conversely, asking too few questions may give students the message that a lesson or activity is unimportant. The proper number of questions should be determined by the involvement of children in the activity as well as the content of the lesson.

Sensing when to ask a question is a skill well worth developing. Interrupting activities with questions is often disruptive. However, a well-timed question may redirect the learner's attention or clarify fuzzy information. Sensing when to ask questions and how many to ask takes professional judgment developed through experience.

The effectiveness of questioning is also influenced by the length of time children have to respond (Rowe, 1978). Rowe's research revealed two types of wait-times, each of which can positively influence inquiry and creativeness. The first wait-time is the duration of time between when a teacher finishes posing a question and when he or she either comments or calls on another student. What would be your estimate of this time span? Rowe found it to average *less than one and one half seconds!* When that wait-time increased to three seconds, students' responses became longer, more students responded, speculative thinking increased, and contributions from slow students increased.

The second wait-time is the period from when students complete their responses to the moment any additional talking occurs. Increasing this wait-time encourages students to expand or modify their responses, and promotes increased student interaction.

In asking questions that require higher level thinking skills, it may be helpful to consider the taxonomy suggested by Hunkings (1972). This taxonomy is similar to Bloom's (1956) categories of objectives; a brief description and example of each type of question is presented in Table 3.3.

The most common types of questions asked by teachers are knowledge, comprehension, and application level questions. It takes time to acquire the skills needed to ask analysis, synthesis, and evaluation

TABLE 3.3. LEVELS OF QUESTIONS

Question	Description	Sample
Knowledge	Recall of specific information	What is the instrument used to measure temperature?
Comprehension	Changing information into a different symbolic form or language (restating something)	Label five parts of the flower on the drawing. Give a definition of gravity in your own words.
Application	The use of abstractions in a concrete situation or in solving a problem (applying a rule or a skill or applying knowledge to a new setting)	How many liters of water would be in a gallon of water (applying the equivalancy between liter and quart)? How would you connect the wires to a dry cell to complete the electric circuit?
Analysis	Breaking a problem into its component parts; Sanders (1966) states that this level of questioning requires a knowledge of reasoning for it to be effective	Look at this white powder. It is a combination of three different powders you have observed before. What are the powders in this mixture?
Synthesis	Putting together the elements or parts to form a whole	You place corn and tomatoes in a nutrient solution rather than growing them in soil. For which plant, tomato or corn, is the water concentration likely to need closer observation? What data from your transpiration investigations support your answer?
Evaluation	Making a judgment according to a standard	Judging from developments and technology derived from man's trip to the moon, was the cost of the trip justified?

level questions. It is beyond the scope of this book to treat the three higher level questioning skills, but you may wish to do some personal reading about developing these higher level skills. Two references are useful: Hunkings (1972) and Sanders (1966).

Teachers are not the only question askers in a classroom. Children should be taught to ask questions also. They should be encouraged to ask questions about the science activities they are conducting as well as about science content. In fact, some activities may be designed specifically to arouse curiosity and elicit questions. For instance, children observe the teacher holding a paper cup over an open flame; the cup begins to burn. A second paper cup, partially filled with water, is held over the open flame but does not burn. The event immediately prompts questions from the children: "Why didn't the second cup burn?" "Are the two cups the same?" (NOTE: If you try this activity with paper cups, you should wear safety goggles and have a pail of water handy in which to drop the first cup after it ignites. Use tongs to hold the cup over the open flame.)

Great care must be exercised in responding to children's questions if you want them to ask more. Consider the first question about why one cup burns while the other does not. One teacher might respond, "The second cup has water in it and the water prevented the paper from reaching its kindling temperature." A second teacher might respond, "What differences in the two cups do you observe?" After the children respond, the teacher might continue, "Did the paper in the two cups seem to be the same? How could you find out if the water may have prevented the second cup from burning?"

The first teacher was prepared to answer the question he or she anticipated the children would ask. This brought immediate closure to the questioning. As a result, the children were not provided with the opportunity to solve the problem for themselves. Notice, by contrast, that the second teacher set up a dialogue of questioning that encouraged the children to participate in the problem solving. (Which students will ask more questions next time?)

During their school careers, children often experience deterrents to questioning. One is simply lack of opportunity. Frequently, teachers ask so many questions that children have little or no time to ask any of their own. Some children are exposed to only one type of question: the knowledge question. As a result, they may not look on the act of questioning as interesting or provocative. Nor do they have a good model for learning to formulate intriguing questions. In addition, some children's questions are ignored by peers and teacher. Such children may become inhibited about asking questions at all. Experiences that encourage questioning include listening to a speaker, viewing a videotape, watching demonstrations, viewing a film, or using a software package. Once the stimulus for questioning has been provided, children must be given the time and encouragement to ask questions. Just saying "What are your questions?" or "Do you have any questions?" tends to be nonproductive. Modeling may be necessary: for example, "How many of you wondered about . . . ?" Stimulating children to ask appropriate questions is an important accomplishment for a teacher.

Like teachers, children need to learn effective questioning skills. Some questions children ask may be vague. Again, guidance is necessary in helping children rephrase questions so they can be answered. For instance, suppose a child asks, "How do animals live?" Such a question is not answerable until it's made more specific. The teacher may have to question the child to determine the intent of the original question: "Are you curious about a particular animal? Would you like to know *where* it lives? Or are you wondering what it eats?"

Questioning is vital to classroom inquiry. Mechanically conducted science activities raise few questions in the learner's mind. Yet questions are the key to thinking. Given the time and opportunity to do so, children are generally eager to help find answers to their own questions. And this questioning, problem-solving approach is the very essence of scientific inquiry.

Reinforcing

When a child performs as teacher expects, desires, or anticipates, the child is frequently rewarded with such phrases as "That's good," "That's right," "OK," or some other nebulous term. Such evaluative responses tend to encourage children to perform for the teacher's approval, rather than for personal satisfaction.

Rowe's (1978) research on verbal rewards indicates that nonevaluative rewards may be more suitable for most inquiry based elementary science programs. She found that children who received verbal rewards frequently tended to make more errors, repeated more steps, checked with the teacher more frequently, and displayed less self-confidence than children who experienced a low reward schedule. She also found that children on a frequent reward schedule tended to respond to the teacher in short phrases with only brief explanations, and that they seemed to be conducting science activities for teacher reward, not personal learning.

Probably the most effective reinforcement for completing a task is the opportunity to share it with others. This internal reinforcement is generally more effective than if it came from some external source.

Discussing

Classroom discussions include both formal and informal question and answer sessions as well as incidental conversations between teacher and child. Discussions are useful with large groups, such as the entire class, small groups, or individuals. Some discussions may help in summarizing a lesson, clarifying results of an activity, or exchanging observations.

A question-answer discussion is one way for the teacher to obtain information from children quickly and identify problems children are experiencing. This kind of discussion is intended primarily for retrieving information. Another type of discussion seeks to develop thought and interaction among children. The teacher asks a question, a child responds, and other children are encouraged to offer additional comments. This type of discussion leads to an exchange of ideas rather than mere information retrieval.

Planning for discussion sessions is somewhat different from planning for other activities. For one thing, a discussion may move in unanticipated directions. Still, if the end point is carefully thought out, key questions can help focus the discussion or at least give it a central theme.

During a discussion, it's important to maintain focus. Straying from the topic can be easy, interesting, and useful at times—particularly if children are openly sharing experiences. But it may be difficult to get back on track. Well-phrased, carefully timed questions can help return the discussion to the desired topic without placing the teacher in an authoritarian role.

Discussion may also reveal something about students as individuals. Many times, children share information that sheds light upon difficulties they may be experiencing. Teachers who are good listeners and who avoid expressing judgments will tend to draw out such information.

The format of a discussion strongly influences its effectiveness. The purpose—such as facilitating the exchange of information derived from investigations—should be clear. The discussion should be long enough to accomplish the expressed purpose, but once that end is achieved, the discussion should be terminated. Prolonging the discussion beyond the children's attention span usually causes the discussion to degenerate into a teacher monologue.

Leading a discussion well requires sensitive leadership. A good discussion leader keeps the discussion moving without losing focus. In addition, a good leader encourages *all* children to participate—through selective questioning or by asking one child to respond to another's observation. The leader should not interrupt children when they are talking unless they are offering unrelated information.

INTERACTIONS BETWEEN LEARNER AND CONTENT

Content is usually presented through four strategies: concept development, guided discovery, personalizing instruction, and investigation. Each encourages interaction between content and learner.

Concept Development

For the purpose of this discussion, a concept may be thought of as a mental structure or idea which results from combining related information into a special framework useful in processing future information.

Concept development usually begins as children make observations about the environment, either as a class, within a small group, or individually. These observations may result from manipulating objects or watching an event. For the young child, most learning occurs within an environment comprising familiar objects with obvious attributes. As the child matures, that environment expands with more detailed observations aided by scientific equipment. In addition, as the child matures, he or she becomes more skilled at identifying interrelationships among components within the learning environment. Thus, concepts develop as a direct result of interaction between the child and the learning environment. The following example illustrates the beginning of concept development—sometimes referred to as a "preconcept." A child begins to acquire a concept of "dogness" through many experiences with a dog, perhaps the family pet. Initially, the concept of dogness may consist of an object with four legs, covered with hair. It has a tail that wags, it barks, it's friendly and fun to play with, it sleeps with the child, and it welcomes snacks under the table. The concept of dogness is further expanded as the dog is observed with the hair on the back of the neck raised and teeth bared, making a sound quite different from those it makes when it wants to play or go out-of-doors. These latter characteristics are observed as a stranger approaches the dog. The dog does not seem at all friendly now. In fact, the entire series of observations associated with "dog" may involve some contradictions, yet all be of a "dog." Observations of a dog reveal that the thing called "dog" has short legs and is close to the ground, is brown, has a pointed nose and long floppy ears. Another thing called "dog" is tall, has long legs and has short, pointed ears. Additional observations reveal that the word "dog" applies to animals with short hair and long hair; long tails, short tails, or no tails; loud barks and soft barks; friendly and not-so-friendly habits.

Enter another creature. This one has four legs, is covered with fur, is soft to the touch, likes to be petted, and is black and white. It doesn't quite look like a dog, doesn't run and play, likes to be by itself at times and doesn't seem to like dogs. It just doesn't look like a dog or act like a dog. Is it a dog? Further observation is necessary to determine whether this new creature fits the concept of "dogness."

Notice that once concept formation has started, additional observations may be processed in one of two ways: They may be incorporated into existing concepts (assimilated) or they may be accommodated. Incorporating observations extends, refines, or enriches earlier concepts. For instance, when the name "dog" is incorporated in the learner's thinking, other information is either processed into the concept, or excluded from the concept. When an animal is viewed in a zoo, the information processed or incorporated into the concept "dogness" is used to place the animal in the category of "dog" or "not dog." As the child has more experiences with animals, the concept is expanded or altered. Note that the concept "dogness" is initiated through interactions with the dog and with events (playing, feeding). Although the objects or events may not occur in the classroom, they are still part of the learning environment.

When the observations do not fit the current concept, that concept may be accommodated. Accommodating works like this: The knowledge of the observer is challenged (the second creature the child saw had some characteristics of a dog, but also had other characteristics which did not fit the dog concept). Alterations must be made in the concept (all creatures with four legs, hair/fur, and pointed ears are not dogs). A restructured concept results as children return to mental equilibrium (some creatures are dogs and some are not).

Some accommodating may not occur so rapidly; lack of experience or mental maturity can interfere with this process. For example, a child observes that objects fall toward the earth when they are not supported. This observation seems consistent for all objects until, on one occasion, the child is holding two balloons. One is inflated with air, the other with helium. Both balloons are released. The helium-inflated balloon floats off into the atmosphere, while the other falls to the earth. Past experience suggests that both balloons should have fallen to earth. The concept of gravity held by the child did not function in this case. Thus, the child may temporarily conclude that these observations are unrelated to the effects of gravity. Time is needed for the child to accommodate the concept of gravitation to accept the new observations.

Two interactive techniques assist students in concept formation. Both use examples of the concept and a rule by which the concept is defined; however, they differ in the sequence in which the examples and rules are presented.

The first technique follows the sequence example-example-rule-example. An illustration of this sequence is rubbing an inflated balloon over a piece of nylon cloth and watching it attract pieces of paper (example); running a comb through the hair rapidly and watching as it attracts pieces of cereal (example); giving a name to the cause of the attraction—static electricity (rule); rubbing a plastic rod over a sweater and watching it attract small pieces of a plastic bag (example). The second technique follows the sequence rule-example-example. An illustration of this latter technique would be defining static electricity as electrical charges that attract objects (rule); running a comb through the hair and watching it attract pieces of paper (example); rubbing a balloon with a piece of nylon cloth and finding that the balloon was attracted to a wall (example).

It may also be effective to use nonexamples. Imagine trying to help someone learn the concept of dogness if that person had never had any experience with other animals; or the concept of "green" if that were the only color in existence; or "rough," if no other texture were available. Concept formation is enhanced by the use of carefully selected nonexamples that help students learn discrimination. As concepts are expanded, refined, and restructured, children begin to recognize relationships among concepts. From these recognitions generalizations evolve.

A generalization may be described as a collection of concepts that characterize some aspect of the environment or relationships among aspects of the environment. For example, the generalization "Magnets attract some metal objects" requires understanding of several concepts: magnet, attraction, and metal. To move from concept development to the formation of generalizations demands a wide range of experience—in other words, intensive interaction between learner and content. Teachers can help provide this experience through learning activities, audiovisual aids, field trips, visits from guest speakers, textbooks, and reference materials. These diverse means of interacting demand a wide repertoire of instructional strategies. And the effectiveness of each depends upon the security of the teacher, purpose of the lesson, characteristics of the learners, and available resources.

Concept formation is a very complex function of the human brain. We hope this discussion provides some insight into the mental processes through which humans translate observations into concepts, and concepts into generalizations.

Guided Discovery

Discovery is frequently defined as becoming aware of something new, be it information, relationships, or events. Discoveries are usually cognitive in nature, although they may relate to the affective or psychomotor domains.

Discovery may arise from random or planned activities. Guided discovery is planned, implemented, and assisted by a teacher—who may very well know in advance what it is he or she wants students to discover.

Several types of guided discovery experiences—ranging from highly structured to minimally structured—can be used in the classroom. These include whole class discovery lessons, guided discovery with minimal structure, and self-initiated discovery. Regardless of the structure of the guided discovery, active participation by the learner is mandatory. The teacher's primary responsibility is to guide the learner in a way that fosters cognitive development.

Whole-class guided discovery is very common. It is a strategy suggested in many elementary school science textbooks, and begins with an announcement—either by the teacher or within the text itself—of what is to be discovered. A teaching plan is then developed to guide children toward this discovery. Activities and experiences are designed so that the probability that the discovery will occur. Otherwise, the lesson proceeds as usual.

The following lesson, selected from *Heath Science,* a level five textbook, illustrates guided discovery (Barufaldi, Ladd, & Moses, 1985). The lesson is taken from Chapter 2 on cells. The general topic is "Making Things Look Bigger."

LESSON: MAKING THINGS LOOK BIGGER

Vocabulary:	Lens, magnification
Main Idea:	A microscope is an instrument (containing lenses) that is used to magnify images of objects.
Objective:	The student should be able to *describe* how a microscope is used to magnify the image of an object.
Content:	**Learning Activities**
Lenses	1. Read the following paragraph. How does a microscope make things look bigger? You may have discovered something about microscopes when you looked at a drop of water on a leaf [A picture of a grass leaf with drops of water on it is beside this passage. The drops of water magnify the leaf surface underneath them].
	2. *Activity:* Here is a simple way to see how a water-drop magnifier works. You will need an eyedropper, some water, an index card, some clear plastic wrap, and tape. Cut a hole in the middle of the card about the size of a quarter. Tape a piece of plastic wrap over the hole. Fold each edge of the card about 1 cm. Place a drop of water on the plastic. Place your magnifier on top of a printed page and look at the letters through the water drop. What happens?
Micro-scopes	3. Read the following: Water-drop microscopes are easy to make, but they do not last long. We need something that does not evaporate. Should it be able to hold its shape? Should you be able to see through it? Should it be a round

shape like a water drop? The answer to all these questions is yes.

We can find all of these properties in glass. Many microscopes have curved glass *lenses* . . . to make things look bigger. A microscope is made with at least two lenses, one at each end of the tube. The two lenses work together. Sometimes a microscope may have more than one lens at the bottom. In this way, it is possible to change the *magnification*. . . . The magnification is how many times something is made to look bigger, compared to its real size.

4. *Activity:* You can see how a microscope works. You will need a microscope, some slides, several cover glasses, and a hair from your head. You will also need a few grains of salt, a few grains of pepper, and a feather. Your teacher will show you how to use a microscope.

   To the Teacher: Provide assistance as the students prepare their slides. Explain and demonstrate how to focus the microscope. Have the students begin with the lowest power objective lens. They should bring the objective lens as close to the slide as possible, <u>watching from the side</u> so as not to damage the lens or the slide. Then, looking through the microscope and using the large knob, they can move the lenses <u>up and away</u> from the slide to focus. Then have the students use the smaller knob to sharpen the image. Students may need help in adjusting the mirror to get enough light and in focusing. [A picture of a microscope with the parts labeled is provided in Heath Science.]

5. Always remember to begin with the lowest lens. Slowly bring the lens close to the slide. Be careful not to damage the slide with the lens. When you can clearly see the object under low power, then you can change to a higher power lens. How does the view of each thing change under different magnifications?

   To the Teacher: Discuss the students' observations of various objects viewed through a microscope. Encourage them to observe the objects under various magnifications. Check to make sure that they are viewing the materials correctly.

6. Read the following: Now let's look at some pictures of everyday things. [Pictures of objects under the microscope are included.] The pictures were made through a microscope. Can you guess what the things are? Under each picture is a number and an "x." For example, 100x means you are seeing something 100 times larger than it really is. The magnification is said to be 100.

To the Teacher: As a final check, ask "How does a microscope work?"

7. Follow-up: Look at additional objects under the microscope and calculate the magnification for each. [Directions for calculating magnification are given.]

The following questions are intended to assist you in analyzing the preceding lesson:

1. What was the intent of the lesson?

a. To learn how to use a microscope
b. To observe that a drop of water magnifies objects
c. To learn what magnification is

Response **a** was not the intent of the lesson. It is a skill necessary for the lesson to be taught. Observing that the drop of water magnifies objects **b** sensitizes the students to the concept of magnification, but is not the intent of the lesson.

To learn what magnification is **c** is the intent of the lesson. Note that care is taken throughout the lesson to state that lenses make objects *look* bigger; they do not make objects bigger.

2. Why was the water-drop microscope used in the lesson?

a. Because it is readily available
b. Because it illustrates magnification
c. Because it is easy to use

All three responses are applicable. It is something that is readily available and children can use it easily. The magnification of objects through water is readily observable. Using the water-drop microscope could sensitize students to the phenomenon of magnification which is to be discovered.

3. With which teaching activity was the discovery likely to be made?

a. Focusing the microscope
b. Looking at an object under the microscope
c. Looking at pictures of objects taken through the microscope

Focusing the microscope **a** is a skill necessary to observe magnification, but has little to do with the phenomenon of objects appearing larger. When the student looks at an object under the microscope **b**, that is the most likely moment of discovery. Then text then gives a name to the phenomenon of making things look bigger. Looking at pictures of objects **c** reinforces the idea of magnification.

4. With which teaching activity could the discovery be reinforced and expanded?

    a. With the discussion of students' observations
    b. Answering questions about what the microscope does
    c. Identifying what 100x means

Response **a** provides opportunities for the idea of magnification to be explained in terms of the activities the students conducted. This is the opportunity for students to learn about the finer points of magnification and the significance of their observations. Answering questions **b** does not directly reinforce the idea of magnification, though it may provide valuable information. Calculating degree of magnification **c** helps students refine their definition of the word *magnification.*

This lesson was designed to help students discover the meaning of a word, then refine that definition using additional information gained through experience. The instructional activities were carefully sequenced: providing an experiential background for understanding the word (using the water-drop microscope), presenting the word (magnification), extending the definition (discussion, calculating the amount of magnification, and observing additional objects under the microscope). Although students may have looked through lenses previously and made random observations, the idea of magnification and its application may not have been presented. (Which technique for concept building discussed earlier was used in this lesson?)

A second type of guided discovery is much less formal, but nonetheless important. It consists of helping learners become discoverers, that is, they make their own discoveries. The discovery may arise from a child's question or observation that is of interest. They may pursue this new-found interest and discover information that they did not know previously. During the process of discovery children may encounter an obstacle; they may need additional information or assistance with some laboratory technique or equipment. With the guidance of the teacher, the student can overcome the obstacle quickly and move on toward the discovery.

Guided discovery is also important in helping learners discover relationships among ideas, facts, concepts, or observations. Through discussions, questions, demonstrations, and laboratory activities, the teacher can help the learner become more adept at applying inquiry skills. For instance, a black hole in space may seem mysterious to the student who is trying to reconcile this new concept with a definition of black learned much earlier. Stars in space emit light. During the star's existence something happens that causes the star to explode *inward* on itself. As the atoms and molecules in the star move closer together, the star compresses, and eventually, it no longer emits light. Instead, there is a black hole in space where the star was. Given this explanation, the student can apply the definition of black learned earlier to the concept of an exploded star no longer capable of emitting light. (The illustration of the formation of a black hole is overly simplified. It is intended only to serve as an example of an application of a term to an event.)

Limited guided discovery has an affective component, too. As the learner becomes more of a discoverer, self-confidence develops. The purpose of learning becomes more for oneself than for the teacher, more internal than external. It seems likely that the affective development would have a positive influence on the cognitive development.

A teacher may wonder when to use limited guided discovery. Textbooks do not indicate when to use it, curriculum guides fail to suggest when to use it, and students may not ask for it directly. Actually, there is no definite answer. With experience, teachers learn to recognize important indicators: children's comments and questions, their frustrations, the books they read for pleasure, the computer software they enjoy, and the games they play. For instance, a third-grade teacher asked the class where chickens came from. The response was that they came from the supermarket. With probing, the children continued to be vague about the source of chickens. The teacher bought thirty-three fertilized eggs, one for each child and three extras, and set up an incubator. In the required time, the chickens hatched. The children were amazed and related this to their previous study of birds being hatched from eggs. All thirty-three eggs hatched. Each child was given a chick to take home. (Although the parents were pleased that the teacher provided the experience for the children, they were less than enthusiastic about becoming owners of chickens.) Teachers who work closely with children—like the teacher in the chicken story—quickly learn to tell when children are ready for guided discovery.

Do not assume that only children with high ability need limited guided discovery. *All* children—creative, gifted, disadvantaged, and mentally or physically handicapped—benefit from this strategy.

Self-initiated guided discovery may arise from the children themselves, rather than from the teacher. As children study a science lesson, several may wish to pursue the topic in greater depth. The teacher can suggest resources or appropriate experiences, offering support and encouragement as the child continues to inquire. Using this strategy, of course, requires that a teacher respond to individual needs.

Personalized Instruction

It has been suggested that if teachers had more time to work with children individually and if a learning program were available for each child, instruction would be more effective. Such ideals are unlikely to materialize. However, personalizing instruction is an attainable goal. Personalizing consists of designing the instruction and the instructional site so children may work as rapidly as their ability permits and may interact with the teacher on a one-to-one basis as the need arises. Although children are permitted to work individually, there are times when large-group and small-group instruction are included in the curriculum.

When directions or information must be given to all learners, large-group instruction saves time. The instructor must be careful, however, not to present too much information at one time, and not to offer directions too far in advance of activities.

Learning centers are helpful in personalizing instruction. Several work stations within a learning center may be planned, each dealing with one aspect of the topic under study. Although not mandatory, preassessment may also assist the teacher in designing and pacing a lesson to suit students' knowledge and skill levels.

With a personalized approach, each learner works as rapidly as possible. The teacher interacts with each learner as the need arises, freed from the need to focus on large-group instruction at all times. Teachers generally enjoy the opportunity to interact with each child and to observe his or her work in some detail during the lesson. Students, in turn, enjoy the relaxed atmosphere in the classroom.

Frequently, the learning center is envisioned as a place in the classroom where all instructions are given, where equipment and materials are kept, and where all work is done. If space is limited, a work station may be set up anywhere space is available. Equipment, materials, and instruction may be obtained from a central location and taken to a counter or table—even an open area on the floor—where work can be completed. Although setting up and using learning centers requires more planning than large-group instruction, it is worthwhile for both the teacher and the learner. (A detailed description of a personalized lesson is found in Chapter 6.)

Evaluating the results of personalized instruction does not lend itself to traditional testing. Personalized instruction calls for personalized evaluation of each student's work. This approach offers several advantages to teachers. For one thing, the teacher does not have to construct a formal test each time a lesson is planned. On a daily basis, the teacher has the work of only a few children to review. And when responses are written, the teacher has only a few papers to analyze. Further, with the usual concern about testing alleviated, students are more relaxed. Interestingly, personalized evaluation appears to improve performance; thus grades rise.

Once several children have completed learning center activities, it is well to bring them together to discuss and share their observations. Children need this summarization as an indication that their work is acceptable. In addition, it serves as a time to ask questions. The teacher can use this time to determine whether children are grasping the significance of the topic, and also to offer additional information.

Investigation

Investigation is not an isolated strategy, but rather an appropriate, integral part of every instructional strategy used in teaching children science. Stated simply, investigating is a way of finding an answer to a question.

Various levels of investigation are appropriate for elementary school science. Although all investigations have structure, the extent of the structure varies with the maturity and needs of the student—the investigator.

Investigations begin with a question that can be answered or a problem that can be solved. The result of any investigation must be an answer or solution, sometimes complete and sometimes partial. Such questions as "Why does the sun rise?" are impractical. Certainly the learner may collect information about the movement of the Earth in relation to the sun, but no such observations will clearly answer the question *why*. Consider this question: "Does the time of sunrise vary with the season?" This question can be answered through observation, by recording the times of sunrise for a season. Similarly, the question "Why is chlorophyll green?" cannot be answered by observation. However, the question "What pigments exist in a leaf?" *can* be answered by observation, either by pigment extraction or by observations of leaves throughout summer and fall accompanied by some research on the causes of differences in leaf colors.

Good investigative questions account for the variables involved. In every investigation, something is changed; this is called the manipulated or independent variable. The change may be instigated or only observed by the investigator. The responding or dependent variable is the one affected by change in the independent or manipulated variable. Controlled variables are those that do not change. There are many controlled variables in every investigation. Except for the responding and manipulated variables, the investigator tries to keep all conditions the same as much as possible in all investigations. Allowing controlled variables to change undermines the success of any investigation.

Once variables are identified, the next step is to plan the investigation. Planning includes defining any terms that will be used or that will have some special meaning within the investigation. For example, in a magnet investigation, the term *attract* needs to be defined. For purposes of the investigation, does *attract* imply that the paper clip will be held in one spot by the magnet or that the paper clip will move when the magnet moves? Or that the paper clip will be held in place but later fall from the paper?

In addition, investigators should ensure that any manipulated or responding variables are measurable. The plan should state what is to be measured, how it is to be measured, and how the information is to be reported. Frequently, a graph or chart is used to record measurements.

After the investigation is completed, the question is answered or a conclusion is drawn. The investigator must be able to give information or evidence to support the answer or solution to the problem.

Investigations are fun for both teacher and learner. They add excitement to science classes and enhance learning. Children tend to learn investigative procedures quickly, and they can be effective with any instructional strategy.

Learning Theories

The theories of four researchers—David Ausubel, Jerome Bruner, Robert Gagné, and Jean Piaget—have contributed greatly to the development of elementary science programs.

Ausubel's (1963) research, for example, yielded the concept of advance organizers. An advance organizer is an introduction to content that precedes instruction. It is usually given orally. Advance organizers may serve two purposes: One is to introduce the points to be presented during a lesson before that lesson is taught. This is appropriate when students have little or no knowledge of a topic. A second purpose is to relate new information to what the student already knows. Since advance organizers are usually delivered as lectures, a wide range of content may be presented quickly.

Remember the textbook lesson on "Making Things Look Bigger" (page 72)? The first activity in that lesson served as an advance organizer. Although advance organizers are usually oral, the one in that lesson was written. Defining terms that will be used in a lesson or showing a film prior to a lesson are other examples of using advance organizers.

Jerome Bruner's (1962) research suggests that while children mature at varying rates, they go through observable stages of development in the same sequence, and no child skips a stage. He characterizes the stages as follows:

- Inactive (birth to approximately three): The child learns about the environment by interacting with it perceptionally.

- Iconic (from age three to age seven or eight): The child develops the ability to make mental pictures about experiences that he or she has had. Children at this age are egocentric, which may color their perceptions, and they may view the world inconsistently.
- Symbolic (ages seven or eight to adulthood): During this stage the child develops the ability to use words and symbols for actual experiences. He or she is able to represent thoughts through words and to understand advanced relationships about scientific phenomena.

One of Bruner's major contributions to educational theory is discovery learning. Discovery learning is characterized by the student's active involvement in the learning process. The teacher's role is that of a guide rather than a dispenser of information. Students learn the discovery process through hands-on interaction with the environment. Through the thrill of discovering, the reward for learning becomes internal rather than external. With a discovery approach, the understanding of science content increases—as does the ability to investigate. Bruner strongly urges teachers to use their knowledge about discovery learning to teach children, and urges children to view each discovery as a step toward making others.

Robert Gagné's (1965) work has taken a different direction from that of Ausubel and Bruner. Gagné's theories deal with the effects of instruction on the cognitive processes of the learner. He suggests that as information is taught, it is processed in several ways by the child. The ultimate goal of such processing is the development of an ability to apply new information and concepts to other science concepts, principles and ultimately, inquiry skills. Within this framework, mental events are perceived as transformations of information from stimuli to responses. The process is designated as information processing. For further information, refer to Gagné at the end of the chapter.

The theoretical framework of information processing sheds some light upon the thinking process. Imagine the thinking process working something like a computer program. The brain proceeds through a well-defined sequence of mental activities in processing information. The result is an approximation of reality as the person perceives it. The brain processes the information in the most effective and efficient manner for storage. Piaget theorizes that children's ability to use various mental operations depends upon their cognitive maturity (Ginsburg & Opper, 1969). He also theorizes that they develop at varying rates through a series of invariant steps. All children pass through the same sequences of stages as they mature mentally. Children are held biologically in a developmental stage until their maturation releases them. Much of Piaget's work is based upon the idea that children's thinking is expanded through further interaction with objects, events, and social experiences.

Piaget has identified four stages of development: sensory motor, preoperational, concrete operational, and formal operational. Although Piaget suggests that children tend to remain at stages for a period of time, some ongoing maturation occurs throughout each stage, preparing the child for the next stage.

These brief descriptions can only suggest the influence these four researchers and theorists have had on the teaching of science. The chapters of this book reflect much of what they theorize. The *Looking Forward* section that precedes each chapter serves as an advance organizer. The previous section on investigation illustrates some of the theories of Bruner. Many of the sample activities are based upon Gagné's work. Chapter 2 reflects many of the ideas of Piaget. As you read the following chapters, you may perceive the influence of these four researchers on the authors. Additional information on learning theories is suggested in the references.

NEEDS OF CHILDREN AND TEACHERS

Thus far, most of our attention has been focused upon science and how it is taught. A few additional nuts and bolts of the teaching-learning process remain to be discussed—including the needs of children and teachers and the role science plays in meeting these needs.

Needs of Children

Concern for the needs of students is an inherent part of teaching. Effective teaching requires identifying children's needs and planning instruction to meet those needs.

Needs differ somewhat according to age and maturity level. And a variety of instructional techniques must be used to fulfill children's diverse needs. Various needs of children and suggestions for meeting them are listed in Table 3.4. This list is intended to be illustrative, not exhaustive. Note that many of the identified needs relate to the affective domain, to feelings, values, and self-concept. These needs require teaching techniques that develop and nurture positive human relationships. Another way to look at it is that sometimes you use science instruction as a means of meeting needs, rather than simply teaching science.

Needs of Teachers

Teachers have needs, too. And if their needs are not met, they may find it difficult to effectively utilize instructional strategies, plan lessons,

TABLE 3.4. NEEDS OF CHILDREN

Needs	*Meeting Needs*
Developing an understanding of words and concepts	Helping children describe objects, feelings, and thoughts
Exploring the environment perceptually	Using proper terminology to help children build associations
Forming concepts based upon experiences with concrete objects	Providing opportunities for children to manipulate equipment and ideas
Developing feelings of security in manipulating equipment	Providing opportunities for children to assimilate and accommodate observations
Developing feelings of self-worth	
Beginning to think logically, to give a rationale for ideas	Teaching children to observe critically using all senses
Feeling accepted by teacher and peers	Providing time for children to think when questions are asked
Developing a background of scientific information	Providing opportunities for children to communicate with others
Engaging in interactions with concrete objects rather than abstractions	Using a variety of instructional strategies and techniques
Experiencing a range of learning activities dealing with each science topic or concept introduced	Interacting positively with learners, providing positive reenforcement, and giving assistance when a child becomes frustrated
	Teaching content appropriate for the cognitive maturity of the learner

establish positive human relations, and meet the needs of learners. The prominent need of teachers is really a search for effectiveness and security. Security, in part, is characterized by the following:

- Ability to use a variety of instructional strategies.
- Knowledge of a wide variety of learning activities for various science topics.
- Knowledge of which science topics to teach at various grade levels.
- Availability of equipment and resources for teaching children science.
- Ability to design activity-oriented science lessons.
- Knowledge of modern science programs for the elementary school.
- Ability to manage an investigative science lesson.

Note that many of these needs tend to deal with mechanics of teaching. This is primarily because in learning content and learning about equipment and resources, teachers increase their feelings of security and confidence.

——————— *LOOKING BACK* ———————————————————————

1. Of what practical importance to teachers is considering the act of teaching as an art and a science?
2. Of what significance is the interaction between teacher and student in an effective science program?
3. What unique qualities of interaction between student and content affect the teaching of science in the elementary school?
4. What rationale could you offer for considering needs of teachers when science instructional methodology is discussed?

ACTIVITIES

1. Read the following questions to determine if each is managerial, rhetorical, closed, or open.
   a. What did adding two dry cells to an electric circuit do to the brightness of the light?
   b. Of what significance is the evidence that some substances prevent viruses from attaching themselves to the membrane of an animal cell?
   c. Did everyone see the cross section of the leaf under the microscope?
   d. Isn't it wonderful that green plants make their own food?

   Question a is closed. It asks the student to recall an observation. Question b is open. It is intended to promote discussion. This question differs from the rhetorical question in that some information about the effects of the virus attaching itself to the cell membrane is available; however, there are questions that are not answered.

   Question c is managerial. The teacher is determining whether all learners have seen what was intended.

   Question d is rhetorical. The teacher asked a question with no answer expected from the children.

2. Background: You have just completed a lesson with your class on the properties of leaves. The children went outside and collected leaves from a variety of plants and then listed properties of leaves. The concluding discussion aims at helping students to identify one list of properties that can be used to classify leaves into different groups.

Direction: Write questions which use the content of the lesson described above as a focus and which elicit student response at each of these three levels:

- Recall (knowledge)
- Comprehension
- Application

Your questions could take a variety of forms. The following examples may help you assess your efforts. Recall: Jimmy, will you name a property of this leaf, please? Comprehension: What properties would you feel are essential in identifying an object as a leaf? Application: [Holding up a paper cutout of a leaf] Does this drawing have the characteristics common to most leaves?

In your interactions with students you should strive to utilize a mix of questions at different levels and types and avoid using a preponderance of knowledge (recall) questions.

3. Obtain an audiotape of one half hour of your teaching or the teaching of another. Analyze it for the following points:

   a. Number of questions asked by teacher and children.
   b. Time given for children to respond to questions.
   c. Type of questions asked.

   You may wish to refer to some of the information about questions given earlier. Do the questions appear to encourage children to respond? If not, what changes could you suggest? If this is your own teaching, implement the changes and record and analyze the tape again. Were the desired results evident?

4. Identify the manipulated and/or responding variable in the following activities:

   a. The effect of varying amounts of fertilizer upon the rate of plant growth.
   b. The effects of exercise (e.g., jumping jacks) on pulse rate.
   c. The effects of different kinds of music.
   d. The results of identifying different odors.
   e. The path of light transmitted through plexiglass.

   Option **a** has both a manipulated variable (varying amounts of fertilizer) and a responding variable (changes in growth rate).

   Option **b** has a manipulated variable (number of jumping jacks) and a responding variable (pulse rate).

   Option **c** has only a manipulated variable (effects of different kinds of music).

   Option **d** has only a responding variable (identify different odors).

   Option **e** has no variables. It is merely a description of a possible observation and is not set up as an investigative activity.

REFERENCES

Aschner, M. J. (1961). Asking questions to trigger thinking. *NEA Journal, 50.*

Barufaldi, James P., Ladd, George, and Moses, Alice (1985). *Science* (Teachers edition, Level 5). Lexington, MA: D.C. Heath & Co.

Bruner, Jerome S. (1962). *The process of education.* Cambridge, MA: Harvard University Press.

Bloom, B., et al. (1956). *Taxonomy of educational objectives: Handbook I.* New York: David McKay Co.

Blosser, P. E. (1975). *How to ask the right questions.* Washington, DC: National Science Teachers Association.

Carin, A. A. (1970). Techniques for developing discovery questioning skill. *Science and Children 7(7).*

Gagné, Robert M. (1965). *The conditions of learning.* New York: Holt, Rinehart and Winston.

Ginsburg H., and Opper S. (1969). *Piaget's theory of intellectual development.* Englewood Cliffs, N.J.: Prentice-Hall.

Hunkings, F. P. (1972). *Questioning strategies and techniques.* Boston: Allyn and Bacon.

Hyman, R. T. (1974). *Ways of teaching.* Philadelphia: J. P. Lippincott Co.

Rowe, M. B. (1978). *Teaching science as continuous inquiry: A basic 2-E.* New York: McGraw-Hill.

Sanders, N. M. (1966). *Classroom questioning, what kind.* New York: Harper and Row.

4

Integrating Science Content, Inquiry Skills, and Attitudes

Objectives

1. To describe at least three characteristics of contemporary science content.
2. To identify several ways in which new science content may be integrated into a science program.
3. To identify characteristics of inquiry skills and their effect in a science program.
4. To describe the relationship between science content and inquiry skills.
5. To specify the role of science in the development of scientific attitudes.

LOOKING FORWARD

Discussions of contemporary elementary school science frequently deal with science content and inquiry skills. Development of scientific attitude is seldom stressed. This chapter examines the interrelationships among science content, inquiry skills, and attitude. The interrelationships are discussed within the framework of grade levels.

Science content may be thought of as the topics taught at a specified grade level. Inquiry is the means of exploring those topics. Scientific attitudes characterize how children view their science experience. And those attitudes tend to evolve throughout life.

Within this chapter, procedures for integrating the three aspects of contemporary elementary school science are examined. We'll consider this integration within the context of three broad categories of science: physical, biological, and earth/space science.

The chapter also presents topics that are generally used for teaching inquiry skills and helping children develop positive attitudes. Although many science textbook series are currently in use, the information provided should be compatible with most series.

In this age of rapidly expanding knowledge, many teachers may question which science textbook is appropriate for the elementary school. They may also question whether science textbooks and programs reflect new information. In this chapter we attempt to answer two important questions: First, what science curriculum is appropriate for the contemporary elementary school? And second, what is the purpose of studying science in the elementary school?

CONTEMPORARY ELEMENTARY SCHOOL SCIENCE

Contemporary elementary school science is much more encompassing than topics contained in a textbook. It comprises not only information, but also inquiry skills, concepts, attitudes, and relationships among these elements.

For many years, elementary school science programs were limited to the information in textbooks. But the emphasis now is on active involvement—by students and teachers. Science has become a verb rather than a noun.

With the current knowledge explosion, teachers are no longer expected to know all the facts of science. Much of what they learned themselves as students may be outdated. Thus, they must rely upon current sources of information, and must feel secure enough to admit that they don't know all the answers to children's questions. Teachers need not know all the facts to be effective or to present science dynamically. All of us are better versed in science than we realize; all of us can learn a great deal of science through reading, informal experience, and careful observation of our environment. The quest for scientific knowledge is exciting, both personally and professionally.

SCIENCE CONTENT

Science content, of course, is critical as the basis for discovering additional information. This was true in the distant past and will be true in the distant future—regardless of whether that information comes from casual observation, from formal instruction, or from planned experiences.

Sometimes unplanned events can teach us a lot. Children who witness a tornado or hurricane, or its aftermath, may have many questions about the storm, the forces that destroyed property and injured people, weather prediction, or safety. The death of a pet or classroom animal may trigger questions on the meaning of death, or the results of death. Unanticipated events may or may not relate to the current topic under study. Either way, it is worthwhile to discuss the events during science class—either formally or informally—to take advantage of children's curiosity and readiness for further inquiry.

To derive maximum benefit from these discussions, it is most helpful to question children about their observations, their interpretations of the observations, and their way of relating these observations to previous knowledge or concepts. The following example illustrates methods for using incidental content.

Scenario

During the middle of March, six inches of snow fell in central Georgia. This much snow is unusual anytime in central Georgia, but is certainly unexpected in mid-March. The school was closed for a day while roads were cleared and transportation problems were solved. When the children returned to school they were excited about their experiences with the snow. Second-grade teachers responded to the children's excitement by encouraging them to discuss their experiences, carefully guiding the discussion with questions. The children were asked whether they knew what snow was. In response to several questions, children brought a sample of snow into the classroom and watched it melt. Once the snow had melted, they quickly discovered that it was a form of water. One teacher asked them if they knew what a snowflake looked like. No one had closely observed just one snowflake. The children were taken outside where the temperature was near freezing (32° Fahrenheit or 0° Celsius). The teacher found one flake, and placed it upon a thin piece of transparent plastic that had been chilled on top of the snow. The children looked at the snowflake through a hand lens. They were amazed at its delicate structure. When the flake melted, the teacher placed another on the plastic, and asked the children to describe it. Although they found this task difficult, they did notice that all the snowflakes had six sides and that no two snowflakes looked alike.

Following their observations, the teachers and children went back inside and discussed their observations of snowflakes; they also discussed changes the snow caused in people's daily routines. The children recalled playing in the snow and riding down slopes on sheets of corrugated cardboard or any other object that could be found. They concluded that packed snow was slippery. The teacher asked if they had any idea why sand was spread over the walkways to the school. No one had an idea. They were taken outside a second time. On this trip, they took an empty paper box with them, and placed it on the walkway that was covered by sand and packed snow. A small child sat in the box as the other children took turns pushing it. Later, they moved to an area covered by packed snow but no sand. Again a small child sat in the box while the other children pushed it. The children quickly discovered that the box was easier to push where there was no sand. The children were asked where they would rather walk to avoid falling. They agreed they would be less likely to fall on the sanded walks—although walking there would not be as much fun.

This experience took a great deal of time, but it was worthwhile. The children later wrote creative stories about their experiences. Some hunted through the library in search of information about people and places where snow is common. These teachers had succeeded. They took advantage of an event when it occurred to provide effective instruction that increased students' inquiry skills and gave them a positive attitude toward science instruction.

While experience is invaluable, another important source of science content is the elementary science textbook. A review of science textbooks for children reveals much variation among topics and content areas. However, there are some similarities in topics at various grade levels. Representative content for various grade levels is presented in Table 4.1.

In the past, the science topics taught in elementary school tended to be somewhat stable. Most textbooks covered electricity, magnetism, plants, animals, heat, light, and sound. Furthermore, information about these topics tended to be standard. That is no longer the case. With the recent expansion of scientific knowledge, many new topics have been added to the science program. Some examples are presented in Table 4.2.

TABLE 4.1. REPRESENTATIVE TOPICS IN SCIENCE TEXTBOOKS

Grade Level	Categories of Topics		
	Life Science	Physical Science	Earth/Space Science
K	Five senses Plant parts Animals Seeds Parts of the human body	Properties of objects Changes in objects Objects in the environment	Seasonal changes Weather Moon Shadows
1	Living and nonliving things Structure of animals Nutrition Kinds of living organisms Classifying animals	Sinking objects Temperature Magnets Heat Light Motion Focus	Changes in shadows Rocks Moon Mars Changes in rocks
4	Insects Green plants Population Ocean life Human skeleton Nutrition Ecology Environmental quality Microscopic organisms	Changes in phases of matter Physical changes Chemical changes Heat	Solar system Atmosphere Rocks Natural resources Plants Water cycle Earth
5	Cells of living organisms Changes in organisms over time Animal behavior Systems of the human body The senses Plant studies Reproduction Genetics Health Life cycles Carbon dioxide cycle Microscopic life	Measuring matter Light Sound Electricity Floating matter Energy transfer Forces Magnetic forces Energy transfer Physical properties	Changes in the earth Energy source Fossils Rocks Forces Gravitation Black holes Binary stars Heat and motion

TABLE 4.2. NEW TOPICS IN SCIENCE TEXTBOOKS

Categories of Topics	New Topics
Physical sciences Metric measurement	Exclusive use of metric units
Energy	Fission and fusion Nuclear energy Alternate sources of energy Solar, geothermal, wind, and tidal energy
Matter	Crystalline structure
Electronics	Transistors
Radiation	Semiconductors Electromagnetic spectrum Ultraviolet radiation Infrared radiation
Light	Holography Lasers
Earth/space sciences Geological timetables	Radiometric dating Half-life of elements Plate tectonics Seismology Greenhouse effect Ozone layer Renewable natural resources Nuclear waste disposal Environmental quality Water management Acid rain
The universe	Binary stars Black holes Characteristics of planets Quasars Quarks
Biological sciences	Food supply and distribution Overpopulation Death education Noise pollution
Societal topics	Genetic engineering Disease control and treatment
Health	Recreation Drug and alcohol abuse Smoking Personal maintenance Mental health World health problems Immunology
Biological energy sources	Biomass Photosynthesis

Information on many of these topics is available from newspapers and magazines, news broadcasts and television documentaries, political debates involving scientists, and various other sources. Although the topics are new, they now have a permanent place in the science curriculum—as will additional topics that continue to be introduced at a rapid rate.

INQUIRY SKILLS

While the term *inquiry skills* may be new to you, you have been using them most of your life. Inquiry skills permit you to make discoveries about objects and events in your environment. Inquiry skills involve observations, manipulations, restructuring of events, and interpretation of events. Briefly, inquiry skills develop as we *learn how to learn.*

The ability to use inquiry skills is related to mental maturity. Younger children, grades K through 3, can be taught to use those skills that rely heavily on perception and require limited cognitive action. Children in grades 4 through 6 can be taught to use skills demanding higher cognitive processes as well as perceptual components. (You may wish to reread that section of Chapter 2 covering the cognitive abilities of the developing learner.)

Inquiry skills of the sort covered in the following add a dynamic quality to science instruction. They encourage children to investigate, to use prior knowledge in making discoveries, and to communicate their new knowledge to others. Although inquiring requires more time than reading about and discussing science, the children who are participants in their own learning and the teachers who witness firsthand their joy of discovery agree that it's time well spent.

Observing

The process of observing is as old as history, yet we continue to learn more about it. Observing requires the use of the five senses to identify attributes of or changes in objects and events, and to interpret the meanings of those changes. For instance, children who observe changes in leaf color from green to yellow or red may interpret that change in color as indicating a change of season. Colors are identified through sight, shapes and sizes through sight or touch. Sounds are identified mainly through hearing—though visual association (e.g., seeing a book fall on the floor) may also play a part. Many objects are identified through the sense of smell. Identifying characteristics like *sweet* or *salty* requires the sense of taste. Determining smoothness or roughness requires the sense of touch.

The art left by past civilizations offers evidence that observation and interpretation are not new skills. Drawings of animals and hunting scenes that cover the walls of caves suggest that ancient man, much like the young science investigators of today, tended to focus on the immediate environment. Children, from the time of birth, observe the objects and events in their immediate surroundings. As they mature, their observation skills become refined, and the need for detail increases—often forcing them to rely on scientific instruments to make very precise observations.

LESSON ON TEXTURE

Suppose children are learning about textures. Would the following activity be satisfactory? Let's say they are given a pebble, a broken piece of rock, a plastic pan with water in it, and an index card with a small amount of cooking oil on it. They are asked to identify the textures of the objects. After touching the objects, they say the pebble is smooth, the broken piece of rock is sharp, the wet plastic pan is slippery, and the index card is oily or slippery. Note that of all the terms used to describe what the children feel, only one relates to texture: *smooth.* There is some confusion between texture as a rough or smooth surface, and texture as a word commonly used to describe a variety of "feels." There are only two textures but an infinite number of "feels."

LESSON USING TWO SENSES

Children observe through all their senses, and often through a combination of senses. For instance, suppose a child is given a box containing several objects which cannot be seen, then asked to make observations about those objects using the senses of touch and hearing. The child might shake the box, listening to sounds the objects make as they move, or feel the box as objects move. Children can feel heavy objects as they hit the side of the box or can feel objects rolling. Using just these two senses, the child would be able to determine that there were several objects in the box, to identify the shape of the objects, approximate the weight of some of the objects, and describe the composition of the objects. If a child offered no observations, the teacher might ask questions that would encourage him or her to listen to and feel the objects in the box as it was tilted.

Children frequently misinterpret the intent of making observations. In the example above, for instance, they might feel it was paramount to name the objects rather than describe their characteristics. Identifying such attributes as shape, weight, and size takes careful observation and concentration. Simply naming the objects with those attributes misses the purpose of the activity. Since many objects may have the same attributes, it is not possible for the children to know whether they have named the objects correctly unless the box is opened. If this is done, forget about observing with the senses of touch and hearing and concentrate on visual observations.

Teaching children to observe encourages them to concentrate on the *attributes* of objects and events. For instance, young children may be given a magnet and told to find out all they can about it. Through exploration, the children discover the texture, dimensions, color, and shape of the object. They also discover that it will stick to paper clips, thumbtacks, and the metal band on a ball point pen—but that it will not stick to paper, plastic, or wood. It will "pull" objects through a leaf, a sheet of plastic, the petals of a flower, paper, hair, cloth, or a rubber band. Children encouraged to develop observational skills learn to teach themselves about the world.

Observational skills for children at higher grade levels continue to be perceptual. However, their observations tend to be goal-directed, rather than random. For instance, let's say children are to observe which objects placed in an electric circuit will permit electricity to pass over them. They may try such objects as paper, pencils, pans, fingernails, aluminum foil, rubber bands, and the metal wire in spiral notebooks. All their efforts are directed toward answering a specific question: Which objects will complete the circuit?

Or, as part of another activity, they may rub the "green stuff" (pigments) from maple leaves on the paper towel strip about 2 centimeters from the end and place the paper towel in isopropyl alcohol with the green section sticking out. As the alcohol moves up the paper towel and past the green spot, children observe not only the green color, but also some yellow and reddish brown. They observe that parts of the color, which came from the green spot, were not all green. These observations raise questions about the composition of colors.

In a third activity, children mix plaster of paris with water in a container they hold in their hands. As the water and plaster of paris mix, they feel heat—which they may correctly interpret as a chemical change. This observation has extended their knowledge about the nature of chemical change.

Notice that in all three activities, the children used their perceptual skills. But they used them in a very directed and focused way, rather than simply (like the younger students) to make random observations.

Inferring

A skill closely allied with observing is inferring. Inferring consists of making a series of observations, combining and categorizing them, and finally attempting to interpret them. Distinguishing between observations and inferences is important. Observations are perceptual, while inferences are interpretive.

Inferring is a vital process in the study of science because much that cannot be perceived directly can be inferred from evidence or observations made using scientific instruments. For instance, the existence and location of subatomic particles have been identified from X-ray diffraction. The existence of black holes has been inferred from evidence gathered by astronomers. As scientific knowledge expands, inferences become increasingly important.

Measuring

Measuring is the skill of quantifying observations, frequently using numbers. Distances, time, volumes, and temperature are some of the observations which can be quantified either with standard or nonstandard units. If you were to measure distance using a pencil, hold two objects to find which was heavier, or give a friend a "handful" of candy, you would be using nonstandard units. If you used some measuring instrument such as a meter stick, a thermometer, a metric measuring cup, or a balance, you would be measuring in standard units. Unlike nonstandard units, standard units do not change. Pencils come in many sizes. But a centimeter is the same length all over the world and on through time.

In addition to quantifying some attributes, an observer may need to arrange the attributes according to the degree to which some characteristic is displayed. For instance, crayons may be put in order according to length; leaves may be placed in some order according to surface area. Colored objects may be arranged from light to dark, rocks from rough to smooth.

Placing objects and events in ordered sequence is called *seriation*. Some events, such as seasons, may be seriated in a recurring cycle. The life cycles for some insects—from egg to larva to pupa to adult—may also be seriated in this way. Numbers are sequenced too, as are letters of the alphabet.

Learning to use measurements is important both for professional scientists and young learners. Children are often asked questions that require measurements, but are not given the opportunity to do the measuring. For instance, suppose they are asked how rapidly a dye dissolved in water travels through a celery rib. If they have not been taught to use measurements dealing with centimeters and minutes, this question will be difficult to answer in any precise way. Or, they may be asked how rapidly ice melts under certain conditions. This will be simpler if they have been instructed in procedures for weighing or finding the volume of liquid water in specified units of time. Children must be taught to measure using such quantities as length, time, volume, weight, and size. They must also be taught to measure changes in these quantities in specific units of time such as seconds, minutes, hours, and days. They must also learn to express observed, measurable changes in such units as centimeters per minute, milliliters per second, and so forth. You may wish to review the activity with colored water and celery in Chapter 1. Your measuring skills can be used to determine how rapidly colored water moves through a celery rib.

Classifying

Classifying incorporates several subskills. One is sorting a set of objects into subgroups, so that members of each subgroup share a common characteristic unique to that subgroup. For example, if very young children are given a set of red, blue, yellow, and green paper squares, they could be asked to place the squares in subgroups by color.

Sometimes classifying calls for selecting a characteristic, then creating two subgroups—one with the characteristic, one without. If children were to create a classification scheme based on the color red, all members of one subgroup would be red, while the members of the second subgroup would be any color except red. This is a classification scheme used frequently for classifying plants and animals.

Occasionally children are asked to construct groups based upon a characteristic that has little meaning except in relation to some standard. For instance, they may be asked to group objects as *large* or *small*. Without some definition or example to go by, it is really not possible to say which objects are *large* and which are *small*. Other nebulous characteristics are hard and soft, hot and cold, more and less, light and heavy, and short and long. Relative characteristics can only be stated in comparative terms (e.g., this rock is small compared to that one). To remedy the situation some standard is needed. If objects are to be grouped according to length (long and short), the members of one group may be shorter than the child's finger while members of the other group are longer than the child's finger. The finger in this example is used as a standard of measurement.

Using a standard is a valuable technique for scientists. Chemists wishing to measure a quantity of a substance accurately would use a set of standard weights. Scientists wishing to measure the quantity of a liquid would use a graduated cylinder. (*Graduated* meaning that there are marks on the cylinder at regular intervals to indicate quantity.)

In another kind of subgrouping, certain characteristics are specified, and any object having those characteristics is said to be a member of that group. For instance, if an animal is covered with scales, lives in water, and has gills, it is classified as a fish. If a plant has leaves that look like needles, does not lose all its leaves in winter, and produces cones, it is classified as a conifer.

Classification requires careful observation. It is an excellent way to encourage children to observe attributes; it is an experience that many children enjoy.

Manipulating and Controlling Variables

The process of manipulating a variable begins when the investigator selects a variable to be changed or observed. For example, suppose an investigator wishes to determine if adding differing amounts of fertilizer to the water used in watering plants has any effect upon changes in stem length. The manipulated variable is the amount of fertilizer. The investigator is the one making the change; he or she determines the amount of fertilizer that will be dissolved in the water for the various plants.

Another investigator wishes to determine whether there is any change over time in the length of a shadow cast by a stick. The shadow is measured at noon each week over a period of six weeks. The manipulated or selected variable is the six-week period; however, it is a variable that the investigator did not intrinsically change. It is a variable that changes independently.

In any investigation only one variable should be manipulated at a time. If more than one variable is manipulated, the investigator cannot determine which variable produced a given result, or whether some combination of variables produced a result. For instance, if an investigator varied the amount of fertilizer *and* the amount of water that plants received, it would not be possible to determine which variable might have accounted for differences in rates of growth.

Aside from the one variable selected for change, the investigator has a responsibility to see that as many other variables as possible are unchanged. This is known as controlling variables. In the plant investigation example some of the variables that may have been controlled include using only one kind of plant, giving the same amount of water to each plant, measuring the amounts of fertilizer given to each plant, keeping all plants in the same place to ensure consistent light and temperature, and watering all the plants on the same schedule.

Interpreting Data

During science activities much information is collected, organized, and graphed. But if stockpiling information is all that happens, an experience is of little value. Information must be interpreted to provide insight. Frequently the term "interpreting" means asking the question "What do the data and information mean?"

Defining Operationally

An operational definition is one designed by the investigator to clarify his or her meaning for terms, actions, conditions, or results within the scope of an investigation. For instance, the term *healthy* could be defined operationally as describing a specified change in a plant's stem length over a given period. Frequently operational definitions can be illustrated as well as verbalized. For instance, gravity can be described as the attraction of the earth for objects as well as illustrated by dropping an object and noting the direction it falls.

Formulating Hypotheses

A hypothesis is a statement of a relationship which may exist between two variables. A hypothesis is more formal than an investigative question. The hypothesis states that a relationship is likely; the investigative question merely asks whether any relationship exists. In formulating a hypothesis, investigators call upon their background knowledge and experience as well as information from other investigations. A hypothesis gives direction to the investigation itself and to later interpretation of data.

Communication

One secret to effective communication is understanding scientific terminology. This must not be construed to mean that children should memorize terms. However, if they understand the meaning of terms used in context, they can describe interactions between objects or the results of actions. This is another way of saying that they need to feel comfortable using operational definitions.

Students who work with numbers must learn to read—and sometimes construct—graphs. Graphing communicates a relationship between two variables or conditions. A bar graph may state a relationship between flavors of ice cream and the number of people who like each flavor. It may express the relationship between the quantity of a substance dissolved in water and the time required for the water to freeze. Graphing and interpreting relationships can help answer investigative questions. For instance: What is the relationship between the amount of salt dissolved in a cup of water and the amount of time required for the water to freeze? The investigator might construct any hypothesis—but perhaps the graphed results would prove surprising. (You may wish to try this investigation.) Note that the investigator is assuming that some relationship exists between the amount of salt and freezing time. This is the beginning of formulating a hypothesis. The hypothesis is further defined when the investigator specifies the relationship that is anticipated.

Making Predictions

Children are able to predict based on their background experiences. For instance, they may predict that a car will crash if it travels at excessive speeds around a turn. They may also predict that rain will fall if there are dark clouds in the sky, if thunder is heard, and if there is wind. Prediction is the process of identifying the *likelihood* rather than the certainty of an event.

INTEGRATING INQUIRY SKILLS AND CONTENT

Inquiry skills are frequently taught in isolation from science content. However, they are best considered as a means of asking and answering questions about scientific information, by learning science content, and by developing thinking skills. Children do not learn effectively at a distance. They learn about magnification by looking through a lens, not by memorizing information about magnification. They learn molecular structure by making a model of a molecule with gumdrops and toothpicks, or about chemical change by observing a release of gas, a release of energy, a color change, and the formation of a precipitate. The mysteries of rocks are revealed as samples are broken and examined, and as acids produce bubbling on some samples and not others. Children do not need to memorize which rocks will withstand scratching by nails. They can experiment for themselves and record their observations about scratching rocks.

When presented with fine white powders and given a lens, iodine solution, vinegar, water, and matches, children are able to answer the question "What are the characteristics of each powder that makes it different from the other powders?" They can later use their skills to determine whether unlabeled mixtures contain any of the original powders.

When presented with a box containing four different shapes (square, parallelogram, triangle, and circle) in two different sizes and four different colors, they can draw the shapes out one by one and arrange them in some pattern as they are drawn from the box. As the pattern develops, the children can use it to predict which shapes remain in the box. Eventually, they have enough information through experience and inference to answer this question: "Does the box contain a large yellow triangle or a smaller green circle?" Through inquiry skills children are able to answer a wide array of investigative questions.

Although very young children are generally considered incapable of logical thinking, many researchers believe that children are capable of logical thinking that deals with the here and now, with an object or event with which they are interacting at the present time. Here is an illustration.

Scenario

In a kindergarten classroom, a group of five-year-olds were investigating the effect of adding weight to a toy truck on the distance it could travel when placed on a ramp and released. One end of a ramp was 2 decimeters from the floor. A truck was placed at the top of the ramp and released. This was repeated five times and the distance was measured each time. The children observed that the truck did not travel exactly the same distance each time. The teacher explained that it would be difficult to try to compare five different distances that the truck traveled without weights. Therefore, the teacher calculated the average of the five distances and marked the distance on the floor with tape.

Next the truck was placed on the ramp and a 50-gram weight was placed in it. It was released five times and the distances were averaged. Again the distance the weighted truck traveled was marked on the floor with tape. The average travel distance for the unweighted truck was compared with the average travel distance for the weighted truck. The children observed that the truck traveled farther with the weight than without the weight.

As the distances were being measured, one boy observed that the truck appeared to travel the distance of the ramp each time. He suggested that the distance of the ramp be measured and added to the distance the truck traveled on the floor. The teacher asked the boy why this should be done. He replied that the truck started from the same place on the ramp each time and always traveled the entire length of the ramp. This procedure was followed thereafter each time the truck was released on the ramp.

When this activity was completed, several children asked what would happen to the distance the truck traveled if the ramp were raised. The teacher reminded them that they should be comparing distances with an unweighted truck each time. Overall, the truck investigation required a greal deal of logical thinking to plan, conduct, and interpret.

The preceding classroom example required a great deal of information (content) as well as a means of getting and interpreting information (inquiry skills). Can you identify where children used content and inquiry skills in the toy truck scenario? The following examples from the life, physical, and earth sciences for young children (grades K through 3) and older children (grades 4 through 6) should help familiarize you with methods for integrating content and process.

Grades K Through 3

Since younger learners are activity-oriented, why not capitalize on their active nature? Several appropriate activities utilizing inquiry skills follow. (Although the activities are designed for children, you may wish to conduct them before presenting them to students.)

LIFE SCIENCE LESSON: BODY PARTS OF AN INSECT

Give children a collection of insects (fly, wasp or bee, grasshopper, ant, beetle, butterfly, moth or any insects you can obtain. Ask children to look at the insects and count the legs and wings (observation, using numbers). Ask them to look at the body of the insect (observing), count the body parts (using numbers), and name any they know. Holding up a butterfly, point to the head. Ask if anyone knows the name of this body part. If no one knows, tell the children that is the *head.* Point to the next part just back of the head. Ask if anyone knows the name of this part. If not, give the name *thorax.* Point to the third part of the insect body. Ask if anyone knows the name of that part. If not, give the name *abdomen.* Give the children paper circles 2 inches in diameter and elliptical paper shapes 2 inches long. Some paper circles should be red and others yellow. The elliptical shapes should be blue. The red circle is a head, the blue circle is the thorax, and the elliptical shape is the abdomen. Ask the children to place the three body parts in the same order they are in on the insect's body. Ask children to name and point to the body parts of an insect by using the paper shapes (communicating).

This activity could be continued by asking children to construct an insect from parts that you supply and comparing their constructed insect with a real insect. Depending upon the maturity of the children, you may want to include the antennae.

PHYSICAL SCIENCE LESSON: LIGHTS AND SHADOWS

Ask the children to go outside to a paved area of the playground. The children stand in the sunlight; they observe their shadows. They draw outlines of their feet with chalk and write their names next to the outlines. Next, outlines of their shadows are drawn by the teacher. They are asked to look at shadows of other children and to tell if they are different or alike (observing). How are they different and alike (observing)? They are asked to return to the place where they stood, standing in the marked feet outlines and see if they can make a shadow that is longer than the original shadow (measuring); a shadow that is wider than the original shadow (measuring); a shadow that is smaller than the original shadow (measuring).

The lesson may be continued by observing changes in shadows throughout the day. If a study were continued over a longer period of time—say, a matter of months—records could be made of weekly changes in shadows, with observations made at the same time of day.

EARTH SCIENCE LESSON: PARTICLES IN THE ATMOSPHERE

Children are given 5-centimeter squares of transparent hard plastic. Then a light coating of petroleum jelly is rubbed over each square. Several children place their squares in the classroom. Others place their squares near an unpaved area on the school campus where softball, baseball, and basketball are played. A third set of squares is placed outside in a protected area. Before the squares are placed, they are laid on white paper and a photo is taken of them. The squares are left in place for a week. When the squares are collected, they are compared with the photo to determine the amount of particulate matter on the squares (observing). The squares from the three sites are then placed over newsprint to compare the relative clarity (observing). The squares are put in order from those having the least amount of particulate matter to those having the most (seriating). Children are asked to explain the differences they observed (inferring).

The lesson may be expanded by placing the squares in a variety of places. (You may also wish to read several activities in science textbooks for grades K through 3 and identify the inquiry skills children must use to complete each activity.)

Grades 4 Through 6

Children in grades 4 through 6 may use any inquiry skill which is appropriate. Sometimes the skills are used separately, and other times they are used in combination. As the learner matures, higher level skills are used. Although many of the skills involve manipulations, cognition becomes more prominent. (You may wish to refer to Chapter 2 to review the cognitive abilities displayed by children as they mature.) In the following sample activities, inquiry skills are used to develop understanding of science content.

PHYSICAL SCIENCE LESSON

This lesson deals with density of objects. Each child is given a metric ruler, a container half full of water, blocks of wood, an iron magnet, 10 grams of plasticene clay, and a bar of soap. Several balances and metric weights are available. Children are to test each object by placing it in the water to determine if it sinks or floats (a). The children construct a table on which to record the names of the objects, and their mass, volume, and density. The masses of the objects are found by weighing them (b). The amount of the mass, in grams, is written in the table (c). Next, using the ruler, the children calculate the volume of each object (b). The volumes are also written in the table (c). Using the formula *Density = Mass / Volume,* the students calculate the density of each object. They are told that the density of water is 1 gram of mass for each milliliter of volume. They are asked to refer back to their observations about objects which sank and which floated. They are instructed to look at the table and compare the density of objects that sank with the density of water (d). They are also asked to compare the densities of objects that floated with the density of water (d). They are then asked to describe the relationship between sinking and floating as a function of relative (to water) density (e).

You might follow this activity by giving the children other objects and materials such as cooking oil, honey, a ceramic tile, and a glass, then asking them to measure the mass and volume and calculate the density. Finally, ask them to predict whether the objects will sink or float (e).

Can you name the inquiry skills (a through e) indicated in the example? The inquiry skills are: (a) observing; (b) measuring, using numbers; (c) communicating; (d) interpreting data; (e) hypothesizing.

Through the use of inquiry skills, children may become proficient in measuring mass and volume, calculating densities of objects (solids, liquids, and gases), interpreting data, and generating hypotheses. As this example shows, the study of density can be an active process with some problem-solving elements, not just a routine mathematical exercise.

BIOLOGICAL SCIENCE LESSON

For this lesson, the class is divided into pairs of students. Each pair is given a box containing the cleaned and bleached bones of an animal skeleton and an empty box approximately 45 centimeters wide, 65 centimeters long, and 5 centimeters high. A piece of felt or burlap is placed at the bottom of the empty box. The children are then asked to assemble the bones of the animal. They are instructed to take the bones from the box and lay them where they can be seen easily. Children look at the bones carefully (a). They then refer to a picture of a mounted skeleton. Some groups begin by separating the vertebrae and skull from the other bones; other groups begin to separate ribs or bones of appendages (b). As the groups begin to assemble the bones, a variety of skills are used. (Note: This lesson requires several days.)

What inquiry skills are used?

The inquiry skills here are: (a) observing; (b) interpreting data. This lesson may be followed by individual work on another animal skeleton or by an activity in which students study one bone from an animal and draw whatever inferences they can about the animal.

EARTH SCIENCE LESSON

This lesson deals with the release of lava from an active volcano. (The nature of this lesson dictates that much of the information be presented through resource materials and analogies.) The class is divided into five or six groups; each group is assigned to review volcanic activity in various places in the earth such as the Hawaiian Islands, the West Coast of the United States, Mexico, Southeast Asia, and the floor of the Pacific Ocean.

They are to collect information about volcanoes, both active and dormant, in the assigned geographic area. Each group is to construct a model of an inactive or presently active volcano in the assigned area, showing such events as the path of lava flow, the extent of lava flow, the environmental alterations, descriptions of lava as it is spewing in the air, the appearance of the land following a lava flow (the Forest of Devastation on the Big Island in Hawaii is an excellent example), and other factors of interest (a). Models of active volcanoes such as Mount St. Helens or Kilowea may be kept and lava flows added; future changes of the environment may be predicted as a result of investigations concerning lava flow (b).

The inquiry skills used are (a) observing; (b) hypothesizing. Since volcanic events tend to be unpredictable, the models may be kept and updated. This lesson may be followed by further research on the environmental advantages and disadvantages of lava flows. Such factors as the effects on land, people, vegetation, air quality, and economic conditions may be investigated.

SCIENTIFIC ATTITUDES

Much has been written about scientific attitudes. But while virtually everyone agrees that the development of a positive scientific attitude is a worthwhile goal, it is difficult to define and equally difficult to emphasize in an elementary science lesson.

Developing Scientific Attitudes

Positive scientific attitudes have been diversely characterized as enthusiasm for science, willingness to share opinions and beliefs, curiosity, ability to base judgments upon evidence, open-mindedness, and objectivity. Regardless of their specific nature, scientific attitudes are personal qualities that require some time to develop.

Frequently, teachers are role models whose attitudes may be emulated by the children they teach. Therefore, the actions of teachers in the classroom should reflect a positive disposition toward science. We live in a scientific and technological age, with every promise that it will become more so. It is imperative, therefore, that teachers look upon the discipline of science as a basic subject. Specifically, teachers can encourage positive attitudes by showing that they are eager and willing to learn, and that they value the power of science to improve the quality of our lives. Consider the possibilities for curing cancer through the analysis of blood with magnetic resonance, or the possibility that additional planets exist in our solar system, that we will better understand the mechanism of human genetics through the study of yeast cells, or that someone will develop a polyester sweetener that is not absorbed by the human body—thus helping reduce human weight problems.

Admittedly, many teachers associate science with negative experiences they had as students. They may have left the science course uninspired, disinterested, fearful of science, and totally convinced they were incapable of learning or understanding science—much less teaching it. These experiences should not overshadow all the positive aspects of science. If you're like most of us, perhaps you recall times when you felt that you would never be able to parallel-park. But most likely, you did not let one set of negative experiences prevent you from reaching your ultimate goal: driving a car well.

In order to serve as good role models for students, teachers must be willing to base judgments upon evidence, must invite and compare opposing opinions, constantly inquire about the world around them, and feel secure in encouraging children who may know more than they do about technology. These expressions offer very powerful models for children. You may feel that encouraging children to develop positive attitudes will be too difficult, or that it will take too long. Keep in mind that developing positive attitudes takes time. Enjoy your teaching and the learning that goes with it. Let students see how pleased you are by each success, each new discovery. Your enthusiasm will be more contagious than you imagine.

Depending upon the grade level of the child, there are several methods for initiating and reinforcing behaviors indicative of positive scientific attitudes.

VALUES AND CONTROVERSIAL TOPICS

Controversy over the teaching of certain science-related topics is not new. Proponents for and against such topics as the theory of evolution, creationism, and human secularism have exerted great influence upon school curriculum. Recently, litigation has been initiated seeking either to emphasize or eliminate some topics from public school curricula. The results of such actions are unclear at this time.

Much traditional school curriculum is in a state of flux. The community, together with legislators and various national groups, frequently seek to bring their own values to bear in determining what is taught in the schools or presented in textbooks. You may wish to inquire about local school policies and community standards as you begin planning for teaching children science. Guidance from administrators may be helpful in those situations where it is unclear how much influence various value systems should or do exert over instructional approaches and content.

_____ *LOOKING BACK* _____

1. How can a teacher determine the appropriateness of content for the science program being used?
2. How many changes can be made in science content to reflect contemporary information?
3. What contributions do inquiry skills make to a science program?
4. What relationships seem to exist between science content and inquiry skills?
5. How does the study of science influence attitudinal development?

ACTIVITIES

1. Get a candle and light it. Make as many observations about the burning candle as you can. List your observations. What observations did you make using the senses of sight, touch, hearing, and smell? From your observations, answer the following questions:
   a. Is the flame one color or several colors?
   b. What happens to the melted wax?
   c. How high is the flame?
   d. What happens to the wick as the candle burns?
   e. How fast does the candle burn?
   f. Does the wax melt evenly around the outside of the candle?
   g. How long does it take for the melted wax to solidify?
   h. How high above the candle can heat from the flame be felt?
   i. Does the flame of the candle always point away from the earth?
   j. When a jar is put over the candle flame briefly, is the flame extinguished?

2. Read the following statements and determine if each is an observation or an inference.
   a. Leaves fall from trees in autumn.
   b. Simple machines make work seem easier.
   c. Mars is a planet with a reddish color.
   d. Dogs and wolves are similar in appearance.
   e. Insects have compound eyes.
   f. All green plants produce flowers.
   g. Magnets will attract objects through parts of the human body.
   h. Some seeds will not germinate immediately after being taken from the fruit.

i. Few women become scientists.

j. All human organs can be transplanted.

Statement **a** is an inference. Although you may have observed that leaves fall from trees in autumn, they may fall at other times. Leaves will fall from some trees during the summer if the tree gets very little water. Other trees lose their leaves a few at a time throughout the year.

Statement **b** is an inference. People use simple machines to assist them with tasks. But while individual tasks can be observed, the concept of work "being made easier" cannot be observed. It is an interpretation of observations.

Statement **c** is an observation. The color of Mars can be observed through the sense of sight.

Statement **d** is an observation. Why?

Statement **e** is an observation. Why?

Statement **f** is an inference. Why?

Statement **g** is an observation. An example of this is an earring being held in place on the ear lobe with a magnet.

Statement **h** is an observation. Why?

Statement **i** is an inference. Why?

Statement **j** is an inference. Why?

3. Measure the distance from one side of a room to another using a nonstandard unit of your choice. Do this several times. Are your measurements the same each time? [Tell another person the distance you measured in terms of nonstandard units. Does the other person understand the distance you measured?] Use a meterstick to measure the same distance. Do you have difficulty communicating the distance in terms of metric units?

4. Lay out a collection of objects from a purse, a kitchen drawer, or laboratory storage area. Select one object and set it aside; it will be used later. When all the objects are collected (except the one set aside) sort them into two groups on the basis of a characteristic and the lack of this characteristic. After this is done, place the object which was set aside in one of the groups. If the classifying was done properly, you should be able to place the object in *one* group without any problem.

   Now that you have two subgroups, sort each subgroup into two smaller subgroups according to the presence or absence of an attribute of your choice.

5. Read the following investigative questions. For each question, select the manipulated variable, if there is one, and name at least two variables that should be controlled during the investigation.

   a. What effect will adding increasing numbers of ice cubes, one at a time, to water have upon the rate at which the temperature of the water decreases?

     b. What factors cause salt to dissolve faster?

     c. What effect will adding differing amounts of sugar to water have upon the time required for the water to boil?

     d. What causes plants to be healthy?

     e. What is the effect of breaking rocks?

Question **a:** The variable the investigator manipulates or changes is the number of ice cubes. Some of the controlled variables are the size of the ice cubes, stirring the water after the ice cubes are added, using the same amounts of water, and using the same thermometer to measure the temperature. You may be able to think of many others.

Question **b:** There is no manipulated variable. There are a number of factors that could cause salt to dissolve, none of which are specified. The term "faster" is undefined also; the basis for comparison is undefined. This is not an investigative question.

Question **c:** The manipulated variable is the amount of sugar added to the water. Some of the controlled variables may be the amount of water to which sugar is added, the heat source used for heating the water, and the watch or timing device used to measure the time required for the water to boil.

Question **d:** This question is not an investigative question; there is no manipulated variable. A second problem is that the term "healthy" needs to be defined specifically.

Question **e:** The manipulated variable is breaking rocks. However, this is not an investigative question. Why? If you are not sure, review Chapter 3. Since this is not an investigative question, there are no controlled variables.

5

Contemporary Science Materials and Units

Objectives

1. To review features of contemporary elementary school science programs.
2. To identify three levels of plans necessary for the development of a school system's science program.
3. To identify characteristics which distinguish among types of prepared instructional units.
4. To apply criteria for evaluating an effective prepared unit.
5. To identify at least two advantages and disadvantages of each of the three types of prepared units.

_____ *LOOKING FORWARD* _____

Many teachers who would prefer to plan their own science programs find themselves pressed for time. As a result, most work with the programs developed by school systems and the textbook series adopted by the local district. This does not mean, however, that the instructor cannot innovate or personalize the instruction. On the contrary. In this chapter, we offer suggestions for using various types of contemporary science instructional materials and programs.

Three types of contemporary science instructional materials are discussed: textbook series, innovative programs selected from several sources, and prepared science units.

Mention a science textbook and many teachers think at once of a "read about-talk about" science program. Fortunately, however, contemporary elementary school science textbooks no longer fit this conceptualization. They tend to provide the teacher with topics, information, and activities that encourage an active science program.

Several types of prepared units are also available for teachers. The unique features of each are discussed, together with criteria for evaluating each instructional unit. The chapter closes with some suggestions for using prepared instructional units.

A welcome ferment is becoming evident in contemporary elementary school science. Nationally, educators are expressing concern about the quantity and quality of science instruction at the elementary level. In response to those concerns, publishers and curriculum developers are designing new, innovative science programs. Many state departments of education are working to improve science instruction, to assess the quality of local science instruction, and to develop resource materials that will help science teachers become more effective. Many universities and colleges are offering workshops and courses in teaching science. Local school systems are designing staff development programs to meet the needs of science teachers. It is beyond the scope of this chapter to describe all of these developments, but we will try to cover enough to give you a sense of why this is an exciting time to be teaching science.

One national initiative that deserves particular attention is the Search for Excellence in Science Education (SESE), which operates under the auspices of the National Science Teachers Association. This group identified criteria for excellence relating to both students and programs, then conducted a national search for elementary school science programs which met the criteria.

The criteria for excellence in students include the following:

- To exhibit effective consumer behavior.
- To use effective personal health practices.
- To learn when presented with new ideas and data.
- To recognize that the individual is influenced by the environment.
- To recognize each individual as unique.
- To recognize that a solution to a problem may present new problems.
- To recognize that data may be interpreted from a variety of viewpoints.
- To recognize that science processes are required to resolve problems rather than to solve them.
- To develop an understanding of information and concepts from a wide variety of topics selected from the life, earth, and physical sciences.
- To recognize that scientists have individual human and personal characteristics.

The criteria for excellence in programs include the following:

- Alternatives exist for solving a problem.
- Students are presented with realistic problems that can be solved.
- Students are actively involved in gathering data.
- A variety of means is used to present information to students.
- Information presented is cognitively appropriate.
- Science programs are interdisciplinary.
- Decisions are based on information and values, and their consequences for others in the community are evaluated.

These criteria are likely to have far-reaching effects since they were distributed widely during the national search. Schools which met the criteria were representative of all regions of the country. Together they provide a standard for judging other elementary school science programs.

This *is* a very exciting time to be teaching science in the elementary school. The modern science instructional materials now available add interest and excitement and open a range of new options.

Because contemporary science instructional materials are used in the many methods courses for teacher preparation, preservice teachers have the opportunity to review these materials and to use them during their student teaching.

Textbook authors have also become increasingly sensitive to the problems of teaching children science. In the past, science classes tended to be similar to reading lessons, in which children were assigned a portion of the textbook to be read and discussed the following day. On occasion, demonstrations or token student activities were provided to verify that the information in the textbook was accurate. The curriculum reforms of the 1960s and early 1970s suggested a new, dynamic approach to teaching science. The science curricula were often published as articulated programs. Several of the curricula were so highly structured that even teachers with limited science background could teach them effectively. The early science curriculum reforms had an effect on contemporary science textbooks. Some of these richer, more diverse curricula are now being revised for use with textbook series.

Although a school system may have an adopted science program, teachers may be permitted to adapt or alter some portion or unit of the program to fit their needs. But in order to make good choices, teachers need to be aware of what's available—the characteristics, advantages, limitations, and sources of effective programs and materials. Providing that background information is the primary focus of this chapter.

CONTEMPORARY SCIENCE MATERIALS

A wide variety of science materials is now available for elementary school teachers. We will offer representative examples as illustrations.

Contemporary Textbooks

Many changes in the teaching of science have been attributed to contemporary science textbooks. These positive changes are largely the result of a new way of presenting science content.

The teacher's edition frequently contains information about the textbook content, along with suggestions for teaching science through an activity-oriented or investigative approach, and questions designed to encourage student thinking. Many of the activities illustrate the content and incorporate scientific terminology. Although teachers continue to need some background in science, they may also become learners along with the children as the activities are conducted. Teachers no longer need to be authorities on science. They are now free to serve as facilitators of learning, assisting children in making discoveries. Activities using inquiry skills abound in today's textbooks.

Just as the role of the teacher shifts—from science expert to facilitator—so the role of the child changes from that of passive information receiver to active investigator, user, and sharer of information.

Analyzing Student and Teacher Sections of a Science Lesson

The following lesson illustrates a contemporary approach. It is taken from the teacher's edition of *Heath Science,* to which we have previously referred (the lesson is from Grade 3, pp. 67–70). The title of the chapter is "Investigating Living Things and Environments," and in its original form was illustrated by photographs of woods, fungi growing on fallen trees, children investigating the processes of decay, etc. The focus of the lesson is the community. Read the excerpt; then complete the inquiries that follow.

LESSON: SOIL-MAKERS (GRADE 3)

A few years ago, something happened here. With a loud crash, a dead tree fell to the ground. This was not the first time that such a thing happened. The community has been here a long time. Many, many trees have lived and grown and died here. Where are they now? [*in the soil*] What happened to them? [*they decayed*]

Look at what the children have found! They have found some plants, but the plants are not green. They do not make food like green plants. Like all living things, though, these plants need food. They use the energy they get from food to live. Where do you think these plants get energy? [*from the log*]

Look closely at these plants. Where are they growing? [*on a log*] These plants get food from the log. The log used to be part of a green plant. When it was alive, it got energy from the food it made. These plants change the log into soil by breaking it into many pieces. Sometimes these plants get food from animals that have died. Plants that get energy in this way are called **soil-makers** [*soyl-MAY-kuhrz*].

Soil-makers slowly break down things that have died and make them part of the soil. Can you think how animals could also break down a log and make it part of the soil? Some ants make their home in logs. They chew the logs and lay their eggs there. Birds may peck holes in the log. The holes let air and water inside. The log gets soft and breaks apart.

Soil is made in still another way. When an animal dies, other animals feed on its body. The parts that are not eaten right away mix with the soil and become part of it.

Soil-makers are at work all around you. Sometimes they even grow on different kinds of foods. Living things that grow on food such as bread, fruits, vegetables, and cheese are called **molds** [*mohldz*].

Activity

Let's find out more about one kind of soil-maker. You will need a piece of bread, some water, and a bag that you can see through.

Put a few drops of water on the piece of bread. Then put the bread in the bag. Wait a few days. Look at the bread. What color is it? [*Molds may have several colors.*] Does it have an odor? [*Yes, it smells bad.*] The living thing feeding on the bread is called a mold. A mold is one kind of soil-maker.

What do you think will happen to the bread after a while? [*It will completely decompose.*] What do you think will happen to the dead log in time? [*It will completely decompose.*]

LESSON: SOIL-MAKERS (TEACHER SECTION)

Vocabulary

soil-makers
molds

Main Ideas

- Some nongreen plants feed on dead plants and animals.
- Soil-makers are organisms that break down dead organisms and change them into soil.

Objectives

The child should be able to:

- describe soil-makers such as mushrooms, fungi, and molds
- describe the activities of soil-makers
- tell what a mold is

Lesson Plan

1. Have the children read the first paragraph and look at the top picture [*of a dead tree*]. Ask them what they think happened to the tree. (It died; it was struck by lightning; etc.) Discuss the questions. [*Any answers are acceptable at this time.*] Tell the children that they will learn about what happens to dead trees in this lesson.

2. Ask the children to read the second paragraph and look at the bottom picture [*of children studying forest plant life*]. Have them point out the nongreen plants in the picture. Ask them if they are familiar with any of them. They may have eaten mushrooms. Discuss the question in the text. [*Any answer is acceptable.*]

   Caution: Tell the children that many mushrooms growing in the woods are poisonous and can kill people who eat them.

3. Have the class read page 68 and look at the picture [*of fungi*]. Ask the children where these nongreen plants get their food [*from the log*]. Ask them what these plants are doing to the log [*breaking it down into smaller pieces and making it into soil*].

4. Write the word *soil-makers* on the chalkboard. Help the children pronounce it. Ask them what the word refers to [*nongreen plants that get their food from dead plants*]. Ask them if they think it is a good name for these nongreen plants. [*yes*]

5. Ask the children to observe the two pictures near the top of page 69. Ask them to describe the activity of the animals in the pictures [*ants crawling along a log; bird pecking at a dead log*]. Have the children describe how these activities make the log part of the soil. [*Ants chew holes in the log. The bird pecks holes. Both of these help to break the wood into little bits.*]

6. Tell the children to read the first paragraph on page 69. Ask them what name they would give to the ants and birds [*soil-makers*].

7. Ask the children to read the second paragraph on page 69 and look at the bottom picture. Ask them to describe the picture. [*A dead animal is breaking up into soil.*]

8. Have the children read the last paragraph on page 69. Ask them what molds will grow on [*cheese, fruit, vegetables, and bread*]. Write the word **mold** on the chalkboard. Help the children to pronounce it. Ask them what a mold is [*a nongreen plant that is also a soil-maker*].

9. Activity—Growing Bread Mold

a. Have the children read the first two paragraphs on page 70. Make sure they understand what to do. Distribute the necessary materials to each group. Have them follow the directions for the first day. Some children may be allergic to certain kinds of molds. It might be best for them not to participate in the activity.

b. After several days, tell the children to observe the bread. Discuss the questions with them.

c. Have the children read the last paragraphs. Discuss the questions with them. Continue to observe the bread mold for several weeks.

d. Have the children compare the breakdown of the bread and the log. [*They are the same.*]

Lesson Follow-Up

Enrichment (*Observing Mold Under a Microscope*)

Provide children with some bread mold, a microscope, glass slides, and cover glasses. Have them put a small piece of mold and a drop of water onto a slide and cover it with a cover glass. Have them observe it under a microscope. Have the children draw pictures of their observations. Make sure they notice the cottony appearance of the mold and the small black round spores. Under proper conditions, each spore could grow a new mold plant.

Tie-in *(Language Arts/Listening Skills)*
Read to the class *Let's Learn About Mushrooms*, by Phyllis J. Perry (New York: Harvey House, 1974). This book discusses commercially grown mushrooms as well as those found in the wild.

Note the interesting developmental writing style used in the narrative. Factual information need not be presented in a dry discourse that lulls students to sleep. Instead, here's a lesson in which the writing style does the topic justice. Note also that photos are carefully chosen to illustrate the information in the narrative, one photo for each topic discussed.

- Note the correspondence between the main ideas and the objectives.
- Can you find where each objective is addressed in the narrative?
- Do the objectives deal with memorizing information or do they require the learners to think? What is the basis for your answer?
- How does the first activity in the lesson plan require children to think? What technique is used to capture the children's interest? In activities 2 through 8, what techniques are used to involve children in the lesson—that is, to make them active learners rather than memorizers of data?
- Read the directions for the follow-up activity. Would you be able to complete the activity? If possible, get the equipment and mold and conduct the activity. Were the proper items of equipment listed? Were the procedures easy to follow? What would be the purpose for asking children to draw pictures of their observations? (Trying the activity is a very valuable technique to use when a teacher is unable to observe what the children observe.)
- Could you think of tie-ins with other subjects, such as reading, art, or mathematics?
- How does the activity "Growing Bread Mold" relate to the information in the lesson? How is transfer of information incorporated? (If you wish to try this activity yourself, grow mold on cheese rather than on bread. DO NOT remove the food and mold from the container. If you wish to look at the mold under a microscope, secure a small amount of it with a toothpick and place it on a microscope slide.)

How would you characterize the lesson?

a. A high-interest narrative with much information for the learner to memorize and recall.
b. A high-interest narrative with many activities included to show that the information is accurate.
c. A high-interest narrative with a variety of activities that are likely to challenge the learner to think and to develop an understanding of some of the soil-making processes.

If you selected **a**, you need to reread the lesson. There are few places where information is to be recalled.

If you selected **b**, reread the activities in the narrative and teaching plan. Although the activities deal with information in the narrative, they are not intended to validate the accuracy of the information.

If you selected **c**, you have made a wise choice. The questions require thinking before a learner can answer them; the activities illustrate the information in the narrative but there is no indication of the "right" observation or result of an activity. Using this approach, the teacher becomes a guide or facilitator of learning rather than the authority with *the* answer.

INQUIRY-ORIENTED SCIENCE PROGRAMS

A new type of science program under development consists of a series of modules emphasizing inquiry. A module may be defined as a self-contained instructional unit. The modules have some features in common with textbooks: an overview, a time schedule, a listing of activities, an evaluation strategy, a glossary, and pupil worksheets. But among their unique features is a problem-solving approach. Children are taught to solve problems through experience: they learn to deal with discrepancies, to raise (and answer) questions, and to use inquiry skills in defining and resolving problems. The inquiry model used in these modules consists of a series of steps: planning; collecting and organizing data; generalizing from the data; and ultimately, arriving at a decision. Activities are arranged in a logical sequence that supports conceptual development of a science topic.

The following sample lesson from an inquiry-oriented science program illustrates a modular approach to teaching science. The module is adapted from *Meet the Mealworm* published by Delta Education, 1987, Nashua, NH.

Read the following module and complete the inquiries.

SAMPLE LESSON: FOOD CHOICES

Focus

- To predict what food mealworms prefer
- To state generalizations from observations and data collected on the food eaten by mealworms

Vocabulary

generalization

Materials

mealworms
shoe box
piece of raw potato
bran
other foods as needed

Teaching Suggestions

1. Ask, "What does a mealworm prefer to eat?"
2. As a demonstration, place in a shoe box twenty mealworms, a piece of raw potato, bran flakes, and other foods the students think might be appropriate.
3. Ask the students to predict which food(s) the mealworms will prefer.
4. By the end of the day have the students observe the demonstration again. Discuss the foods the mealworms seem to prefer. Ask the students to generalize about the food that all mealworms prefer, based on the data collected in this experiment.

Optional Activities

- Have interested students generate a list of five foods and poll all your science students to determine preferences for these foods. Make a bulletin board histogram of the collected data (Figure 5.1).

You may have noticed that the sequence of activities includes asking what the children thought the mealworms would eat, testing their suggestions, predicting which foods the mealworms would eat, and observing the worms to verify the predictions. There is also an opportunity for children to summarize their observations in graphic form. Each lesson in the module specifies a focus objective, required vocabulary, needed materials, teaching suggestions, and some optional activities.

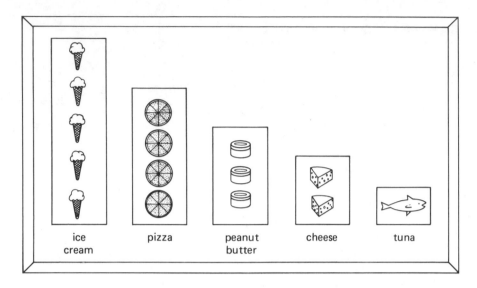

Figure 5.1. Histogram of Food Choices

PLANNING FOR INSTRUCTION

Although most school systems provide a science program, teachers may not know how the components of the program were selected. A school science program usually begins with a general plan that includes identification of available resources. Such a plan is necessary for a coordinated, articulated science program.

At one level, planning consists of adopting contemporary materials, such as those described earlier, either as they are published or in some adapted form as a curriculum guide. Planning at this level includes listing science topics for each grade level and specifying goals for the entire science program. Teachers' participation at this level usually involves serving on a textbook selection or curriculum development committee.

At another level, administrators and teachers define objectives for the science program within the local school. They may also lay out the sequence of topics for each grade level, and identify some means of assessing the program's effectiveness. Most of the instructional staff participate in this level of planning.

At the third level, individual classroom teachers develop plans for teaching children science and assessing the effectiveness of their own instruction.

Table 5.1 illustrates the goals, methods, and sample content outcomes which result from planning at these three levels.

A comparison of several aspects of the three levels of planning follows.

TABLE 5.1. LEVELS OF PLANNING FOR A SCIENCE PROGRAM

	District Level	School Level	Classroom Level
Goals/Objectives	To become scientifically literate To solve problems To base opinions on information and evidence	To develop the facility to use scientific processes To develop skills in using scientific instruments	To construct a complete electric circuit To identify at least one variable that affects the pulse rate in humans
Methods of Instruction	Use methods which are activity oriented Use a variety of instructional resources	Use a variety of instructional strategies Involve children in planning a lesson	Construct a learning center to teach a science lesson Have children in groups of three or four construct a diorama of the surface of the moon
Science Content	Topics for Grade 3 • Electricity • Animals • Magnetism • Space	Sequence of topics for Grade 3 • Magnetism • Electricity • Animals • Space	Subtopics for Grade 3 • Electromagnets • Electric circuits • Habitats • Surface of the moon

THE PREPARED INSTRUCTIONAL UNIT

The term *unit* may designate any of several types of instructional plans. A unit may offer an overall instructional plan, or a self-paced, personalized learning experience dealing with one science topic.

But regardless of form or purpose, instructional units usually consist of a set of objectives; an outline of content; initiating, learning, and culminating activities; a plan for pre- and post-assessment; and a list of resources to support the learning activities.

Using a prepared instructional unit offers the busy teacher several advantages. First, the objectives, content, learning activities, and (often) resources are already specified—a real plus for a teacher with limited time or limited background in teaching science. Teachers can use the time they save collecting resources. Further, a written unit can be reviewed for completeness and consistency—and altered if necessary.

Prepared units also present several disadvantages. No consistency may be evident among objectives, content, learning activities, and assessment. Some units specify objectives, but fail to outline any learning activities or content based on those objectives. Often, units provide little opportunity for teachers to include their own ideas.

Following is an excerpt from a prepared teaching unit. Read the objectives and learning activities carefully and complete the questions that follow. (*Note:* This is an activity that may be used when a unit on electric circuitry or magnetism is taught.)

LESSON: CONSTRUCTING ELECTROMAGNETS WHICH VARY IN STRENGTH (Grades 4–6)

Objectives

1. To construct an electromagnet
2. To identify two variables that affect the strength of an electromagnet

Learning Activities

1. Use an iron nail, 1.5 meters of No. 24 insulated bell wire, a dry cell, and a box of paper clips. Remove 3 centimeters of insulation from the ends of the wire. Beginning about 5 centimeters from one end of the wire, wind 1 meter of wire around the nail to within 5 centimeters of the other end. Attach the ends of the exposed wire to the dry cell. Dip one end of the electromagnet in the box of paper clips.

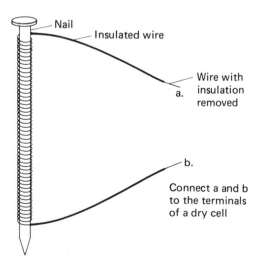

Figure 5.2. Electromagnet

2. Count the number of paper clips attracted to the end of the electromagnet. Now do this ten times and calculate the average number of clips attracted.

3. Use 2 meters of wire to construct an electromagnet as described above. Dip one end of the electromagnet in the box of paper clips ten times, and calculate the average number of clips attracted. (*Note:* Disconnect the electromagnet from the dry cell as soon as possible.) Compare these results with those recorded in **b**.

4. Find examples of electromagnets in the home and report to the class.

Questions

1. What actions are learners expected to perform and how would you, as a teacher, determine if children could perform the actions specified?
2. Which objective does each learning activity teach?

Answers

Objective **1** specifies that the learner construct an electromagnet. This means that after following the directions given in the learning activities, the learner should have an electromagnet that will attract whatever objects magnets usually attract. You would observe the completed magnet as it attracted objects when connected to the dry cell.

Objective **2** specifies that the learner communicate, and frequently illustrate, two variables that affect the strength of an electromagnet. If the learner is requested to illustrate the two variables, he or she might be given a box of paper clips and asked to illustrate the variable by demonstrating how many clips will be attracted after each variable is manipulated. You would observe this demonstration.

Learning activities **1** and **2** deal with constructing and testing an electromagnet that teaches objective **1**. Activity **3** relates to both objectives **1** and **2**.

Activity **4** is unrelated to either objective. The fourth activity neither requests that the learner construct an electromagnet nor that he or she identify variables affecting the strength of the electromagnet. This activity may be quite appropriate for an objective requesting the learner to identify electromagnets, but it is out of place in this lesson.

The prepared unit may facilitate planning by identifying a time schedule for the lesson. If the time available for a science class is forty minutes, daily activities are usually scheduled for completion within that time. An alternative is scheduling activities that can be carried over into subsequent days without losing continuity. Even with the best planning, unexpected events may disrupt a schedule. Be flexible. For example, if a gerbil gives birth to a litter during a science class on constructing electromagnets, do not relinquish the teachable moment on the birth process for the sake of preserving continuity in the electro-magnets lesson.

Keeping in mind that some children learn most effectively with one instructional strategy, others with another. Some children prefer visual experiences while others prefer auditory experiences; some children have difficulty reading while others have difficulty following written directions. A unit should be sufficiently diverse to include a variety of instructional techniques.

TYPES OF PREPARED INSTRUCTIONAL UNITS

Units may be classified as three types: the resource unit, the teaching unit, and the module. Although these units share many common characteristics, each has unique features. A brief description and illustration of each type of unit follows.

Resource Units

Resource units usually consist of a statement of objectives, an outline of science content, suggested teaching activities, a list of resources and equipment, and suggested assessment techniques. A unique feature of the resource unit is its comprehensiveness. It is not intended for classroom use per se, but as a basis for the development of other types of units. A teacher may, for instance, select content, learning activities, resources, and assessment techniques all from the resource unit. Portions of an abbreviated resource unit follow. (Parts of this and subsequent sample units have been omitted from the illustrations that follow in the interest of saving space.)

AN ABBREVIATED RESOURCE UNIT: CHANGES WITH GEOLOGIC TIME

Topic: Geological Timetable

Objectives

1. To categorize the history of the earth into six eras
2. To identify one type of animal living in each of the three most recent eras: a) Paleozoic, b) Mesozoic, and c) Cenozoic
3. To identify one change in structure in plants and animals through geologic time

4. To identify five physical changes in humans during their time on earth

5. To identify at least one way scientists use to learn about the earth's past

6. To identify types of tasks geologists do and fields of geology

Content: Geologic Time

Teaching Activities

1. Make a timeline for the wall. Use a sheet of wrapping paper 10 feet long to represent 5 billion years—the approximate age of the earth.

   a. Starting at the left, measure off 8 feet and draw a vertical line. At this point (1 billion years ago), primitive one-celled life appeared on earth.

   b. Measure to the right 1 foot and draw a second vertical line. This line represents when fish first appeared in the oceans (half a billion years ago).

   c. Draw a line 7 inches from the right end of the timeline to represent the appearance of reptiles (300 million years ago).

   d. Draw the last line 1½ inches from the right end of the timeline to represent the appearance of mammals (60 million years ago).

   e. Draw a line approximately 1/20,000 of an inch thick on the right end of the timeline to represent the point when humans appeared on earth (2 to 5 million years ago).

   f. If space permits, a 20-foot timeline may be constructed by doubling each dimension in (a) through (e).

   g. Additional points may be added as the teacher chooses.

Content: Geologic Eras

Teaching Activities

1. Explain *geologic era* as an extremely long period of time during which both the earth and life on earth have evolved.

2. Use a chart to illustrate geologic eras—a) Cenozoic, b) Mesozoic, c) Paleozoic, d) Archeozoic, e) Azoic.

3. Start a chart of geologic eras by adding the name of each era as it is studied.

4. Have students search the library for names of the geologic eras and their meanings.

5. Ask them to make oral and/or written reports on topics pertaining to different eras: e.g., What was the earth like? What was life like at that time?

6. Make a six-shelf display to represent the geological eras. As you study each era, place dioramas, models, and/or specimens on the appropriate shelves. (Use the information from activity 5).

Content: Studying the Earth's Past
Teaching Activities

1. Discuss scientists who study the earth's history: geologists, archaeologists, paleontologists.
2. Make plaster casts of fossils and animal tracks.
3. Examine and discuss fossils.
4. Construct a display of fossils and note their approximate ages.
5. Visit exhibits of fossils at a museum or the geology department at a nearby college.
6. Make imprints using such objects as twigs, rocks, hands, and feet. (This can be done by placing a layer of soft modeling clay on a cookie sheet and making overlapping imprints using several objects in a sequence. Have the students study the model and decide on the sequence in which the imprints were made. The way imprints overlay each other makes it possible to determine the time order of events.)
7. Invite a speaker on archaeology to visit the classroom.
8. Invite a speaker on paleontology to visit the classroom.
9. Discuss radioactive dating as used by scientists.

Content: Characteristics of the Paleozoic Era
Teaching Activities

1. Define *paleo* as old or ancient.
2. Assign groups to find specific information about the Paleozoic era, and to make presentations to the class following the format of a drama, television documentary, or radio program.
3. Determine the approximate time of this period based on students' research.
4. Discuss: Why might this be called the Age of Fishes? Marine Invertebrates? Spore-Bearing Plants? Marine Plants?
5. Construct models of organisms from the Paleozoic era for the classroom. Add these to the appropriate shelf.
6. Create a bulletin board display using students' drawings of plant and animal life found during this period.
7. Using an overhead or opaque projector; have students design a picture of Paleozoic era ecology.
8. Show some films on prehistoric life.

Content: Changes During the Paleozoic Era

Teaching Activities

1. Using a time chart of the Paleozoic era, note changes in climate, land areas, and living organisms.
2. Explain that the Paleozoic era is especially memorable because the first vertebrate animals, first land plants, and first land animals appeared during this era.
3. Bring in liverworts and mosses to exemplify two early primitive land plants which still exist. Compare these with primitive mosses and liverworts shown in pictures.
4. Point out the gingko tree is an example of an ancient plant from this period.
5. Bring in examples of the first land animals—snails, spiders, scorpions.
6. Bring in examples of the kinds of plants from which coal formed (tree ferns, horsetails, club mosses).

Content: Flying Reptiles

Teaching Activities

1. Show pictures of flying reptiles and birds.
2. List differences between flying reptiles and birds:
   a. Birds have feathers; reptiles have scales.
   b. Birds are warm-blooded; reptiles are cold-blooded.
3. List likenesses between flying reptiles and birds:
   a. The first birds had no bills.
   b. The first birds had claws at the ends of their wings.
4. Conduct research on flying reptiles (particularly the model recently constructed which crashed in flight).
5. Request oral reports from students and add materials to the shelf.
6. Look at chicken feathers and legs under a microscope and a lens. You will find both have scales. This suggests some relationship between reptiles and birds.

Evaluation

1. Show pictures of animals from each of the three most recent geological eras and ask students to place animals in the proper era. Ask them to cite the characteristics used for categorizing.
2. Ask students to list the three most recent geologic eras in order of occurrence, beginning with the oldest of the three. Ask them to enumerate differences among the eras.
3. Ask students to identify changes in plants and animals from one era to the next.

4. Ask students to arrange pictures of humans in order of their appearance on earth.

Materials and Equipment

Roll of paper for timeline
Magic markers
Illustrations
Materials for dioramas and bulletin board
Opaque projector
Plaster of paris
Clay
Shelving
Objects for making "fossil" imprints

The preceding resource unit, designed for use with sixth graders, covers a variety of concepts relating to geological timetables. While several objectives are suggested, a teacher may use other objectives with the learning activities. Content is specified. And a variety of learning activities is included to accommodate differing learning styles. Post assessment tasks are also suggested. Remember, teachers need not include every element specified. They can select and adapt.

Resource units tend to be rich and diverse in content because they draw from many sources: textbooks, curriculum studies and guides, independent teaching units, and teachers' own experiences. They're designed to prompt new ideas and to save teachers a great deal of time.

Teaching Units

Teaching units are intended for use as daily lesson plans. They may be based on resource units, textbooks, the teacher's own experience, or some combination of these. For instance, a teaching unit based upon a textbook may be limited in depth, and the number of learning activities inappropriate for the learners. Thus, additional or alternate activities may be needed. Such additions might be taken from another textbook or resource unit. It is important to select learning experiences appropriate for children. For example, if Ann has a fear of snakes, she might learn more from photos than from direct observation—at least at first. If her fear persists, an alternate activity unrelated to snakes might be provided. Similarly, if John lacks the small-muscle coordination to focus a microscope, someone could focus it for him, a microprojector could be used to project the image on a screen, or a microphoto of the object could be made for him.

Think of ways you might use or adapt components from the abbreviated teaching unit below.

AN ABBREVIATED TEACHING UNIT: OCEANS—CHARACTERISTICS AND EFFECTS

Topic: Origins, Climate, Movement of Oceans

Objectives

1. Each student will be able to identify one hypothesis regarding the origin of the present oceans.
2. Each student will be able to demonstrate three ways in which ocean water moves.
3. Each student will be able to identify the effect of ocean currents on land temperature and climate.

Content: Ratio of Water Surface to Land Surface

Teaching Activities

Divide the class into small groups. Provide each group with a copy of the world map, and enough rice to cover all the water areas of the map. (Students need only identify land and water masses on the map.) Have students estimate how much of the rice can be placed within the boundary lines of the land masses. No rice should be placed on the map if it will not fit within these lines. Have students place the rice on the land masses. Small areas of land will remain uncovered. The procedure should then be repeated with the areas of water. When the students have estimated how much rice was required to cover each area, a ratio of water surface to land surface can be calculated. The ratios found by each group should then be compared.

Content: Oceans That Originated Several Billion Years Ago

Teaching Activities

1. Discuss the following hypotheses, using library resources to support or refute each hypothesis:
    a. When the earth was formed some 3 to 5 billion years ago, it was a molten ball. It cooled like a drying orange, its skin becoming more and more wrinkled as the interior shrank. This is one manner in which the ocean basins were formed (this may be illustrated).
    b. The moon was formed when the earth spun off a part of its mass during this cooling period, and the scar of that giant upheaval is the basin of the Pacific Ocean.
    c. The continents of the world are forever receding from one another or moving close together. The ocean basins are created as this vast motion (continental drift) takes place.
2. Invite a speaker from a college or university geology department to discuss the above hypotheses.

3. Ask students for any hypotheses they may have and any scientific support they can offer for their hypotheses.
4. Creative writing: "How do you think the oceans originated?" Defend your answer.

Content: Warm water, cold water, convection

Teaching Activity

Get two quart jars. Fill one with hot water (add enough red ink to color the water) and set it in a pan. Fill the other with very cold water. Cover the jar of cold water with a piece of thin cardboard. Keeping your hand on the cardboard, turn the jar of cold water upside down and set it on the bottle of hot water. Be sure the tops of the two jars are in line. Carefully take away the cardboard. Which of the bottles contains the *denser* water? (The cold clear water is denser.) What do you predict will happen? Make and test an inference about the movement of water.

Content: Water Density and Ocean Currents

Teaching Activity

Take out two quart jars; add a few tablespoons of salt mixed with water to one jar. Shake the jar to dissolve the salt. Keep adding salt until no more will dissolve. To the other jar, add enough red food coloring to color the water. Put the jar of colored fresh water in a pan. Cover the jar of salty water with a piece of thick cardboard. Turn the jar of salty water over the jar of water without salt. Carefully take away the cardboard. Which bottle contains the *denser* water? (Salt-free water.) What do you predict will happen this time?

Content: Effect of the Earth's Rotation on Ocean Currents

Teaching Activities

1. Obtain a spinning globe of the earth. Mix a small amount of fairly thick blue tempera paint. Spin the globe very slowly in a counter-clockwise direction (from west to east). At the same time, pour a small amount of the paint mixture in a thin stream onto the north pole. Notice that as the stream flows down the Northern Hemisphere, it is deflected to the right (east) by the earth's rotation. When the stream crosses the equator and enters the Southern Hemisphere, it is now deflected to the left (west). Likewise, ocean currents moving north are deflected to the right (east) and currents moving south are deflected to the left (west).
2. Observe water going down a drain. This circular motion is identical to that of the ocean currents which affect our hemisphere.

Content: Ocean Waves, Wind, Earth Movements, and Tides

Teaching Activities

This activity demonstrates what water waves are like. (It would be very effective in a learning center.)

Materials needed: large shallow pan, medicine dropper, bits of paper, plastic ruler or straightedge, newspaper, water. Place these directions and questions on chart paper.

1. Cover your desk with newspaper. Put a pan on the newspaper and fill it three-fourths full of water.

2. Put some water in the dropper. Let a drop of water fall into the water in the pan. Look at the shape of the waves that are formed.

3. Blow along the water near one end of the pan. Look at the waves that are formed.

4. Put a few very small bits of paper on the water. Be sure they are near the middle of the pan. Put an edge of the ruler in the water at one end of the pan. Quickly lift the ruler straight up. Waves will be formed. Watch the bits of paper as the waves pass under them. Do this several times.

5. Discuss these questions:

   a. Any moving object has energy. A falling drop of water has energy. What happened to this energy when the drop hit the water?

   b. When the drop hit the water, did the water move?

   c. What happened when you blew across the water? How could you measure your observations?

   d. Do you think much water travels across the pan with each wave? Explain your answer.

Evaluation

1. Ask each student to identify one hypothesis regarding the origin of the oceans and offer a rationale for that hypothesis.

2. Each student will demonstrate three ways that ocean water moves, and will cite evidence for the energy transfer.

3. Each student will identify one effect of ocean currents on land temperature and climate by constructing a map depicting ocean currents and the temperatures of nearby land masses.

The preceding teaching unit is not as extensive as the resource unit. However, it contains learning activities for all children in a class, as well as alternate activities for certain children. All assessment tasks are intended to be used at the culmination of the lesson. Teaching units are usually developed to teach concepts, factual information, and use of scientific processes.

The Prerequisite Unit

At times teachers find that children lack some vital skills. For instance, they may be unable to observe critically, using all senses, to follow directions or to use scientific equipment. A mini-unit emphasizing these skills may be helpful. For instance, a unit on using all the five senses in observations, or on distinguishing between observations and inferences might be developed for children in grades 4 or 5. A unit on using balances, measuring volumes, or focusing a microscope might be necessary for children at any level who have not had an earlier opportunity to develop these skills.

Modules

Modules may be characterized as a set of learning activities intended to facilitate student's achievement of an objective or objectives. The major focus of the module is on the needs of the learner and attainment of objectives through participation in activities. A module consists of a statement of objectives, identification of prerequisite knowledge and skills (the preassessment), instructional activities, a plan for postassessment, and suggestions for remediation if necessary. Although all three types of teaching units have similar goals, the major emphases of the resource and teaching units are frequently on teaching science *content* to students. Modules also emphasize content; however, the major thrust is on adapting instruction to meet learners' needs. In other words, modules allow for personalized instruction (see Chapter 3).

Objectives for a module are usually stated in behavioral terms. Children are expected to demonstrate that they have met the objective by performing some task. For example, if the objective states that a child will construct a graph, the learner is given graph paper and data and asked to construct a graph.

Objectives must be appropriate for the developmental level of the learner. For instance, a kindergarten child may be requested to identify the color or shape of a given object. An older child may be asked to select an object that meets specified criteria for color or shape (e.g., Find the blue triangle).

Preassessment indicates what a child already knows and gives the teacher valuable feedback on which prerequisite skills of learners have already developed. Usually, preassessment is administered at least two weeks before a module is initiated. Children who already know the lesson content and can perform acceptably on the postassessment may omit a lesson. However, children who know only some of the content should participate in selected activities to form linkages between prior knowledge and new information. Preassessment should be used to identify both weak areas and strengths.

Instructional activities consist of individualized learning experiences designed to assist the learner in meeting stated objectives. Every learner is not required to participate in every activity. Rather, learning activities should be carefully selected based upon each child's preassessment performance (cognitive needs, affective needs, attitudes) and learning styles. At times, students may have the opportunity to select from a variety of activities.

Postassessment gives the learner an opportunity to display the behaviors specified by the objectives. These behaviors may be demonstrated in a variety of ways. For example, suppose the objective reads "To identify the shapes *square, circle,* and *rectangle* by sight." The student may identify shapes by naming them, pointing to examples, or describing where a shape could be found.

Remediation may be required for some children. Two alternatives are available: (1) To recycle the learner through the lesson; or (2) To provide some (alternative) remediation activities. Unfortunately, the first alternative is selected all too frequently. The second alternative offers the advantage of repeating content while varying the approach—and it may be the approach that caused problems the first time through. Repetition per se is not always sufficient for remediation.

The following module, developed by Ruby Stapleton, illustrates the various components we've just described and consists of seven work stations. Read through the module and complete the inquiries.

SAMPLE MODULE: COMPARING LENGTHS

Objectives

1. To sort objects into sets in which all objects of one set are of equal length.
2. To order objects by length, from shortest to longest, or longest to shortest.
3. To determine that one object is the same length as another object by showing that both are the same length as a third (a = b; b = c; therefore, a = c).

Materials for Work Stations

Introduction: Dowels—10 cm, 11 cm, 12 cm, 13 cm, 14 cm, 15 cm, 16 cm, 17 cm (one set of each length)

Station 1: Dowels—10 cm, 11 cm, 12 cm, 13 cm, 14 cm, 15 cm, 16 cm, 17 cm (three of each)
Poster board, one sheet
Plastic cup, small box or glass
Glue

Station 2: Dowels—10 cm, 14 cm, 17 cm (one each)
Filefolder

Station 3: Dowels—10 cm, 11 cm, 12 cm, 13 cm (one each)
Filefolder

Station 4: Filefolder
Yarn
Paper clips (at least 25)

Station 5:   Worksheets
              ¼" x 2" red posterboard strips (25–30)
Station 6:   Assortment of pencils, chalk, crayons, small
                 paint brushes, erasers, straws
              Posterboard (one sheet)
              Worksheets (one for each child)
              Glue
Station 7:   Four sets of crayons (three crayons to a set,
                 each set containing crayons of the same
                 length but different colors, and each set dif-
                 fering in length from the other three sets).
              Answer sheet
              Audiotape, tape player
              Box of crayons

Introduction (Preassessment)

1. Give each child a set of dowels.

2. Ask children to make sets of dowels, grouping the dowels by length.

3. Now ask children to order the dowels by length, longest set to shortest set.

4. Scramble in a pile three or four dowels from each of the eight sets of identical dowels listed under *Materials.* Ask a child to select one dowel from the pile. Then ask him or her to select another dowel that he or she believes is the same length. Compare the lengths of the dowels. Then ask the child to replace both dowels and try again several times. Encourage each student to try this during free time.

5. Record the performance of each child (acceptable measuring). Keep this record to compare with the postassessment.

Activities

Station 1

On a large piece of posterboard, glue one dowel from each set of dowels listed under *Materials.* Leave at least 3 inches between dowels. Prepare an instructions card like that shown in Figure 5.3, and place it beside the posterboard. There is no need for a checking device at this station since the result can be checked visually.

Station 2

Prepare a filefolder to be used at this station. Outline the rectangular lengths of pairs of the 10 cm, 14 cm, 17 cm dowels. Add interest by coloring the rectangles with felt tip pens. Label each rectangle with a letter of the alphabet. Make a pocket out of paper, an envelope, or wallpaper scraps. This will hold the dowels when they are not in use. On the back of the folder make a checking device by matching the correct colored labeled rectangles. (See Figure 5.4.)

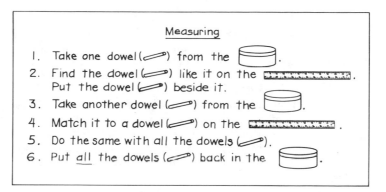

Figure 5.3. Directions Card

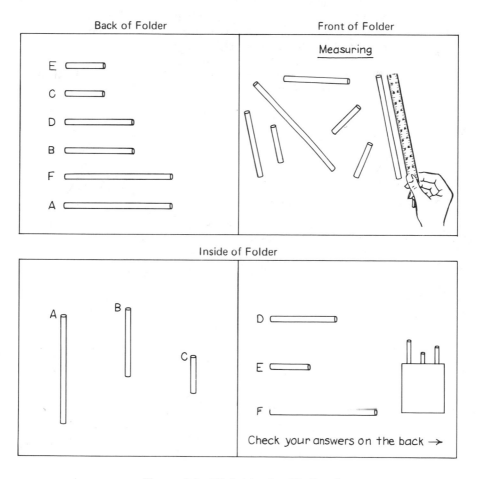

Figure 5.4. Filefolder for Station 2

Station 5

As another enrichment activity, prepare and display the following worksheet. Have at least one sheet per child. Have on hand at least 25 ¼″ × 2″ red posterboard strips. (Figure 5.5.)

Station 7 (Postassessment)

Prepare four sets of crayons of unequal lengths. Crayons in each set should be of equal length. Using the numbers 1 through 12, label each crayon. Make a note of which crayons (by number) are the same length. Example: Are crayons #1, #5, #7 all the same length? Scramble the crayons so the children have an unsorted pile from which to draw crayons of equal length.

Prepare the following audiotape with an answer sheet. (See Figure 5.6 for a sample student worksheet.)

Audiotape Script

Show me what you have learned about measuring. Look at the twelve crayons in front of you. Sort the crayons into sets in which each crayon is of the same length. Stop the tape until you have finished sorting the crayons. Then turn the tape recorder back on.

Look at one group of crayons. Each crayon has a number on it. Write the number of each crayon in Circle A on your answer sheet. Stop the tape until you finish writing.

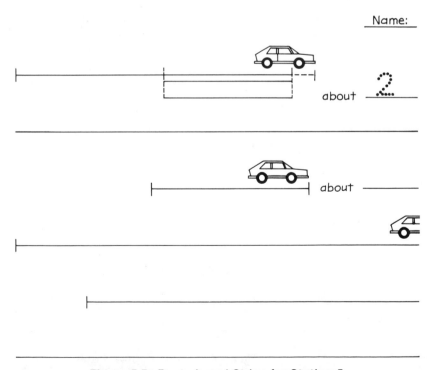

Figure 5.5. Posterboard Strips for Station 5

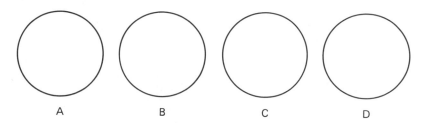

Figure 5.6. Worksheet for Station 7

Put the crayons marked in Circle A into the box on the table. Now look at another group of crayons. Write the number of each crayon in Circle B on your answer sheet. Stop the tape until you finish writing.

Now put the crayons from Circle B into the box with the other crayons. Look at another group. Write the number of each crayon in Circle C on your answer sheet. Stop the tape until you finish writing.

Put the Circle C crayons in the box with the others. Look at your last group of crayons. Write the number of each crayon in Circle D on your answer sheet. Stop the tape until you finish writing. Then put those crayons in the box with the others.

Using duplicate work stations helps avoid overcrowding. Limiting the number of students who work at each station at any one time is another useful management technique. It also helps to space work stations throughout the classroom. And some may even be located outside the classroom. In that case, children could obtain needed equipment and directions from a central storage area and take them to wherever space was available—a corridor, the cafeteria, library, or even the playground. In order for work stations outside the classroom to run efficiently, directions must be clear, conduct rules agreed upon, and some form of supervision must be provided. If an aide or parent volunteer is not available, the teacher must maintain close contact with all groups to ensure that students are on task and not experiencing difficulty.

Notice that a work station is constructed for each activity, as well as for the postassessment. Children may progress through the work stations as rapidly as their ability permits. These work stations are intended to be used in sequence.

Directions at each work station can be provided orally, in writing, via audiotape, or through modeling or pictures. Sketches or audiotapes may be especially useful with younger children or those who have reading difficulties.

Work stations encourage personalized teaching. They offer an approach that (1) recognizes each child's existing skills and knowledge; (2) allows learners to work through activities at their own pace; (3) uses alternate means for communication between learner and teacher; (4) allows extensive one-to-one interaction between student and teacher; (5) lets children who prefer it to work independently—while offering structure to learners who favor that style; and (6) draws children into large-group or small-group discussions when appropriate.

_____ *LOOKING BACK* _____

1. How would traditional instructional approaches have to change to accommodate contemporary materials?
2. How might a teacher who was unfamiliar with contemporary science materials prepare to use them?
3. What advantages do contemporary science materials offer both teacher and learner?
4. What is a rationale for a teacher using a resource unit?
5. What is a rationale for a teacher developing planning skills if a local school system already has a curriculum guide, textbook series, and prepared instructional units available?
6. Many teachers find that preparing a module is very time-consuming; yet they prefer to use it. Why might this be so?

ACTIVITIES

1. Select an elementary science textbook and read one lesson from the book. Does the lesson emphasize recall? What role would the teacher play in the presentation of the lesson?
2. Interview an inservice elementary school teacher to determine his or her role in planning the science program. What input did the teacher have in textbook selection? Did the teacher feel an integral part of the decision-making process?
3. What type of unit would you prefer in teaching science to children? Give your rationale for the type of unit selected.

6

Adapting Instructional Materials

Objectives

1. To formulate a rationale for adapting a prepared unit.
2. To identify major and minor adaptations that may be made in a prepared unit.
3. To identify sources of educational information that might be used for adapting a unit.
4. To describe the process of adapting a prepared unit.

_____ *LOOKING FORWARD* _____

Occasionally teachers find that changing prepared teaching materials increases their effectiveness. Such changes might include simplifying the materials, adding interest, or simply making the materials more suitable for children. In this chapter, the advantages and disadvantages of adapting teaching materials are discussed.

Adaptations in units may be minor—adding an activity or an item of content. Or they may be quite extensive—substituting or deleting several content items or objectives, or altering the sequence of learning activities. At times, integrating portions of a new unit into the prepared unit may also increase the effectiveness of the original unit. Several of these adaptations are discussed and illustrated in the chapter.

Teachers also need sources of information for adapting units. Many are described in this chapter.

In addition, we'll discuss the process of adapting. It isn't as difficult as you might think. In fact, many teachers find it a rewarding way to design an instructional approach that's truly their own.

The chapter closes with an example of how a teacher might incorporate a major part of one unit into another prepared unit—an exciting and challenging task.

At first glance a prepared science unit may appear ideal for teaching a topic. However, as the unit is reviewed, it becomes evident that it will not meet many needs of the class. What are the alternatives? One is to write a new unit. A second is to omit the unit. And a third is to adapt the unit so that it meets the children's needs better. Which alternative would you select?

The first alternative—writing a new unit—might be satisfactory if the teacher had time for planning, defining objectives, selecting content and activities, formulating assessment procedures, and identifying resources. Many busy teachers would not select this alternative.

The second alternative would not be acceptable. If the unit were omitted, the content of that unit might never be taught. This could have serious and disruptive implications for the total effectiveness of the science program.

Many teachers would select the third alternative—and it's a wise choice. Adapting a prepared unit for a class does not require a great deal of time. Such units frequently contain background information and suggestions useful in making modifications. They also generally contain many components that require little or no modification.

Various adaptations are possible. These may include modifying objectives, changing the sequence in which lessons are taught, adding or deleting content, adding learning activities, and changing assessment techniques. Most of these adaptations may be made quickly.

ADAPTING A TEACHING PLAN

Adding New Information

Science teachers are constantly on the lookout for new information. Fortunately, there are many good sources.

Newspaper articles herald new scientific discoveries or suggest new ways to interpret earlier findings. For instance, a newspaper may report that the world's food supply for humans and meat-producing animals could be doubled through hydroponics. This information about hydroponics, commonly called "soilless gardening," might make an interesting addition to a science lesson on growing plants or developing food supplies.

Radio and television programs frequently deal with scientific topics. Public Broadcasting System (PBS) regularly presents special programs on wildlife, environmental concerns, technology, space, and a host of other science-related topics. A schedule of radio and television programs will usually reveal numerous potential sources of current information.

A number of popular magazines and journals containing scientific information are listed in Appendix H.

Courses or workshops may be offered by colleges, science teachers associations, or professional scientific societies. Some courses offer personal instruction; others may be televised or computerized. The curriculum director within a school system or at a state agency can usually provide information about such opportunities.

Don't overlook personal experiences. For instance, when visiting a medical doctor's office, you might question the doctor about any equipment or procedures you think students would enjoy knowing more about. Dentists are often very accommodating about sharing information. Some medical doctors or dentists have videotapes on various aspects of health.

Next time you visit the service department of an automobile agency, you might question the service manager or representative about equipment and methods used in repairing automobiles. Have you ever watched an analysis of a car's operation done by computer? Both you and your students might be intrigued by the speed and thoroughness of the process. The point is, everyday experiences provide many opportunities for gaining new information—*if* you ask questions.

Once new information is incorporated into the teaching plan, several questions need to be answered: (1) Does this new content expand information already in the lesson? (2) Will it be most effective where it's placed? (3) Does the teacher understand the new content or is additional background necessary? Assuming that these questions are answered positively, the next step is integrating the new content with that of the original lesson.

One difficulty that children experience with science lessons is that too much information is presented through reading and discussion, only minimal information through activities that enable children to discover things for themselves. Although reading and discussing are vital for effective science instruction, there should be a balance between reading-based and activity-based instruction.

Few humans learn thoroughly from one experience. A variety of activities or a repetition of the same activity several times is more likely to enhance learning. The following activities were selected for addition to science lessons. Read each activity described below and determine if it is appropriate for the intended science lesson and grade level. Construct a rationale for your decision.

Sample Activities

1. In a lesson on observing seasonal changes in a tree, the class adapted an activity to determine the kind of food and the quantity of food birds eat from a feeder. (Grade 1)
2. During a lesson on floating objects, the children were asked to find the density of various objects in a reference book, then give an explanation for cork floating while a nail sank. (Grade 4)
3. In a lesson on electric circuitry, children were asked to look at several drawings of circuits on a computer simulation and select the ones that illustrated closed circuits. They were asked to give a reason for the selection. (Grade 6)
4. Children were studying factors that affected seed germination. During this lesson they were asked to root a cutting from a coleus plant. (Grade 3)

Which of these four activities would be appropriate for the topic under study and for the grade level? Why?

Activity (1) is inappropriate. Although children would be able to measure the quantity of food eaten and observe the kind of food birds ate, it does not relate to seasonal changes in a tree. Observations about bird food are appropriate for a science lesson dealing with birds, not trees.

Activity (2) is appropriate for the children and is consistent with the lesson. In addition to interpreting useful science information, it would provide an experience with using reference material to solve a real problem.

Activity (3) is appropriate. This experience provides children with an opportunity to apply the content taught during the lesson.

Activity (4) is inappropriate. Children might be able to root cuttings of plants, but the lesson deals with germination of seeds rather than producing new plants from cuttings.

Adding Activities

Adapting science lessons by adding activities has the following advantages:

- The lesson can be adapted to the learning style of the children.
- The lesson provides additional experience for children in learning about science content in different contexts.
- Many science activities add interest to science classes.
- As software becomes available, children enjoy using it and being challenged by it.

You should experience little difficulty adapting a lesson by adding activities. Adding activities may be as simple as posing questions that will pique children's curiosity, or by adding a brief description of an appropriate activity to the teaching plan. Remember to list any equipment or resources you will need.

Several examples of adapting conventional activities for teaching plans are found in Table 6.1.

These adaptations help make science interesting for children, but even more important, they relate science content to the environment of the learner. At an early age, children need to explore their environment, to observe it through perceptual modes. The adaptations above, as well as those you make as you gain experience in teaching, encourage exploration of the environment and interpretation of various observations. Science is one of the few subjects in which environmental exploration can play such a key role.

Observations and interpretations not only build knowledge but also encourage thinking. For instance, observing the number of seeds that germinate in a given area may prompt children to ask what would happen on earth if *all* the seedlings matured.

Constructing a mobile to represent our solar system may help children recognize that our common two-dimensional perception of the system is very limited and misleading. Questions indicate thinking. If children are sufficiently curious, they'll seek answers and provide reasonable explanations for the phenomenon.

Adapting Units

Many teachers find that adapting a prepared unit for their classroom saves a great deal of time. It offers the best of both worlds by allowing the teacher to take a personalized approach to a topic, content, learn-

TABLE 6.1. ADAPTING ACTIVITIES FOR A TEACHING PLAN

Science Topic	Adapted Activity
Identifying three-dimensional shapes (primary grades)	Ask children to observe and touch a variety of objects in the classroom and name the three-dimensional shapes which are felt.
Identifying nongreen plants (intermediate grades)	After they have read about nongreen plants in reference books and the textbook, take children to a wooded area that has decaying trees and ask them to name some nongreen plants they may find—e.g., fungi, lichen, and slime molds. (This activity may be conducted over a period of time to observe the changes in the material upon which the nongreen plants grow.)
Reproducing plants from seed (primary grades)	Collect 100 seeds from a tree (black locust or maple) or flower (dandelion or milkweed) and see how many of the seeds germinate. In an area where seeds drop or are scattered by the wind, count the number of seeds that are germinating within a specified area—e.g., one square foot or square yard.
Observing effects of solar heat (primary grades)	Place thermometers under different pieces of construction paper that are the same thickness, but different in color. Place all the papers in direct sunlight. After a specified time, check the papers to determine which color absorbed the most heat.
Exploring uses for simple machines (primary grades)	Show how a tool is used to do some work. Describe some kinds of work that could be done with the tool that would be otherwise impossible to do without it. In a role-playing situation, devise alternatives to simple machines which could be used to do work.
Studying constellations (intermediate grades)	Construct mobiles of constellations and hang them from the ceiling. Arrange the stars in different planes within the constellation. (Most pictures of constellations depict the stars in a constellation in two dimensions and one plane.)
Exploring changes in the earth's surface (primary grades)	Find a small gully on or near the school campus. Place a container at the bottom of the gully to catch soil and other materials that are washed down during a rain. Weigh the material in the container to determine the amount moved.

(cont.)

TABLE 6.1. (Continued)

Science Topic	Adapted Activity
Exploring changes in the earth's surface (intermediate grades)	Observe layers of actual rocks or photos of layers of rocks. The layers should be tilted or uneven. Search reference materials to find how the layers of rock may have become tilted.
Constructing models of chemical compounds (intermediate grades)	Using small gumdrops and toothpicks, construct a molecule of a compound from its formula. Let each color of gumdrop represent atoms of one specific element. For example, to construct a molecule of water (H_2O), let red gumdrops represent hydrogen and yellow gumdrops represent oxygen. Construct the molecule of water by attaching two red gumdrops to one yellow gumdrop with toothpicks. The formula for a compound may be derived from the gumdrop model if a key to the elements is given to the children.
Observing the effects of heat on matter (primary grades)	To determine if heat affects the rate at which ice melts, measure the temperature at several locations in the classroom—such as near a window when there is sunlight, near the ceiling, near a heater, and in a dark corner. Using ice cubes as nearly identical in size as possible, place one in the open where the temperature is high and another in a place where the temperature is low. Observe which ice cube melts first and relate the melting speed to the temperature at that location.
Observing the effects of heat on matter (intermediate grades)	To determine how rapidly heat travels through water, put one quart of water into a one-and-a-half-quart pan and set the pan on a hot plate. Place several thermometers at various depths in the water. Turn on the hot plate. Measure the temperature every three minutes at each depth.
Constructing a model of an insect (primary grades)	Ask children to create the "silliest"-looking insect that they can. Each insect must have three body parts, six legs attached to the proper body part, and two antennae (wings are optional).
Investigating insect populations (intermediate grades)	Take a census of different kinds of insects in a designated area and attempt to find a reason for the size of the insect population.

ing activities, assessment procedures, and teaching suggestions that are already in place.

There are several ways to adapt instructional units. One is to list additions or changes, then simply insert them at appropriate places prior to teaching the unit. The entire unit, including additions and changes, should be reviewed to ensure logical, sequential organization. Another approach is to combine parts of several units. For instance, the topic, objective, and some content may be selected from one unit, while other content, learning activities, and assessment approach are selected from another unit.

A Textbook Unit. Although many textbook series contain well-prepared lesson outlines and teaching suggestions, teachers may still wish to restate objectives in more definitive terms, add or delete content, add learning activities, or develop their own assessment strategies. A science lesson on mixtures and solutions may be adapted as described in the section that follows.

AN ABBREVIATED TEACHING UNIT: ADAPTING A TEXTBOOK LESSON

Original Objectives

1. To identify and describe three differences among materials in a mixture of solids
2. To separate components of a liquid mixture by filtering

Adaptation (Suggestions for additional objectives):
1. To identify components of a gaseous mixture, such as polluted air
2. To construct mixtures of solids, solids in liquids, and gases in gases

Original Vocabulary

- Mixture
- Filter

Adaptation: Add the term *pollutant* to the vocabulary list.

Original Content

A lesson narrative discusses the term *mixture* and describes where mixtures are found. This discussion is accompanied by a picture of smog over an industrial site. Questions about pollutants in the air, the cause of fog, polluted air being a mixture, and pure air being a mixture are suggested. A photo of smog is included. Additional questions and a photo of polluted water are also included. Suggested questions ask children to make observations about the pictures.

Adaptation: Revise the sequence. It may be more logical for the children to conduct one or both of the following activities before any discussion about the pictures.

Original Learning Activities

Two activities are included in the lesson. One consists of asking children to mix powdered iron and salt, then separate the iron from the mixture with a magnet (*Note:* Wrap a magnet with plastic before putting it near the powdered iron). The powdered iron is attracted by the magnet while the salt is not. A second activity asks the children to separate a mixture of sugar, salt, and water through filtration and evaporation. An extension asks children to separate two mixtures—food coloring and poster paint, each dissolved in water—using filter paper.

Adaptation: Consider adding one or more of the following activities. Ask children to (1) construct several mixtures as a review of the concept of a mixture taught previously; (2) observe pollution locally and identify sources of pollutants; (3) identify the presence of an odor in the air although the source cannot be seen; (4) find ways of separating a mixture of salt and sand or sawdust and sand.

Assessment

Paper and pencil test

Adaptation: In addition to the suggested assessment, ask children to demonstrate preparation of a mixture using sugar and water and to separate the suger-water mixture through the most appropriate method (evaporation).

Although most elementary science textbooks differ in the amount of information they provide about teaching the lesson, background information they offer, and the nature of suggested learning experiences, most offer sufficient structure and detail to make adaptation a better choice than starting from scratch.

Once you've selected a unit for adapting, the next task is to decide on the purpose of the unit. For instance, a unit might be used to extend children's knowledge of a topic, to teach inquiry skills, or to correlate the study of a science topic with another subject such as art, social studies, or mathematics. Knowing the overriding purpose will guide you in construction of an outline, which should include objectives, content, learning activities, and assessment procedures. The outline should be flexible to incorporate changes, additions, or deletions that may not occur to you immediately.

Now it's time to get specific. Ideas for adaptations may come from your creativity, or from the suggestions of colleagues, from elementary science textbooks, or curriculum studies. Many teachers find it helpful to look at methods books and independent units available from some publishers or at the materials published by professional organizations such as the National Science Teachers Association. Governmental agencies and utility companies are other sources. Do you work with handicapped students? Then you might check with organizations that specialize in education for handicapped learners (e.g., the American Printing House for the Blind) and with health-related organizations (e.g., the American Heart Association).

Once an outline is completed, it should be reviewed (more than once) to see whether any additional changes should be made. Then, the unit may be written in final form.

Although some teachers prefer to design their own units, adapting a unit is a very workable compromise for the teacher who lacks either time or experience.

You can feel confident about using an adapted unit so long as the goals and objectives are clearly specified, the activities specifically designed to meet the desired objectives, and the instruction carefully sequenced. Planning also ensures that the lessons meet the needs and interests of individual student learners, directly involve learners in the learning process through a variety of experiences, and put learners in touch with their environment.

Attention given to each step in lesson adaptation pays dividends later, particularly when it frees the teacher to work more closely with students, and frees students to participate actively in and take responsibility for their own learning. Teachers who don't have to spend all their time and energy serving as sole sources of information can become learners too. Thus, everyone benefits.

_____ *LOOKING BACK* _____

1. Under what circumstances may a teacher wish to adapt a unit to include new content or additional activities?
2. How does a teacher determine whether new content and additional activities would strengthen a unit?
3. How does adding new content and activities differ from making extensive adaptations in a textbook unit?
4. How are new content and/or additional activities incorporated into a prepared unit?
5. If a teacher wished to adapt a unit, where could he or she obtain information about new content and additional activities?

ACTIVITIES

1. A prepared lesson for kindergarteners on the care of teeth includes the following:
   a. The number of teeth the children have
   b. Sharp edges of teeth used for biting
   c. Blunt edges of teeth used for chewing
   d. Proper care of teeth (including cleaning, dental supervision, diet, and safety)
   e. Adults who help children care for their teeth (including dentists, dental hygienists, nurses, parents, school dieticians, and teachers)
   f. A record of each child's daily oral hygiene.

New information was gained by the teacher during a visit to the dentist; the teacher found that flossing teeth is very important in maintaining healthy gums and teeth. The teacher wished to inform the children about this finding and assist them in learning a proper way of flossing teeth. Consider these questions:

   1. Can the lesson be adapted to include this new information without disrupting the continuity?
   2. If the new information were to be added to the lesson, where should it be placed in the list of original items of content?

If your answer to question 1 is yes, you are right. The lesson does cover proper brushing of teeth. However, flossing is not mentioned. Since flossing is a very beneficial practice, it should be included, and this inclusion will not interrupt the sequence of the lesson.

    If you selected item **d** as the most appropriate place to include information about the benefit of flossing, we agree. That item deals with the proper care of the teeth. Adding information about flossing anywhere else in the lesson would disrupt content development.

2. Select one lesson from a science textbook, any grade level, any topic. It should have one or more activities. List the content items. Then find a parallel lesson in another textbook or similar source (grade level may be slightly higher or lower than that of the original). Select one item of content from the new source to insert in the selected lesson.

   Does the adapted lesson still follow a logical sequence? Does the new content item reinforce, extend, or provide a basis for the preceding item? Have you inserted it at the best spot? You may wish to discuss the new lesson content or sequence with others.

3. Select one activity (not hands-on or concrete) and adapt it to reflect a highly manipulative experience for children.

4. Add new information to a science textbook lesson by updating the content.

Designing a Teaching Unit

7

Objectives

1. To describe two types of teaching plans.
2. To design a teaching unit for classroom use.
3. To apply criteria for evaluating a teaching plan.

_____ *LOOKING FORWARD* _____

Although teachers may be provided with textbook units or may have
proficiency in adapting units, the ability to design a unit from scratch is
a valuable asset. Creating a unit helps teachers recognize the important
interrelationships among planning, instructing, and assessing learning.

In this chapter, you'll have a chance to actually design a unit. The
final product will be an activity-oriented teaching plan. As you progress
through the chapter, you will work through each step in the development
process. When you complete the chapter, you will have a product, a
teaching unit, that can be used in the classroom.

That doesn't mean all your work is finished, however. The unit must
then be evaluated. One of two methods can be used to assess the
effectiveness of a unit. The first is classroom use. Field testing is
effective, but it may be difficult for preservice teachers to implement. An
alternative is to apply evaluative criteria. We'll offer some suggestions
later in the chapter.

The following poem seems to capture the experience of many
teachers as they begin to plan a science unit.

There once was a teacher
Whose principal feature
Was hidden in quite an odd way
  Students by millions
  Or possibly zillions
  Surrounded him all of the day.

When finally seen
By his scholarly dean
And asked how he managed the deed
  He lifted three fingers
  And said, "All you swingers
  Need only to follow my lead."

To rise from a zero
To Big Campus Hero
To answer these questions you'll strive:
  Where am I going,
  How shall I get there, and
  How will I know I've arrived? (Mager, 1968, p. vii)

The teacher's three questions are expanded in Figure 7.1. Although
these questions may seem simple, answering them requires defining a
philosophy that underlies the entire process of education.

Instructional planning must yield more than a list of facts and
questions. It should result in a well-designed educational experience,

Where am I going?
· What are the goals and objectives of
  teaching?
· With what scientific "stuff" will I/my
  students work?
· Who is to learn what and how?

How shall I get there?

· What plans are needed to reach the
  objectives?
· What resources are needed to
  implement the plans?
· What instructional methodology is
  likely to accomplish the objectives?

How will I know I've arrived?
· How will performance be assessed?
· What alternatives exist if I don't get
  where I thought I was going?

Figure 7.1. Three Important
Questions

one with direction, clear content and methodology, and related assessment procedures.

This chapter is intended to assist you in designing such a unit.
When you have finished you should have a better sense of how to answer the three questions in the poem.

TEACHING PLANS

Teaching plans may be of two types. One specifies very broad content
and learning activities. Such a plan usually lists content items to be
presented and activities to accompany those content items. The result
may be a series of daily lesson plans:

Monday:	Read pp. 25–30 in the textbook. Discuss causes of pulse rate in humans.
Tuesday:	Discuss the relationship between pulse rate and physical activity. Ask children to determine their pulse rates when at rest and after running. Compare the different pulse rates.

Because a plan like this is so general in nature, relating learning activities to objectives and to the needs of learners may be difficult.

A second type of plan, the teaching unit, is developed in greater detail. This plan includes specific objectives, stated in measurable terms; sequenced content relating to those objectives; learning activities appropriate for the learners; and relevant assessment techniques for determining whether the learners have met stated objectives. Remedial and enrichment activities may also be included if they are appropriate for some children.

Designing a teaching unit requires more time than simply listing objectives and activities. However, the time investment is well-justified.

DESIGNING A TEACHING UNIT

Many of the resources we've discussed in other chapters are also useful in planning teaching units; resource books, journals, textbooks, curriculum studies, and curriculum guides are a few examples. Of course, to make the best use of these resources, teachers must know how to select, adapt, and alter content or teaching suggestions to suit their own purposes (see Chapter 6). Once you've designed one unit, you have a model for designing additional units.

A teaching unit usually consists of (1) a science topic; (2) a statement of instructional objectives; (3) an outline of content arranged in logical sequence; (4) a list of diverse inquiry-oriented learning activities; (5) several assessment tasks; and (6) a list of resources and equipment needed for the learning activities. You do not *have* to follow this sequence precisely in designing your instructional unit; however, you are likely to find the task much easier if you do. The model is not intended to be inflexible. It allows for many personal decisions. For instance, you select the topic and content. In addition, you select the objectives and learning activities.

(*Note*: As you read the chapter, conduct the activities relevant to each section, rather than waiting until the end of the chapter. Appropriate activities are noted at the end of each section.)

Selecting a Topic

Potential science topics are often suggested by everyday events or casual observations. Sunlight coming through a classroom window may serve as a focus for investigating heat energy, properties of light, the solar system, or nuclear fusion. When practical experience yields nothing of immediate interest, additional ideas for science topics may be found in textbooks, resource and methods books, and professional journals. Sometimes children have suggestions of their own.

Most teachers have little difficulty finding topics. The challenging part of this task is first narrowing a topic down to manageable size, and then finding ways to teach it most effectively.

Other considerations are also important. Can additional topics be added to those in a textbook without disrupting the instructional sequence of the science program? What resources, other than adopted textbooks, provide ideas for teaching children science? How can topics and content be selected to ensure a science program that is scientifically accurate and interesting to children?

Some science topics generally come from the adopted textbook series of the school system. Others are borrowed—from a similar, complementary series, or from a variety of sources.

One problem with using a variety of resources, particularly multiple texts, is that most series are written for a particular grade level and have a reading level and vocabulary appropriate for students at that grade level. Obviously, successful borrowing requires careful scrutiny of sources. You need to consider not only content and objectives, but reading level and comprehension as well. Of course, if you rewrite large sections of the borrowed lessons, reading level may be less a problem, assuming you have the expertise to adjust the vocabulary and syntax appropriately. It takes practice. Don't worry—your students will offer lots of guidance as you begin sharing lessons with them!

DEVELOPING YOUR OWN TEACHING UNIT

If this is your first experience in writing a teaching unit, it may be helpful if you select a topic that is familiar to you. The topic should

- match the teacher's informational background;
- be appropriate for the intended grade level or group of children;
- lend itself to an activity-oriented approach; and
- be narrowly defined so it can be taught effectively.

Some science background is helpful in teaching any topic. This background may be obtained through courses taken at the undergraduate or graduate level for inservice teachers, through staff development programs, or through discussions with secondary school science teachers. Preservice teachers may strengthen their knowledge of science through personal reading or through additional science courses and workshops.

Many new science teachers fear being unable to answer children's questions. Scientific knowledge is expanding so rapidly that even practicing scientists find it difficult to be current. Both scientists and teachers may be asked questions they are unable to answer. If this happens to you, just honestly admit that you do not know the answer, and tell students you will try to obtain the information.

A topic should be one that children are able to understand. Abstract topics should be avoided. Activities stressing hands-on experience promote both learning and interest. For instance, the characteristics of insects can be taught through observing insects and making models. A topic like molecules, by contrast, would be very difficult to teach to young children. They might be able to memorize information about molecules, but conceptualizing molecules would be all but impossible.

Although reading about a topic is vital, children require a variety of activities to develop thorough understanding. Manipulating equipment, hypothesizing, and testing hypotheses are all valuable.

A teacher must understand a topic well enough to choose activities that illustrate important concepts well. For example, suppose you ask a child to place a card over a glass filled with water and invert the glass, noting that the water and card remain in place. What will this teach the child about air pressure? Probably very little. The only observation that can be made is that the card and water remain in place; air pressure remains unobservable. However, if some more concrete activities illustrating the results of air pressure such as flying kites, designing and flying paper airplanes had been conducted previously, the activity might present an opportunity for children to hypothesize about air pressure. As the children tested their hypotheses, the phenomenon of the water remaining in the inverted glass would become more understandable. Their understanding would transform the activity from an entertaining event to scientific problem solving.

A topic should be specific. Topics like animals, plants, or electricity are too broad. They lack direction. Selecting such a topic is likely to result in a conglomeration of isolated facts. A topic like the habitats of mammals found in a local area is more suited to development of measurable objectives and relevant learning activities.

When a topic not listed in the science program is selected, take care that it does not disrupt the science program. A topic normally taught at another grade level may be too simple or too difficult; either can diminish students' interest and boost frustration. For example, would the topic of electric circuitry be suitable for kindergarteners? They might learn to connect wires in a circuit consisting of a D-cell, a wire, and an electric lamp, but it is questionable whether they could comprehend that electricity was flowing through the wires.

You have been asked to select a topic for the unit you will write. Begin by selecting five topics that you feel both you and children would enjoy. From these five, eliminate any that you would not feel comfortable or secure teaching. Next, eliminate any for which you feel you could not find sufficient background information. If you question what content will be taught, the topic may be too broad and should be more narrowly defined. At this point, if you have more than one of the five topics remaining, choose the one you find most appealing, and the one for which you feel you can design the most valuable and appropriate learning activities.

If, as you begin work on other parts of the unit, you find that the topic is more challenging than you thought, feel free to change it or redefine it more specifically.

Now that you have selected a topic, let's proceed to define objectives.

DEFINING OBJECTIVES

To begin, let's distinguish between goals and objectives. Objectives are specific. Goals, on the other hand, are broad statements of learning outcomes, which often do not lend themselves to direct assessment. Usually, extensive time is required for a goal to be reached. For instance, consider this goal: To develop a positive scientific attitude. Attaining this goal might require an entire school year. Further, measuring attainment of this goal would be difficult, and would likely call for some reliance on subjective evidence—e.g., opinions. All this is not to say that goals are not important, or that they do not provide important philosophical direction to instruction.

There are several schools of thought about writing objectives. One is that objectives are unnecessary. Another is that only general statements or goals are needed for a unit. A third school of thought is that objectives are needed for every unit and they should be stated in behavioral terms. A fourth school stresses that objectives not only specify the desired behavior, but also the degree of acceptability and the conditions under which the behavior is to be displayed. Units may contain objectives at the level of specificity which suits you.

Behavioral objectives are precise statements of the learner's behavior after instruction. The major components of a behavioral objective are these:

- A description of the behavior the learner is expected to display
- The conditions or circumstances under which the behavior is to be displayed
- A description of the acceptable performance level.

Let's consider these components more thoroughly. First, the performance must be observable by the teacher (or other appropriate evaluator) using one or more senses.

In addition, specifying how and where the intended action is performed must be explicit. For instance, asking children to name three phases of water from memory or to select the three from a list are different tasks. One requires total recall; one provides contextual clues. Requiring a student to construct a graph from data is yet another sort of task—one requiring organization, application, and possibly some interpretation of information. The point here is that the conditions should be designed to elicit the kind of behavior you will want at some point to measure.

The criteria for acceptability define "how well" you expect a student to perform some task. At times a student may be required to perform with 100 percent accuracy: naming three phases of water or identifying ten insects from a collection. At other times, some acceptable level of proficiency may be defined: naming at least five parts of the human heart, or estimating a metric length within half a centimeter either way.

Remember that numbers are specific; terms like *some, several, a few, the most important,* and *the major* are subjective and open to interpretation. For instance, if your objectives call for a student to identify nine planets within the solar system, name five parts of a flower, or specify one manipulated variable, everyone knows what is expected. If an objective states that a child is to list *some* planets of the solar system, or name the *most important* parts of a flower, neither student nor teacher can truly know when the objective has been met.

The three components of an objective are identified in the following table.

TABLE 7.1. COMPONENTS OF AN OBJECTIVE

Student Behavior	Condition	Degree
Select	from a list of five conditions	those which may control the change in plant stem length.
Measure	the length of a distance in cm	to an accuracy of 5 cm.
Match	young animals with their parents	with 100 percent accuracy.

Answering the following four questions will help you in writing objectives:

1. What behavior is requested?
2. What sense is used to identify the behavior?
3. Under what circumstances are the behaviors to be displayed?
4. What is the level of acceptable performance?

The objectives we've been discussing deal with the cognitive domain. However, it is equally important to write objectives dealing with behavior in the affective and psychomotor domains. Like cognitive objectives, affective or psychomotor objectives must specify conditions and outcomes. The following statements are examples of *affective ob-jectives:*

- Students will reduce the noise pollution in their environment by speaking in a low voice in the classroom. (Behavior: Reducing noise level. Condition: Speaking in a low voice.)
- Students will display an interest in science as evidenced by their selection of science books for independent reading. (Behavior: Displaying interest. Condition: Select science books.)
- Students will withhold judgment until evidence is gathered from several sources. (Behavior: Withholding judgment. Condition: Awaiting information from several sources.)

Affective objectives can be difficult to measure. A teacher may want a child to enjoy science, but how do you measure enjoyment? Is it eagerness to participate in class activities or writing a story about a science topic? Sometimes, the best a teacher can do is to note observable performance—participating in class discussions or doing independent reading—and draw reasonable inferences based on that behavior. Keep in mind that such inferences are subjective and open to diverse interpretations. Affective objectives are more challenging to write and to measure than those in the cognitive or psychomotor domains.

Psychomotor objectives require the learner to perform some kind of physical action. This may include building, balancing, demonstrating a procedure, or making a collection. The action is usually readily observable. Conditions may or may not be specified. However, a product or outcome is usually required. The following are examples of psychomotor objectives:

1. Construct an electromagnet.
2. Demonstrate one method for constructing a complete electric circuit.
3. Illustrate a technique for stretching and mounting a butterfly.

In objective 1 the action is constructing and the product is the electromagnet. In objective 2 the action is demonstrating and the product is a complete electric circuit. Note that this objective requests only one method. There may be many methods for constructing a complete electric circuit; the learner has the option of using any one. The criterion of acceptability is completion of the electric circuit. In objective 3 the action is illustrating and the product is the mounted butterfly. Objectives in the psychomotor domain require manipulation in addition to utilization of knowledge.

Several references give further information about writing objectives. (See Appendix I.) Writing sound, measurable objectives takes practice, but working from a specified structure can be helpful.

The use of behavioral objectives is sometimes criticized by those who feel objectives can limit a child's learning or force the child to behave in a structured, inflexible way. However, if care is exercised in translating objectives into learning activities, this need not be the case. For instance, take the objective "To construct a complete electric circuit." The means by which the circuit is constructed is left to the child. One child's circuit may include two pieces of wire, a dry cell, a light socket, and a bulb. Another's may include a dry cell, a bulb, a metal spiral from a notebook, a piece of wire, and a metal watch band. Both children have met the objective. Yet they have done so in creative, independent ways. Each child has had to use his or her thinking skills in solving the problem at hand.

Another objective might ask the learner "To identify and test one solution to a specified problem." This objective permits the child to clarify the parameters of the problem, and plan activities to solve the problem. One child might choose to determine the effects of pollutants in waste water upon plant growth. The child would need to define the problem clearly, identify the pollutants, operationally define *plant growth,* and so on. Meeting this objective, in other words, would require the child to synthesize information and to use a variety of inquiry skills. No two students would likely solve the same problem in the same way. Clearly, providing structure and direction to instruction need not stifle creative thought.

You should specify the objectives for your unit at this time.

Selecting Science Content

Selecting content is a task many teachers fear. They tend to feel that their backgrounds in science are so limited that intelligent decisions will be difficult. Actually many teachers have more scientific knowledge than they realize. Since we are living in a highly technological society, much scientific information is available via radio, television, magazines, and newspapers. Further, it is never too late to take a course or two in science. Many are available through local colleges and technical schools. Both secondary and elementary science textbooks provide valuable background information, too.

Does your school or district offer a staff development program related to science instruction? If not, you might request such a program. Of course, for the teacher who likes to live dangerously, there's always the alternative of learning right along with the children by conducting the same activities.

One way to begin content selection is to list all the content items you can think of dealing with a given topic. Then rearrange the items into subtopic lists that seem to go together. For instance, the topic *light* might include these concepts: reflecting, refracting, traveling in straight paths, traveling in curved paths, angle of incidence, and reflecting, colors, wave length, sources, transparent, opaque, and translucent. Since all these concepts could not be treated in depth in one unit, some reorganization is called for. The following subtopic list shows one alternative: (1) color, wavelength; (2) transparent, translucent, and opaque; (3) reflection, angle of incidence, angle of reflection; (4) traveling in straight and curved paths; (5) sources; (6) refraction.

As a unit is developed, any combination of content items may be used so long as they relate logically to one another. Just selecting items because they deal with a broad topic leads to confusion. Placing content subtopics in closely related groups minimizes confusion.

The following example of content modified from a fifth-grade textbook (Barufaldi et al., Level 5, 1985) illustrates how the authors might group related content items.

UNIT TOPIC: CELLS

Content: Cells as the building blocks of living things.

Related Topics: Appearance of cells
Structure of cells
Functions of cell parts
Division of cells
Single-celled organisms in pond water
Multicellular organisms in pond water
Specialized tasks performed by cells

Note that the items of content are closely related to each other and to the topic. Note also the sequence in which the topics were presented, from an operational definition of a cell to the appearance of a cell to the structure of a cell. The learner is permitted to observe the cell first, then to identify the structures, and finally, to explore the functions of the structures. The topic is expanded to cover the diversity of cells, single-celled organisms, and multicellular organisms. The unit concludes with special functions.

By this point you should have selected a topic, defined objectives, and outlined content. With these tasks done, you have made an excellent start at developing a unit. However, if any part of the task is making you feel uncomfortable, you should get help. Someone experienced in unit writing—perhaps a colleague—may be of assistance to you. Also, be careful not to set your expectations too high. Few teachers can write units with which they feel fully satisfied the first few times. Practice is the key. The reward is the smile on a child's face that says "I understand this."

Selecting Learning Activities

If you are a beginning teacher or one without an extensive science background, don't hesitate to become a borrower. And do not limit yourself to one or two sources. Books, films, people, experiences: all can be valuable. Even for very experienced, confident teachers, outside sources remain necessary. You are encouraged to keep current with new ideas and techniques by subscribing to professional journals, both those related to the discipline of science and those devoted to general education. *Science and Children, Instructor, Teacher, Learning, Science Activities, Childhood Education,* and *Young Children* are a few of the excellent journals that may provide suggestions for your planning and teaching. Computer packets may also be of assistance to you.

Because of the close interrelationship between objectives and learning activities, it may seem tempting to select an exciting activity and worry about writing an appropriate objective later. Avoid this temptation. Objectives provide direction for the entire unit; activities are simply intended to help learners meet those objectives.

Depending upon the developmental level of the students, activities may have several levels of sophistication. Younger children learn most effectively from direct experience, particularly in making observations. Older children may also enjoy interpreting data and making inferences based on their observations.

Activities should be varied to meet the diverse needs of children who are creative, who are logical and methodical, learn rapidly, who learn slowly, or who have perceptual or physical problems. Some active and some passive learning experiences should be included. Manipulation of equipment tends to be more active, discussion and reading more passive.

The following activities illustrate the diversity that can exist in a unit. The activities relate to this objective: To identify at least five observable properties of water.

- In groups of four or five, children are asked to observe a beaker filled with a liquid; they are to make at least five observations.
- In a large-group discussion, the children are asked to share their observations and suggest a name for the liquid. They are asked to give a rationale for the name suggested.
- Children are asked to use a reference to check for agreement between their observations and the suggested name. Based on this information, a name is selected for the liquid.
- Using a medicine dropper, students place drops of water on paper towels, waxed paper, aluminum foil, and on cloth. Observations are made of the interaction between water and the surface material.
- Students are encouraged to put drops of water on other objects and to observe the interaction.

- Students are given containers of cooking oil, alcohol, and water. After observing the liquids, they are asked what they think will happen when all liquids are combined in one container. Before the liquids are combined, equal quantities are measured out and weighed.
- The liquids are combined in a test tube. As children observe the results, they are referred to the weight of equal quantities of liquids. They are referred then to a textbook to read about density.
- Children may mix other liquids following the procedures above.

These activities illustrate a variety of learning experiences, requiring both manipulation and reading. Children may also explore their own ideas, transferring techniques from other activities. Note that the teacher's interaction with the children is not specified in the activities. The teacher's role is one of a guide. He or she does not dominate the activities or the discussion. The emphasis is on the students' interaction with their environment.

The preceding activities also illustrate a learning cycle incorporated into the Science Curriculum Improvement Study (SCIS). This learning cycle has three parts:

Exploration:	The child encounters a new concept through an activity.
Invention:	Once the child has acquired some knowledge about the concept, a name is supplied for the concept.
Discovery:	The child applies the concept in a new situation.

This cycle is designed to maintain the joy of discovery as students encounter new phenomena, observe and investigate, conduct research, and expand their knowledge and capability to form hypotheses or make predictions.

At this time you should begin to select learning activities for your unit. Remember that each unit should include several activities for each item of content, and that activities should be appropriate for a variety of learning styles and abilities.

Note: One method for determining the effectiveness of an activity is to try it yourself before writing it into a unit or using it with students. Having done an activity yourself, you are better prepared to help students work through the activity and learn from it. In addition, doing the activity can help you identify prerequisite skills and knowledge required of learners.

Selecting Alternate Learning Activities. Alternative activities may be required for students with special needs—not only those who are unable to successfully complete the unit, but also those who do well and may wish to explore the topic in greater depth. Remedial activities for children experiencing learning problems frequently consist of the original activities or parallel activities broken into very small steps. More capable students enjoy a challenge; they may require additional equipment and resources to continue their investigations. Alternative activities are intended for a few children with special needs, not for the entire class.

Identifying Resources

A resource list can save you a lot of time. It's much easier to glance at a summary list than to read through an entire unit searching for references to needed supplies. The following activity is presented to assist you in selecting resources for your unit.

Read your list of activities. What equipment and materials are needed for these activities? The following questions may guide your thinking.

- What books, films, and other audiovisual aids will you use?
- Where will you get your equipment and other resources?
- If some equipment or resources are not available, do you know of alternatives?
- What quantities of each resource will you need?
- Do you know how to use the equipment?
- If you have to share, rent, or borrow resources, will they be available when you need them?

DESIGNING ASSESSMENT TECHNIQUES

The term *assessment* is used to connote three types of evaluations frequently incorporated in a unit. One type, frequently omitted from teaching plans, is the *preassessment,* discussed previously. The second is *continuous monitoring* of learning as a unit is being taught, sometimes known as *formative evaluation.* Formative evaluations are seldom written into the unit as specific tasks. Such evaluation may consist of observing a child's work, asking a question, making a comment when the child has met an obstacle, or giving a diagnostic quiz. Since the problems children will encounter during a unit are usually not predictable, it makes little sense to select questions or specify observations or comments in advance.

The third type of assessment is a planned, formal *summative evaluation,* intended to determine if children have met prescribed objectives. Most units specify plans for summative evaluation because it is an important tool for assessing the knowledge and skills a student has acquired through a unit. In addition, summative evaluation results may provide a basis for reporting the progress of children as well as assessing the effectiveness of a unit.

Summative evaluation tasks require students to display the specific actions or behaviors specified by the objectives. For instance, suppose the objective is to list at least five observable properties of water. Evaluation of students' performance on this objective could consist of asking them to list orally or in writing at least five properties of water. Or students could be given a list of sixteen properties and asked to select the five properties describing water. As you may have guessed, a logical time to plan evaluation is when objectives are first being written.

A word of caution: Summative evaluations need not be in paper-and-pencil format. This stereotype is a holdover from the days when testing often tended to stress recall. However, with the new emphasis on behavioral objectives, some testing alternatives should be considered. If a child is expected to construct an electromagnet or complete an electric circuit, paper-and-pencil testing is inadequate. Construction of the circuit is a more reliable measure of the critical objective. In designing summative evaluation tasks, consider the nature of the learning objective being measured. The following information will assist you in selecting summative evaluative tasks for your unit.

Read the objectives for your unit. Select at least three tasks in which learners may demonstrate the action specified by *each* objective. (One task per objective may not be sufficient to provide a reliable picture of performance.) If possible, try out each task with a group of children or peers. Ask them to state their opinions of each task. Answering the following questions may help you assess your evaluation:

- Is the performance observable, or do you have to draw inferences or guess at the child's action?
- What sense(s) do you use in observing the child's performance?
- Is there a good match between task and objective?

CRITERIA FOR EVALUATING A TEACHING UNIT

At this point the initial draft of your unit should be complete, and some thought must be given to evaluating it. Several suggestions are offered in Table 7.2.

Several additional factors should be considered when a unit is developed. First, is there internal consistency in the unit? The unit topic should be descriptive of whatever content or strategy the unit is meant

TABLE 7.2. FEATURES OF EFFECTIVE UNITS

Characteristics	*Indicators of Characteristics*
1. Active involvement of the learner in the learning process	1. A variety of learning experiences are planned for learners with diverse abilities and learning needs.
2. Problem-solving orientation	2. Time is built in for children to identify and discuss problems. Children are encouraged to identify their own problems. Time is available also for problems to be clarified and limited.
3. Relevance to learners' interests and needs	3. Learning experiences allow children to manipulate concrete objects. Abstractions are avoided.
4. Consistency with the underlying goals and philosophy of science education	4. Units are planned so children learn content by using scientific processes. They engage in such activities as observing, measuring, and classifying. Conclusions are based upon as much data as is available, rather than on limited data from one activity.
5. Open-ended nature, free of built-in "correct" solutions	5. Time is provided for the teacher to question each child about observations, rather than saying "That's right," and hurrying on to the next activity.
6. Open approach that allows students freedom to inquire, to develop a personal method of solving the problem, to test the solution and judge its correctness individually without the imposition of an outside judgment from any source—and freedom to be wrong as well as right	6. Children are encouraged to suggest methods for conducting an activity or solving a problem. At times, the child is permitted to make a mistake and retrace the steps in order to identify the error. Above all, the instructor avoids bringing closure to an error by stating "That's wrong," and then continuing with the lesson.
7. A conceptual framework, designed to build knowledge of broad concepts and using specific scientific information	7. Science content is logically arranged. Lesson content may be outlined and all items in the outline relate directly to the topic of the unit. For example, an outline of content for a unit on plant reproduction would include the following items: seeds, cuttings, layering, growing plants from seed, grafting.
8. Continuity with previous and future lessons	8. Skills taught previously, such as observing or measuring, are included. If a lesson relates to a

(cont.)

TABLE 7.2. (Continued)

Characteristics	Indicators of Characteristics
	skill taught previously, the relationship should be identified.
9. Opportunities for each student to succeed as a result of his or her own learning activities	9. Activities appropriate for all children in a classroom should be included. This requires alternate learning activities within each unit.
10. Flexibility	10. The unit should be organized so that it can be altered easily without losing the thread of continuity. Content as well as learning activities may be inserted or deleted. Teaching techniques may be adjusted as necessary. Time schedules as well as the learning site should be capable of some modification.

to teach. Evidence of chemical change is such a topic; it specifies what is to be taught rather than just chemical change. Other examples include *Effects of Fertilizers on Plant Stem Growth, Germination of Seeds,* and *Refraction of Light.* These topics identify functional learning units that teachers can manage. Objectives should derive naturally from the topic. For example, the objective *To identify four foods which promote the development of strong bones* is consistent with a unit on *Selection of Foods.* The objective deals with the utilization of nutrients, an important facet in the selection of foods. In a unit on seed germination the objective *To develop a tomato plant from a cutting* would be inappropriate. Developing plants from cuttings might be a worthwhile activity, but it would not relate directly to the stated objective of the teaching unit.

Second, the content should agree with both topic and objective. An objective for a unit may be *To identify at least four parts of a green plant.* The following items of content might be selected for the unit: root, stem, color of leaves, flowers, germinating seeds, and stems. Since *colors of leaves* and *germinating* are not parts of a plant, they should be eliminated from the list of content items. The root, stem, flower, and leaf *are* parts of a plant and may constitute the content of the unit.

Learning activities should directly relate to content and objectives. These activities may be used to provide information, develop vocabulary, relate one item of content to another subject, or provide a basis for expanding learning. Whatever the purpose for any activity, it must promote mastery of an objective or a prerequisite skill for the unit. For example, a unit on weather might have an activity on reading a thermometer—in this case, a prerequisite skill. The module *Symmetry* (reprinted from *Science: A Process Approach Module 35,* copyright 1984, Delta Education, Nashua, NH) states the following objectives:

   a. Identify objects that have line or plane symmetry.
   b. Demonstrate that some objects can be folded or cut in one or more ways to produce matching halves.
   c. Identify and describe bilateral symmetry.

Note the correlation between the preceding objectives and the following activities from the same module:

Activity 1:	Cutting paper figures to identify bilateral symmetry in as many ways as possible. (Objectives **a, b,** and **c.**)
Activity 2:	Finding lines of symmetry through observation and grouping shapes according to the number of lines of symmetry. (Objectives **b** and **c.**)
Activity 3:	Using real objects and drawings of objects to find lines of symmetry. (Objectives **b** and **c.**)

In the module on symmetry, the following correlation is evident between objectives and evaluation tasks:

Evaluation Task 1:	Choosing shapes that are symmetrical. (Objective **a.**)
Evaluation Task 2:	Testing shapes to demonstrate that they are symmetrical. (Objective **b.**)
Evaluation Task 3:	Identifying shapes that have bilateral symmetry. (Objective **c.**)

Third, as we've already noted, once learning activities are selected, the resources necessary for teaching the unit must also be identified. Resources like reference books and printed materials seldom pose problems. However, not everyone knows how to boot a computer, focus a microscope, or run a film projector. Teachers who are not familiar with certain pieces of audiovisual or science equipment, or with computers, can usually get help or suggestions from other teachers in a school. Personnel from the media departments of colleges or community colleges are often helpful. Many schools have student assistants or paraprofessionals who will demonstrate or even run equipment for you. Or, you may be lucky enough to get a parent volunteer. If several teachers in a school are unfamiliar with the operation of certain items of equipment, they might request a workshop on equipment utilization and operation.

A fourth consideration, arrangement of furniture and facilities, may seem a relatively minor issue, but it can be important. Generally, arrange furniture and facilities so as to minimize children's movements; however, make sure they can move when necessary without crowding or bumping into each other. Children using a learning center should not have to move much to proceed from station to station. And when they move, they should not block walkways or doorways, or interfere with the work of other students. (We discuss this issue in somewhat more detail in Chapter 8.)

Finally, it's important to ask how the content of a science unit may relate to what is being taught in other subject areas. For example, metric measurement may be covered in both the mathematics and science programs. To avoid repetition, it could be taught in just one class. Some science units can provide enrichment experiences for lessons in other subjects. A science unit on the classification of rocks and minerals might supplement a social studies unit on natural resources. Skills generally taught in other subjects may be used in science units. Writing, for example, is traditionally considered a language arts skill. But writing can be a valuable and necessary tool for learning in science classes. Children can write to learn, clarifying and expanding ideas as they prepare notes, journals, and reports. Increasing numbers of science teachers report success in teaching science through writing.

Some attempted links between science and other subjects may be questionable. Singing a song about clouds, plant growth, or friction may have little impact on concept development. On the other hand, listening to various musical sounds might be a fine activity for the unit on pitch and loudness of sound. The point is, contrived relationships should be avoided. If you have to stretch to establish the link, it probably isn't worth the trouble. Given that science touches our everyday lives in profound and expanding ways, the opportunities to capitalize on genuine and important relationships between science and other content areas are numerous.

_____ *LOOKING BACK* _____

1. What advantages and disadvantages can you identify with a broad generic teaching plan vs. a structured teaching plan? Give a rationale for your answer.
2. If you were to write another teaching plan, how might you change your approach in selecting a title, objectives, content, learning activities, assessment procedures, and resources?
3. What changes in your teacher's plan were indicated by the criteria for evaluation?

ACTIVITIES

If you have been completing activities throughout the chapter, in accordance with our suggestions, then some activities in this list will serve primarily as reminders. You might use the list to ensure that you have completed all elements for your science unit.

1. Select a title for your unit using criteria in the chapter.
2. Select the words from the list below which specify an *observable* behavior. List the sense which may be used to observe the behavior:

Behavior	*Sense*	*Behavior*	*Sense*
Name		Construct	
Group		Know	
Conceptualize		Like	
List		Identify	
Understand		Appreciate	

The behaviors *name, construct,* or *identify* may be observed through hearing or sight. The behaviors *know, understand,* and *conceptualize* are not observable; thus they could not be used in behavioral objectives.

3. Write four action words and the senses used to observe them.
4. Five behavioral objectives are written below. Reconstruct the objectives, writing number (1) above the behavior, number (2) above the condition, and number (3) above the word or phrase indicating acceptable level of performance.

a. To construct a graph from a data table listing the average height increases of plants over a two-week period with 100 percent accuracy.

b. To match the names with pictures of eight out of ten trees.

c. To name the colors *red, yellow,* and *blue* on sight.

d. To measure the volume of a liquid within 1 milliliter using a graduated cylinder.

e. To identify from pictures three stages in complete metamorphosis.

Compare your responses with those that follow:

(1)	(2)	(3)
a. Construct a graph	from data ...	100% accuracy
b. Match	common names with pictures	8 out of 10
c. Name	when seen	100% accuracy implied
d. Measure	using graduated cylinder	1 ml
e. Identify	from pictures	100% accuracy implied

5. Write three objectives in the affective domain. Mark the action or behavior with the numeral (1) and the conditions with the numeral (2).

6. Write three objectives in the psychomotor domain. Identify the action and the product (or outcome) for each objective. You may find that such verbs as *construct, demonstrate, illustrate, build,* and *sort* are used frequently.

7. Write from three to five objectives for your unit.

   • Answering the following may help you evaluate your objectives.

   • What behavior is expected from the learner?

   • What is the level of acceptable performance? In other words, what are the indicators that the learner has mastered the objectives?

   • Under what conditions are the behaviors to be displayed?

8. Review the teaching unit in Chapter 5. Based on the content of several science textbooks or curriculum guides, list items you may wish to teach. From this list, select a set of closely related items. Use this list in selecting the content for your unit.

9. Select at least three activities to teach each item of content.

10. Write two evaluative tasks for each objective. Ensure that each task directly measures the behavior or performance specified by the objective.

11. List resources and equipment needed for your unit.

REFERENCES

Barufaldi, James P., Ladd, George, & Moses, Alice (1985). *Science* (Teacher's Edition, Level 5). Lexington, MA: D.C. Heath & Co.

Delta Education (1984). *Symmetry* (Module 35) in *Science: A Process Approach.* Nashua, NH: Delta.

Mager, Robert F. (1968). *Developing attitudes toward learning,* Palo Alto, CA: Fearon Publishers.

Science Curriculum Improvement Study (1970). SCIS Sampler Guide. Chicago: Rand McNally.

8

Creating and Maintaining a Learning Environment

Objectives

1. To identify classroom facilities necessary for effective science lessons.
2. To identify facilities management techniques that enhance science teaching and learning.
3. To identify resource management techniques that enhance science teaching and learning.
4. To identify important safety procedures for a science classroom.

_____ *LOOKING FORWARD* _____

Science is a little different from some subjects in that it demands some special facilities and equipment. It's only natural for teachers to be concerned about managing the equipment and facilities effectively. What if something gets broken, damaged, lost, or stolen? Suppose there's no real order and the whole facility reverts to chaos? These fears are real and they're not uncommon. But careful planning can put you in control of good classroom management. Of course, proper distribution, retrieval, inventorying, and replacing of equipment is time-consuming. So is the design and arrangement of an inviting, stimulating classroom environment. You could have the finest equipment and resources in the world, but if they were not arranged so that children could get at them and make good use of them, what would be the point?

Safety in the classroom concerns everyone associated with education of children: teachers, parents, administrators, and children themselves. In this chapter, we'll offer some suggestions for the safe use of equipment, chemicals, and living organisms (both animals and plants). We'll also alert you to some potential dangers, and offer advice on the supervision of children.

We've emphasized planning to such an extent that at this point you may feel that planning is all a teacher does. Obviously that's not true—yet the success of classroom instruction does depend, to a large extent, upon the depth and quality of a teacher's preparation. Instructional planning alone is not enough, however.

Not even the most comprehensive instructional unit can achieve its full potential in an environment that fails to provoke children's curiosity or that stifles their efforts to explore, to examine, and to discover.

It's no secret by now that we believe in the importance of letting children interact with the environment, utilize resources, manipulate equipment, and explore materials. That doesn't mean that these explorers should head off in all directions, helter skelter. On the contrary, effective exploration, like virtually every endeavor, depends on good management. You, as the instructor-manager, need to set goals and to guide the use of equipment and other resources—to track how it's being used, where, and to what purpose. Careful management helps you not only create a productive learning environment, but expand and enrich that environment for the many learners yet to come.

LEARNING ENVIRONMENTS

A learning environment is any place where children learn. Its features include furniture, people, lighting, noise level, space in which to move, and all the objects, equipment, or resources existing within the environment. The learning environment, then, is the total of all features within a learning setting, both human and physical. Because not all learning occurs in school, children may encounter many different environments, each with its own unique influence upon their education. Let's consider four learning environments a child may experience: home, community, school, and classroom.

Home

The home is the first learning environment for most children. In this setting, the child's first science experiences occur, and curiosity first develops. At home, children have their first opportunities to explore the environment of which they are a part. They touch, see, smell, and taste everything with which they come in contact. Constant manipulation is a way of life for young children; it is their way of learning. And as early environmental explorers, most children are driven to learn. Some children have a wealth of experiences with which to appease their curiosity, while others have only limited experiences. The range and nature of early experiences seem to influence strongly the later learning of the child. As the number of experiences increases and children mature, they begin developing concepts and generalizations about their world.

The home environment is generally rich in materials to manipulate, places to explore, and events to observe. The kitchen is especially attractive to children since pots and pans, measuring cups, and wooden spoons provide interesting textures, shapes, and sources of noises. These objects become whatever a child's imagination makes of them.

Common household objects as well as toys may be managed in one of two ways. In some homes, objects may not be provided or they may be kept in a designated place to maintain a standard of safety or neatness or to protect the objects from potential damage. Some parents may go too far in stripping an environment of potential temptations, perhaps unaware of the vital aspect of play in the cognitive and physical development of the child. However, children explore, whether objects are provided or not. If nothing else is available, they will examine their fingers and toes, furniture, walls, windows, and floors. Their insatiable curiosity drives them to cover every inch of even the most impoverished environment.

A second type of home setting management is one that encourages exploration and investigation. Children are free to interact with objects as their interests dictate. Frequently the learning setting is enriched with the addition of toys, books, puzzles, games, pets, and people. A child in this environment receives a much broader range of stimulation.

Another aspect of home setting management is parental instruction. Parents differ widely in the amount of encouragement, instruction, or modeling they may provide to children in how to interact with the environment. One parent may read stories in books and discuss the pictures. Another may help children assemble puzzles or construct shapes from blocks. However, sometimes the effect of parental instruction is limited. If a child is given a gift wrapped in paper and ribbons, the wrapping may attract attention and the content of the package go ignored. For instance, picture a young child who has just been given a top wrapped in tissue paper. The paper may be removed quickly, torn, wrinkled, squeezed, and put in the child's mouth while the top lies on the floor unnoticed. The parent may show the child how to make the top spin, then hold the child's hand on the top to make it spin. But as soon as the parent releases the child's hand, the top is forgotten. The child returns to the paper. Operating the top is too difficult for the child without help; the paper seems to offer more exciting and satisfying sensory experiences.

There seems to be a definite relationship between home experiences and academic progress. As some educators have noted, children who have been provided with experiences in the home prior to entering school are better prepared for the academic challenges they meet.

Many effective school science activities are based upon common activities in the home setting; sometimes, these experiences may help to compensate for lack of experiences in the home. There is one major difference, however. At home, children may observe, measure, and classify in a random manner. In school, learning activities are usually conducted in group settings and are formally structured.

After the child enters a formal educational setting, the home becomes a place where learning that occurs outside can be reinforced. For this reason, encouragement and support are vital home contributions.

Teachers can do a lot to see that as many children as possible receive support from home. Many parents are interested in their children's elementary school experiences. Others may become interested if they are informed about the topics children are studying and the kinds of activities they are doing. Do not depend on children themselves to communicate this information. First graders using string to construct geometric shapes may describe the activity as "playing with string." If you want parents to appreciate the real purposes and objectives of your instruction, you'll need to take the initiative for sharing that information. You might consider a letter to parents phrased something like this one:

Dear Parents:

For the next three weeks the class will be studying life cycles of plants and animals. If you have a pet at home, your child will already have had an opportunity to see changes in its growth and development. This type of out-of-school experience will help to further illustrate what we are studying in class.

Your cooperation can help us. If you have picture books with stories about baby animals, this would be a good time to read them and discuss the changes that occur as the animals grow up. A visit to a farm or zoo with a discussion of how various animals change as they grow would also be useful and fun for your child.

As always, you are invited to join us in this study by coming to school. If you have some knowledge or skill to share on this topic, I would be grateful for your help.

If you have any questions, please contact me.

Sincerely,
John Marks
Elementary Science Teacher

Sometimes, parents who are informed about science topics can reinforce learning. For example, when a class studies machines, parents who have the opportunity can take their children to construction sites where large machines operate. A unit on plants could be reinforced with visits to parks, national forests, botanical gardens, nature preserves, or plant nurseries. Even careful scrutiny of a back yard or window box can provide a variety of worthwhile observations.

You can also encourage children to repeat activities at home and explain them to parents, brothers or sisters, or other adults. Repetition tends to clarify concepts for the child. Few of these interactions will occur without frequent and continuous communication with the parents. And even then, some compromises often must be made. Not all children live with parents. Not all children have parents or other guardians who are willing or able to make site visits or otherwise share in children's learning experiences. Don't let that discourage you, however. If you can elicit the cooperation of some parents, while remaining sensitive to the needs of the child for whom at-home support is nonexistent, you may be able to establish a positive model others will wish to follow.

Community

Once a child leaves home, a wider environment—the community— opens new doors to learning. In the outside world, children see clouds, feel wind, see machines at work, hear thunder, feel rain, experience new faces and voices, and explore both natural and man-made things on a much broader scale than is possible in the home. They notice that some machines move on large wheels, that water usually feels cool, and that air can be felt but not seen as they run. They discover birds' eggs, watch wasps construct their homes, see snails move their shells, watch worms crawl in the ground, see and smell flowers of different colors and shapes. Small children are fascinated by the wind scattering dandelion seeds or by the sight of a spider's delicate parachute floating along on the breeze. They may see insect larvae eating plant leaves and infer that the plant will be destroyed. Seeing is the first step toward inquiring, toward asking how and why events occur as they do. Guided again by parents, or other adults, children learn the importance of using their observations to form questions—then using more observations to get answers. This multiplicity of experience plays an important part in developing curiosity. The child who learns to ask about the impact of leaf-eating insects may later question the impact of industrial wastes being dumped in water or fumes being released into the atmosphere.

Although a teacher cannot control what occurs in the community, he or she can use these events to reinforce learning. For instance, field trips can supplement the study of a topic or offer examples that could only be read about or described in the classroom.

Making a survey of community resources can be extremely helpful. The survey should be recorded on file cards and kept in a central location accessible to all teachers. Each card should provide information about the place including address and directions, restrictions, a contact person, a general description of the facility, and some evaluative comments.

Field trips aren't the only way of interacting with the community. The community can be brought to the school in the form of displays, exhibits, and speakers. Many companies and government agencies will offer speakers, films, or other presentations if a request is made. Remember though, you can only make good use of the community learning environment by knowing it well yourself. Teachers—like their students—must sometimes learn by exploring.

School

The school building and campus can extend the learning site beyond the classroom. The heating plant and air conditioning units, the cafeteria with its unique noises, odors, and machinery may become learning laboratories. Corridors may become learning sites—as may the library or media center. A nearby forest or nature area—if you're lucky enough to have one—can provide an outdoor laboratory for the study of science topics. The point is, don't feel you have to stay within the walls of a classroom for learning to occur.

Keep in mind too that it isn't always the learning site itself that is critical so much as the way in which children's observations or explorations of that site are guided. Children who are taken to see the heating plant or air conditioning equipment and told that this collection of equipment heats or cools the building are likely to gain little from the experience. However, with some planning, children may have a chance to observe simple machines working together or feel chilled air from an air conditioning unit.

Some science programs encourage a wider use of the school environment. For instance, Unified Science and Mathematics in Elementary School (USMES, 1970, available through Education Development Center, Newton, MA 02160) offers units that utilize much of the school and community environments as a focus of study. With USMES units, children investigate such diverse topics as waste in a cafeteria or safety at school crossings from a scientific and analytical framework. These units deal directly with all aspects of the environment that are related to the problem under study. Thus, a problem may incorporate concepts and content from science, mathematics, social studies, and the language arts.

Classroom

Any definition of a learning environment must include a classroom, whether it be a traditional schoolroom, computer laboratory, natural area or other site. The physical nature of the classroom exerts great influence upon the kinds of activities that can occur there. The out-of-doors classroom, for instance, should provide certain accommodations for both children and teacher. Distractions, such as noise or spectators, should be minimal. Needed equipment should be readily available. For instance, a floating classroom constructed in the Okefenokee Swamp, bordering Florida and Georgia, has seating areas for discussions and table space for activities and demonstrations. It is located in a part of the swamp that is isolated from tourists. Visiting teachers and students can observe such wildlife as alligators, water birds, fish, insects, pitcher plants, sundews, water hyacinths, and cypress trees—all from this outdoor classroom. There are no disturbances except for the alligators sunning themselves, birds feeding, turkey buzzards flying in lazy circles, and hawks searching for food. The classroom is located a safe distance above the water so the alligators cannot join the children; the other animals attempt to stay away from humans. Not everyone has an opportunity to attend school in a swamp, however.

For approximately six hours per day, the traditional school classroom is home for many teachers and students. The physical condition and emotional climate within this room influence how children react to a lesson, to the teacher, and to each other. An attractive classroom in which children feel comfortable tends to encourage learning. The ultra-neat classroom with everything in place well out of children's reach or the haphazard catch-all room with facilities in disarray will not provide this encouragement.

In many ways, a classroom reflects the type of educational program which occurs there. Take a look at Figure 8.1, a classroom in colonial America. What can you observe about the room? What type of learning experiences would you expect to find in such a room? On the basis of what you see here, what inferences might you draw about this teacher's instructional style?

Notice the seating arrangement, the place of the teacher, and the lack of educational equipment. In this classroom, the accepted mode

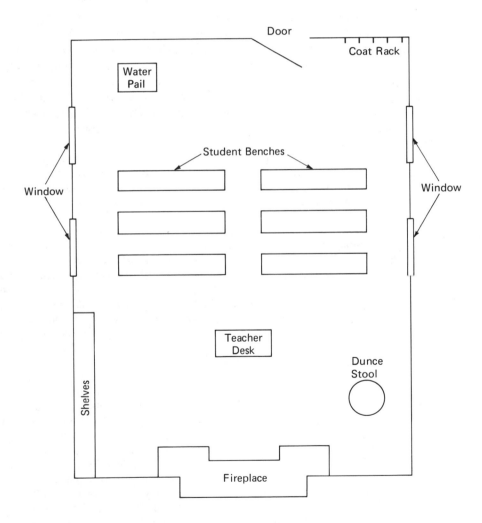

Figure 8.1. Colonial Period Classroom

of learning was memorization and recitation. Lessons were learned by rote and failure to perform acceptably was cause for punishment. The schoolmaster was in complete control and directly guided all learning activities. Every aspect of the classroom emphasized the type of learning that was expected. Colonial schoolmasters had little interest in presenting process-skill-oriented lessons in science; science teaching consisted of discussions. Learning sites were not intended to be pleasant, and the appearance of this room certainly reflected that philosophy.

As American education progressed, classrooms changed. So did curriculum. The classroom of the 1930s placed greater emphasis on students, as shown in Figure 8.2.

How does this classroom differ from the colonial version? Would this type of arrangement be more conducive to presenting the kind of child-centered science lessons this book advocates? Why?

Despite many other changes, notice that the teacher tended to remain in about the same place. Some educators—including John Dewey—were still not convinced that this classroom arrangement was truly functional in teaching children as they should be taught. In his 1902 essay "The School and the Life of the Child" (published in *The School and Society*, 1915) Dewey offered these comments:

> Just as the biologist can take a bone or two and reconstruct the whole animal, so, if we put before the mind's eye the ordinary schoolroom, with its rows of ugly desks placed in geometrical order, crowded together so that there shall be as little moving room as possible, desks almost all the same size, with just space enough to hold books, pencils, and paper, and add a table, some chairs, the bare walls, and possibly a few pictures, we can reconstruct the only educational activity that can possibly go on in such a place. It is all made for listening—because simply studying lessons out of a book is only another kind of listening; it makes the dependency of one kind upon another. The attitude of listening means, comparatively speaking, passivity, absorption; that there are certain ready-made materials which are there, which have been prepared by the school superintendent, the board, the teacher, and of which the child is to take in as much as possible in the least possible time.
>
> There is very little place in the traditional schoolroom for the child to work. The workshop, the laboratory, the materials, the tools with which the child may construct, create, and actively inquire, and even the requisite space, have been for the most part lacking. The things that have to do with these processes have not even a definitely recognized place in education. They are what the educational authorities who write editorials in the daily papers generally term 'fads' and 'frills.' A lady told me yesterday that she had been visiting different schools trying to find one where activity on the part of the children preceded the giving of information on the part of the teacher, or where the children had some motive for demanding the information.

She visited, she said, twenty-four schools before she found her first instance. I may add that this was not in this city.

In pictures of today's open classrooms, Dewey would find room "... for the child to work." In such a classroom, the entire room is structured as a work space, or as a series of work spaces. Furniture and other physical resources are designed for mobility.

Unfortunately, the open classroom is rare. Many teachers continue to be assigned to traditionally arranged and furnished classrooms. Their challenge is to take what is there, alter and adapt it to meet the learning styles they know to be effective. A teacher who wants stu-

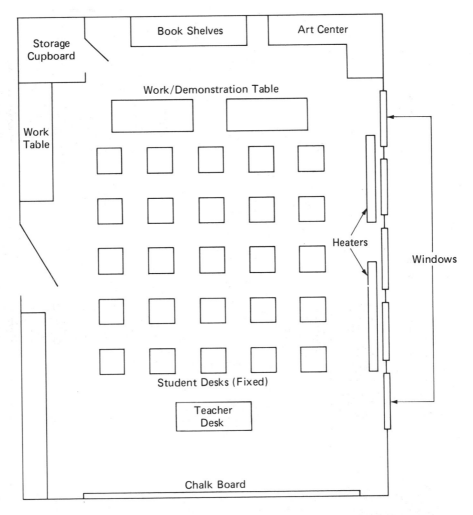

Figure 8.2. Elementary Classroom Circa 1935

dents directly involved in their learning can arrange a classroom to help make that happen.

Even classrooms that are not completely open may provide children with opportunities to follow their interests through extensive use of work areas, learning centers, and movable facilities. If children are to accomplish the goals and objectives established for them, work areas must be arranged to allow freedom, mobility, and varied interaction with the environment. Does the drawing of a partially open classroom (Figure 8.3) look familiar? In fact, many classrooms in use today

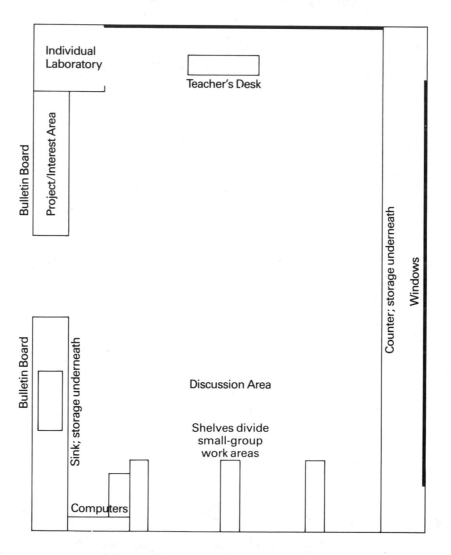

Figure 8.3 A Partially Open Classroom

closely resemble this one. Presenting an active science program in this type of setting requires planning and work—but it can be done.

Compare the three classrooms shown. Then, based on the arrangement of facilities in each classroom, answer the following questions:

- What classroom facilities exist for the comfort of the children?
- Who is the central figure in each classroom?
- What types of lessons might most easily be conducted in each classroom?
- How much student participation would be encouraged in each classroom?
- What teaching strategy would be most appropriate in each classroom?
- What facilities would encourage student investigation?
- Could children move easily around the classroom?
- Are resources for teaching science evident?
- In which classroom would children be most likely to interact with each other and the teacher?

MODERN ELEMENTARY SCHOOL CLASSROOMS

Modern elementary school classrooms include certain basic facilities and equipment for teaching science:

- Bulletin board
- Tables, chairs
- Natural and artificial lighting
- Clock with a second hand
- Storage for equipment and books
- AV equipment
- Water
- Demonstration table
- Electrical outlets
- Chalkboard
- Space for learning and interest centers

The arrangement of these facilities in the classroom is determined partially by the teaching technique used. For instance, tables and chairs can be arranged for a variety of teaching techniques: (1) discussion areas are arranged so that no child need turn to see another child who is talking; (2) small-group areas are located out of the traffic flow, in an area with enough space for children to work or talk quietly; (3) individualized learning centers are located out of traffic patterns or (if all work stations cannot be placed at one table or counter) in some area to which equipment may be easily transported; (4) lecture areas are usually located in the quietest part of the room; (5) demonstration areas are located where children can easily see the demonstration. Some demonstrations require use of an overhead projector or microprojector.

Equipment

Equipment must always be available for student use, which means that the storage area must be convenient for both teacher and children. Suggestions for equipment storage are presented later in this chapter.

If children are expected to get their own equipment from a central location, they need clear access to it. They should be able to move from work site to equipment site and return by different routes so they won't bump into one another. Traffic jams add noise and confusion, and waste time better spent on instruction. Two traffic patterns are illustrated in Figures 8.4 and 8.5.

Both teacher and children may sometimes be responsible for obtaining and returning equipment. Furniture and equipment distribution sites should be arranged so only one trip through the classroom is necessary. Making items of equipment available at several different places in the room also eliminates some traffic problems.

Interest Centers

Interest centers personalize instruction and provide opportunities for extending or remediating learning. An interest center, as its name implies, is designed to lead students into further exploration of some topic or concept. If, for instance, a unit on light were the focus of study, an interest center might contain a series of lenses through which students could observe the refraction of light, or mirrors illustrating reflection principles. In the same way, a unit on flight could include an interest center based on Bernoulli's principle of air pressure and force.

Interest centers may contain items of equipment to be manipulated, objects to be examined, books to be read, or any combination of these. If a center contains equipment, instructions should be provided for its operation. Instructions or suggestions may be written, recorded on audiotapes, or provided through pictures. If objects are included, they might be accompanied by a list of questions directing the observer's attention to some feature.

Interest centers may be started by a teacher and expanded by children. For instance, an insect zoo might contain cages made from milk cartons with nylon stocking covers to keep insects from escaping. As children find various insects, they can add new habitats to the zoo.

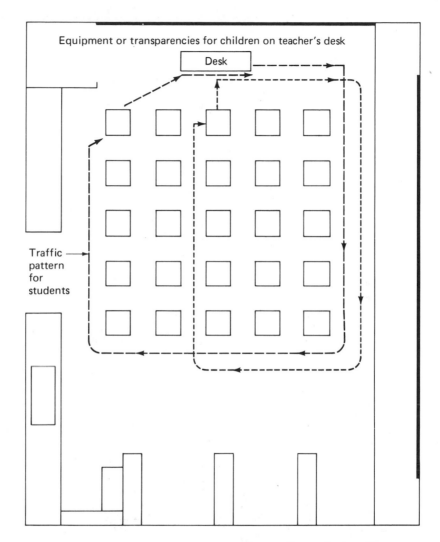

Figure 8.4. Traffic Pattern with Large-Group Instruction

Cards containing information about the insects' habits, food requirements, and life cycles should be placed near each cage.

An interest center can be erected on a library table, window ledge even a corner of the floor. It can focus on any topic that intrigues students. Learning centers that build students' interest and confidence, that make them want to learn more, or that give them a sense of satisfaction about their own participation are meeting important affective objectives.

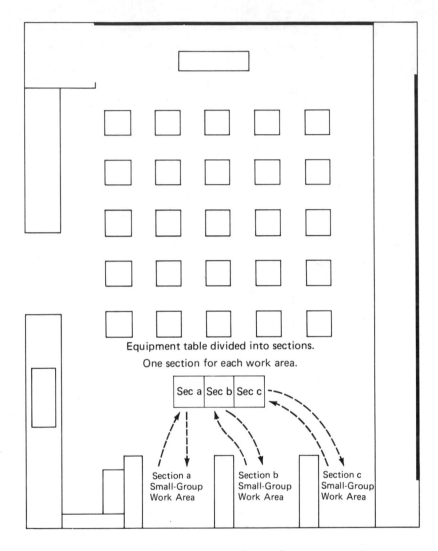

Figure 8.5. Traffic Pattern for Small-Group Instruction

Individual Project Areas

Children need space away from the group, where they can work undisturbed. Imaginative thinking can create many learning areas that allow some measure of privacy right in the heart of a busy classroom:

- A table in the corner of the room marked "Reserved: Please Do Not Feed the Scientists."
- A bathtub for children to sit in as literary research is done. Mark this "Think Tank."

- A large appliance box (refrigerator or washer) in which a table and chair are placed. Mark the box "Laboratory of the Great Wizard."
- A card table under which children work. Mark this "The Hole in the Ground."
- And, if nothing else is available or possible, mark a corner of the room with tape, on the floor, to separate it from other learning areas. Mark this "Admission—One Project."

  In all cases, place this sign near the project area: "Scientist Is In: Please Do Not Disturb."

MANAGING A CLASSROOM

There is no one right way to manage a classroom. It takes trial and error and a lot of planning. Fortunately, you usually have the option to try a new management technique whenever the need arises. What needs attention first? Well, arranging facilities is a logical place to begin.

Planning Facilities in a Classroom

Using the facility management ideas discussed previously, you may be ready to try arranging a classroom for various instructional purposes. Don't experiment with real furniture; you won't feel like changing your mind very often! Instead, make a copy of the floor plan in Figure 8.6 and sketch an arrangement of furniture, equipment, and materials in the room. Experiment. Be innovative. For each of the following situations, arrange the students' desks, teacher's desk, and library table.

- Lecture: Show locations of children and teacher.
- Interest center: Show traffic patterns.
- Learning center with five work stations.
- Small-group activities.
- Discussion: Show locations of children and teacher.

Using another sketch of the floor plan in Figure 8.6, plan for the distribution and retrieval of equipment. Draw lines to indicate traffic patterns as equipment is distributed and returned. Use solid line for the movement of children and a broken line for the movement of the teacher. Incorporate each of the following into your design:

- Equipment distributed by teacher.
- Equipment obtained by children from one location.
- Equipment obtained by children from two locations.

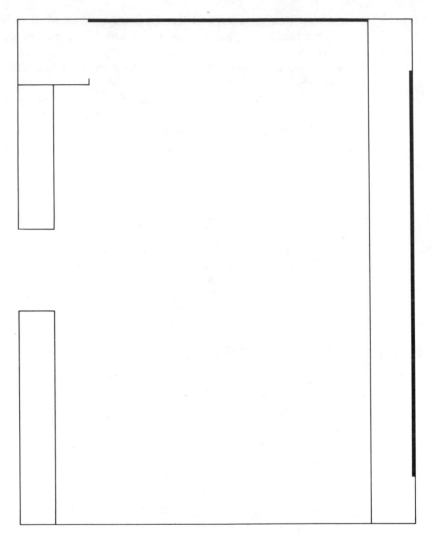

Figure 8.6. Elementary Classroom Floor Plan

- Equipment distributed by student assistants.
- Permanent, nonmovable equipment (e.g., large aquarium).

Children often tend to converge in one place. You can avoid this bunching by planning several activities so children are using different items of equipment at different times. You can also plan shorter activities so that children have time to take turns. A third alternative is to place equipment at the children's desks or tables while they are "on break." A fourth is to ask one member from a group to get equipment for the group.

Getting materials and equipment into the hands of children is only half the problem. Making sure that all equipment is returned is equally important. Magnets and lenses are examples of fascinating, highly portable items that have an affinity for children's pockets. And air pistons (syringes) make super squirtguns. Children often borrow items fully intending to return them—but forget or lose the items. The teacher must devise a system to prevent this, not only because it is a bad precedent for the child, but also because without the equipment, children are unable to repeat activities.

One way to establish a clear understanding about returning equipment is to discuss it openly with children. When students realize that the equipment is really theirs, and that it must be around for use tomorrow and next week, the problem often diminishes of its own accord.

An efficient inventory system is also important. Setting up such a system takes time in the beginning, but saves time in the long run. An inventory system may require numbering items and counting items as they are returned. Small items can be stored in an egg carton, one item to a compartment. Egg cartons can be scanned quickly to check for missing items. Some teachers find it handy to outline pieces of equipment on shelf paper so that each item can be replaced upon its outline. Missing items are easily detected with the outline system. Student assistants can also help count items of equipment as they are collected.

When and if a teacher finds that some item of equipment has not been returned, what should be done? Here is one solution that helped a master teacher handle this difficult situation: The children were called together and told that an item of equipment was missing and had to be found. They were asked to check their pockets, purses, and desks to be sure that one of their friends had not placed the item there as a joke. This approach gave the student who had taken or misplaced the item a way out. No accusations were made, but the children knew the importance of returning the item.

Inventory of Equipment

Nothing is more devastating to the effectiveness of a science lesson than lack of adequate equipment. A continuous inventory of equipment ensures that missing or broken equipment is noted, and that all items are accounted for. Following are some suggestions for maintaining an effective inventory:

- Write names of items to be replaced in a notebook as the need becomes evident. Review this list monthly and annually (at the close of the school year).
- Prepare key sort cards on which items of equipment are listed. The key sort card is made by punching holes at regular intervals

along the margin of a 3 × 5 or 4 × 6 file card. The topic should be written on the card and the name of items used for teaching the topic should be written by each of the holes. As an item of equipment is needed, the hole is notched; cards can then be key-sorted. This method is satisfactory for an annual inventory of needed items.

- List all items of equipment needed to teach each topic. As the need for an item becomes evident, place a check by the item on the list.

Storage of Equipment

Good storage makes efficient use of space. Most commercial kits come packaged in boxes that make storing very convenient. Other equipment might be stored in containers like the following:

- Plastic containers and baby food jars: Many small items of equipment such as nails, washers, electric lamps (bulbs), and animal food may be stored in plastic freezing containers, margarine containers, and baby food jars. Another useful container is a potato chip can.
- Egg cartons: These can be used for storing such items as rock samples, cloth samples, and wood samples.
- Mesh bags: The mesh bags used to package citrus fruit and potatoes in supermarkets may be used to store wood blocks, rock samples, small toys, corks, and pill bottles.
- Envelopes: Small flat items like paper shapes, paper rulers, used aluminum foil, or balloons may be stored in envelopes.
- Pill bottles: Some chemicals may be stored in pill bottles with lids. Items as iron filings, baking soda, corn starch, and puffed cereal may also be stored in these containers.
- Compartmentalized boxes: Milk cases or boxes designed to hold liter bottles of soft drinks may be used to store small items. If space is available, these boxes may be placed on their sides to make shelves for storage.
- Single concept boxes: Supermarket boxes can hold most equipment for the teaching of a specific concept. For example, a "weather" box may include thermometers, rain gauges, blank weather charts, wind vanes, weather maps, and copies of symbols used on weather maps.
- Single-student boxes: Shoe boxes or cigar boxes may hold equipment used by one student. These boxes may be gotten and returned easily by the students with little teacher supervision. This arrangement is especially useful with individualized instruction.

Whatever storage method is used, all containers should be labeled plainly with the topic, items of equipment, quantity of each item, room number, and the teacher's name.

Identifying Facilities and Logistics for a Science Lesson

Another phase of classroom planning deals with analyzing the required facilities, resources, and logistics.

In planning each unit, the teacher must anticipate how children can best be organized for each activity to allow a maximum of freedom and involvement, with enough structure to clarify objectives and to give students a sense of direction. While some structure is desirable for the sake of continuity, too much tends to lessen inquiry and defeat the affective goals of the science experience—including development of self-direction among students.

Consider the following sample planning form (Table 8.1), designed to correspond with a unit on ice cubes. All activities and some facilities and logistics are filled in. Some have been left blank for you to fill in as you consider which might best support each activity.

TABLE 8.1. TEACHER PLANNING FORM:
SAMPLE ACTIVITIES, FACILITIES, AND LOGISTICS: "ICE CUBES"

Activity	Facilities	Logistics
1. Finding how much time is required for ice to melt in air	What facilities would be needed?	Initial discussion with large group Work groups, usually two or three in number Children obtain their own equipment
2. Changing the melting rate of an ice cube in air Constructing a graph from collected data	Work space and materials to conduct a variety of activities Investigation encouraged through questions Clock or timer Furniture placement and work areas planned so that teacher can move around the room easily Ice Containers of various volumes	What logistics are appropriate?

(cont.)

TABLE 8.1. (Continued)

Activity	Facilities	Logistics
3. Making an ice cube melt faster than it does in air	A variety of equipment for children to test their ideas and suggestions Areas in the classroom for children to investigate for a brief period of time (one to two class periods) Newspaper or paper towels to absorb spills	*Grouping of children undefined Movement of children as need for investigations
4. Decreasing the rate of melting	What facilities would be needed?	Children work in small groups at school, and individually at home Large-group discussion to agree on a standard of environmental temperature Competition among children on the effectiveness of their insulators Little fluctuation in the temperature of air in the classroom
5. Making and melting funny-shaped ice	Place for storage of "funny-looking ice cubes" until ready for use (may require several hours) Class determines a standard volume of water to be used to make the "funny" ice cubes Means for preparing "funny" ice cubes at school (dry ice, for example) Food coloring to add to water Place to observe melting for "funny-shaped" ice cubes Timer or clock to measure how long it takes for "funny" ice cubes to melt	Children bringing ice cubes in unusual shapes to school Large-group discussion and observation Large-group observation of water as it freezes Groups undefined for watching "funny" ice cubes melt

Compare your responses with those provided below:

TABLE 8.1. Answers

Activity	Facilities	Logistics
	Suggested Facilities and Logistics for the "Ice Cubes" Lesson	
#1	Equipment available at one location	
	Places for containers of ice	
	Clock or other timing device	
	Introductory questions that encourage investigation	
#2		*Grouping undefined
		Movement as needed
		Students gather for discussion
		Children working at different investigations (All children need not conduct the same investigation)
#3	Nothing to be added	
#4	Equipment and tools to build thermal insulation	
	Space for small groups to construct the thermal insulation	
	Tools and materials in a convenient place	
	Large supply of ice cubes of approximately the same volume	
#5	Nothing to be added	

*Items not listed or suggested in the unit.

CLASSROOM SAFETY

Ideally, neither you nor your students will ever be injured or have an accident in the classroom. The reality is, however, that accidents can and do happen at the most unexpected times and under the most unanticipated circumstances. The safety of children and teachers requires constant vigilance.

An excellent set of safety suggestions and procedures is published by the National Science Teachers Association (NSTA, 1742 Connecticut Ave. N.W., Washington, DC 20009). Much of the information in this section has been adapted from the NSTA brochure, which you may wish to read from cover to cover.

The first step in ensuring students' safety is to survey the classroom for potential hazards. These should be minimized or eliminated to the extent possible. If you aren't sure what to look for, the NSTA brochure will offer some suggestions.

Teachers should consider meeting with the principal and school nurse to outline emergency actions in the event of an accident in the classroom or on a field trip. A list of emergency telephone numbers should be available. Teachers might also review first aid procedures and consider receiving or updating their training in this area. Of course, good common sense is invaluable, and helps teachers identify many preventive measures.

In case of an accident or injury in the classroom, take the following steps immediately: (1) do not panic—one emergency at a time is enough; (2) check the child to determine if there is any possibility of further injury; (3) if there is a danger of a fire, remove any combustible material; (4) if there are objects that could cut a child, remove them; (5) notify the school principal; (6) notify the school nurse; (7) have a properly trained person administer first aid, if it is necessary and if you have parents' approval to do so, and, in any case, notify parents.

If the injury is serious, obtain medical help immediately by calling a predetermined emergency number, the police, or fire department. Never attempt to move an injured child yourself. Contact the parents or guardian as soon as possible and urge that they contact their family physician immediately. If you are unable to contact a parent or guardian, contact the alternate person designated and/or the family physician. If you have parents' written permission, have a properly trained person administer first aid; do not treat the child or provide medication yourself, however. Many schools have emergency phone numbers for parents or alternate persons as well as procedures to follow when there is an accident or injury. Familiarize yourself with these procedures and know where the phone numbers can be found. You may not have time to hunt for them in an emergency. In the sections that follow, we'll discuss safety as it relates to various classroom practices and activities.

Animals in the Classroom

Before introducing animals into the classroom, review the policy of the local school district. When animals are in the classroom, care should be taken to ensure that neither the students nor the animals are harmed. Mammals protect themselves and their young by biting, scratching, and kicking. Pets such as cats, dogs, rabbits, guinea pigs, and gerbils should be handled properly and should not be disturbed while eating. Here are some points to consider:

- Do not permit students to bring live or deceased wild birds, snapping turtles, snakes, insects, or arachnids (spiders, ticks, mites) capable of carrying disease into the classroom.
- Provide proper living quarters. Animals must be kept clean and free from contamination, and must remain in a securely closed cage. Provide for their care during weekends and holidays. (Information about the care of animals in the classroom is found in Appendix E.)
- Obtain all purchased animals from a reputable supply house. Fish should be purchased from tanks in which all fish appear healthy.
- Discourage students from bringing personal pets to school unless you have made prior arrangements. When pets are brought to the classroom, they should be handled only by their owners or under the teacher's guidance, and provisions should be made for their care during the day.
- When observing unfamiliar animals, students should avoid picking them up or touching them.
- Caution students never to tease animals, or to insert their fingers or objects through the cages. Report animal bites and scratches immediately to the school's medical authority.
- Rats, rabbits, hamsters, and mice are best picked up by the scruff of the neck with a hand placed under the body for support. If young animals are to be handled, the mother should be moved to another cage. By nature many mothers are fiercely protective.
- Use heavy gloves for handling animals and have students wash their hands before and after they handle animals.
- Prior to allowing animals to be brought into the classroom, check with school district administrators to determine if there are any local regulations to be observed. Personnel at the local humane society or zoo are often very cooperative in helping teachers create a wholesome animal environment in the classroom.

Plants in the Classroom

Teachers are encouraged to provide plants for students to observe, compare, and classify. Plants used for such purposes should be well-known to the teachers. Avoid those that produce harmful substances.

Since many plants have not been thoroughly researched for their toxicity, you may find it helpful to follow these common rules:

- Never place any part of a plant in the mouth (teachers may want to emphasize the distinction between edible plants, fruits and vegetables, and nonedible plants).

- Never allow any sap or fruit juice to get on the skin.
- Never inhale or expose the skin or eyes to the smoke of any burning plant.
- Never pick any unknown wildflowers, seeds, berries, or cultivated plants.
- Never eat food after handling plants without first washing the hands thoroughly.

Any part of a plant can be relatively toxic, even fatal. Many state departments of forestry, agriculture, or natural resources, as well as county agent offices, have publications identifying poisonous plants of a state or region. Following is a partial list (which teachers may wish to expand) of poisonous plants:

- Plants poisonous to the touch (due to exuded oils):
    Poison ivy
    Poison oak
    Poison sumac
- Plants poisonous when eaten:
    Many fungi
    Belladonna
    Wake robin
    Diffenbachia
    Henbane
    Polk weed
    Caster
    Tansy
    Foxglove
    Jimson weed
- Plants having toxic saps:
    Oleander
    Poinsettia
    Trumpet vine

Eye Protection

Students who work with chemical substances, sharp implements, or any potential eye hazards should be provided with protective devices: goggles, face shields, and safety shields. Realize, however, that such devices may not be 100 percent effective. Appropriate combinations of devices should be used for optimum protection.

To establish an effective eye safety program, teachers should

- orient students to the need for and use of eye protection devices.
- consider eye safety when planning each science activity.

- establish routine procedures for the distribution of individual eye protection devices and for their subsequent return to the storage area.
- maintain strict standards for cleanliness. If some blindfolds are used, they should never be transferred from one child to another without being washed. Eye diseases are highly contagious.
- demonstrate the dangers of eye hazards.
- assure that all persons performing laboratory activities involving hazards to the eyes wear approved eye protection devices. (All persons in dangerous proximity to such activities should be equipped also.)

Field Trips

Field trips are a positive addition to the elementary science program. When the field trip is well organized, the possibility of accidents is greatly reduced. A few relatively simple precautions can ensure safety for all participants.

- Never take anything for granted where students are concerned. Be alert for the unexpected.
- Ask several responsible adults to accompany students on the trip.
- Obtain parental permission before any student is allowed to go on a field trip.
- Send home a list identifying the proper clothing, necessary equipment, and supplies to be taken on the trip.
- To prevent the risk of mite and tick infestation, plant poisoning or scratches, ask students to wear clothing that covers arms, legs, and feet.
- Check first aid kits for essential items, and take several on the trip.
- Do not visit any body of water unless at least one person in the group is familiar with the latest methods of artificial respiration and the rules of ordinary water safety described in first aid handbooks, Scouting manuals, and the American Red Cross Senior Life Saving brochure.
- Before taking students on trips near or into the water of a stream, river, lake, or ocean, be sure they can recognize dangerous aquatic or marine plants and animals common to the area.
- When taking a field trip involving wading, use the buddy system and provide life jackets.
- Ensure that trips to factories and laboratories are well-supervised and ask an experienced plant representative to conduct the tour.

Fire Prevention and Control

It is the responsibility of each teacher to act deliberately and intelligently in the event of a classroom fire. The first concern should be to evacuate the area. Have a plan for doing this quickly and efficiently. It is important that you know not only the location of available fire fighting aids—blanket, fire extinguishers, and fire alarm box—but also how to use them.

It's fairly common for clothes or hair to catch fire when students get too close to an open flame. Water is the most effective remedy, but a fire blanket could be used to smother the fire. Do not use a carbon dioxide extinguisher on a person. A carbon dioxide blast could spread the fire and cause frostbite, thereby compounding the burn.

There are four general classes of fires. Using the proper type of extinguisher for each class will provide the best control.

- *Class A: Fires in wood, textiles, paper, and other ordinary combustibles.* This type of fire is extinguished by cooling with water or a solution containing water (loaded steam), which wets the material and prevents glowing embers from rekindling. A general purpose dry chemical extinguisher is also effective for fusing and insulating.
- *Class B: Fires in gasoline, soil, paint, or other flammable liquids that gasify when heated.* This type of fire is extinguished by smothering, thus shutting off the air supply. Carbon dioxide, dry chemical, and foam are effective on this type of fire. All teachers should learn how to operate the various types of fire extinguishers.
- *Class C: Fires in live electrical equipment.* This type of fire is extinguished by using a nonconductive agent. A carbon dioxide extinguisher smothers the flame without damaging the equipment. A dry chemical extinguisher is also effective. Whenever possible, the electric power to the burning equipment should be disconnected.
- *Class D: Fires in such combustible materials as magnesium, titanium, zirconium, sodium, and potassium.* This new and somewhat specialized classification is extinguished by a special extinguisher powder, unlike dry chemical and general purpose dry chemical, which is applied by a scoop. Dry sand may be used also to extinguish small Class D fires.

Storage and Labeling

One of the most important essentials for classroom safety is adequate, efficiently planned storage. The following should be considered when storing equipment and materials:

1. *Area.* Enough space should be available so that there is no crowding. Shelving should be deep enough that articles are not easily dislodged. A bar on the shelf edge is an added safety measure to prevent items from falling.
2. *Height of Storage Shelves.* Low shelves are safer. Toxic chemicals, large glassware, and heavy articles should always be stored on a lower shelf, but should not be accessible to students. When shelving cannot be easily reached from a standing position, a step-stool should be provided.
3. *Containers.* Materials should be kept in containers which are easily handled: e.g., acids in small bottles rather than large gallon jars.
4. *Placement of Hazardous Materials.* Volatile liquids should be stored away from sunlight, electrical switches, or heat sources. Reacting chemicals should not be stored near one another. Hazardous materials should be kept under separate locks.
5. *Labeling.* At the elementary school level it is prudent to label both the storage area where the equipment and materials are stored as well as the individual items. Marking pens or electric markers may be used to identify equipment by name. Usually temporary typed labels are more appropriate for containers, including those used for dry and liquid chemicals.

   Teachers should dispense substances into temporary marked containers only in quantities that students can use. Pouring dry chemicals or liquids back into the original containers will almost certainly contaminate the entire supply.

   Chemicals should be identified by common name as well as scientific name. The label should also include a formula, precautions for use, and antidote. Substances that have lost their identity labels or about which there is confusion should be carefully discarded. They should never be used in experiments.

   Liquids should be stored in separate storage areas, not near equipment or other materials. Acids, bases, and salts should be placed in separate areas. Volatile substances, if any, should be placed in cool storage areas with proper ventilation.
6. *Transportation and Control.* A system should be developed for transporting equipment and materials to classrooms. A rolling cart with lips on each shelf is highly recommended. Hazardous materials should only be transported through halls under the direct supervision of a teacher. In addition, a method should be established for checking in and out what is needed.

Safe Use of Power Equipment and Materials

Some science activities require power tools. These should never be operated by students except under direct supervision by the teacher. Following is a list of common power tools and related materials with suggestions for safe use:

1. *Sharp Instruments.* Any device which has moving parts, cutting edges, sharp corners, or highly irregular shapes, heating elements, or electrical parts constitutes a potential hazard and should be so considered.
   a. Never grasp any electrical device which has just been used. Most electrical devices remain hot after use and serious burns may result.
   b. Never short-circuit (connect the terminals) dry cells or storage batteries. High temperature developed in the connecting wire can cause serious burns.
   c. In removing an electrical plug from its socket, pull the plug, not the electric cord.
   d. Do not use electrical extensions.
2. *Glassware*
   a. Care should be taken to prevent injuries from sharp edges on mirrors, prisms, and glass plates. Remove sharp edges by grinding them with emery cloth or carborundum stone, or by painting them with quick-drying enamel.
   b. Never attempt to insert glass tubing that has a jagged end into rubber stoppers or tubing. Edges should be fire-polished. Always aim the tubing away from the palm of the hand that holds the stopper or rubber tubing. Lubricate the glass to be inserted with a small quantity of glycerin.
3. *Small Power Tools and Equipment.* A variety of small power tools, appliances, or equipment may be found in laboratories. Three-prong plugs should be used on all power tools to reduce the chance for electrical shock. Extension cords should not be used. Special care should be taken to avoid contact with moving parts or heating elements of any equipment. The following items should be used with special caution: heating elements, small motors, soldering irons, hot plates, and electrical fans.
4. *Hand Tools.* Many hand tools are used in science activities. A work bench provides a suitable work surface and appropriate storage facilities for such tools. Hand tools are designed for specific purposes and should be used only for those purposes.

These are not the only hazards in the classroom. Some activities specify that acids be used. Great care should be exercised with acids when children are around. In most cases, only the teacher should handle the acid, and only with protective gloves. If acids are to be diluted with water, add *ACID TO WATER,* never water to acid; the heat that is generated could be dangerous.

Many common household cleaners are dangerous. Among these are drain cleaners, oven cleaners, and bleaches.

Two liquids that should never be brought into the classroom are mercury and carbon tetrachloride. Mercury is found in thermometers (except those thermometers that have a red liquid in them). If a thermometer with mercury breaks in the classroom, have the children move out of the classroom until the mercury is removed. If carbon tetrachloride (a cleaning fluid for clothing) is spilled in the classroom, evacuate the room until the fluid is removed. Open windows and use fans to remove the fumes.

Safety Checklists

Adhering to the following safety practices can help you prevent accidents and create a safe classroom environment for yourself and your students.

General Safety Practices

- Obtain a copy of the federal, state, and local regulations that relate to school safety, as well as a copy of your school district's policies and procedures.
- Check your classroom on a regular basis to ensure that all possible safety precautions are being taken. Equipment and materials should be properly stored; hazardous materials should not be left exposed in the classroom.
- Before handling equipment and materials, thoroughly familiarize yourself with possible hazards.
- Be extra cautious when dealing with fire and instruct your students to take appropriate precautions.
- Be familiar with your school's fire regulations, evacuation procedures, and the location and use of fire fighting equipment.
- Know your school's policies and procedures in case of accidents.
- At the start of each science activity, instruct students regarding potential hazards and important precautions.
- Limit groups to the number of students who can safely work on an activity without causing confusion or accidents.
- Allow sufficient time for students to complete activities, clean up, and properly store equipment and materials after use.
- Instruct students never to taste or touch substances in the science classroom without first obtaining specific instructions from the teacher.
- Instruct students to report all accidents or injuries—no matter how small—immediately.
- Instruct students that it is unsafe to touch the face, mouth, eyes, and other parts of the body while working with plants,

animals, or chemical substances until they have washed their hands and cleaned their nails.

Chemicals

- Never mix chemicals "just to see what happens."
- Never taste chemicals.
- Wash hands after handling any chemicals.
- Do not allow elementary school students to mix acid and water.
- Store combustible materials in a locked metal cabinet.
- Store chemicals under separate lock in a cool, dry place—but not in a refrigerator.
- Store only minimum amounts of chemicals in the classroom. Any materials not used in a given period should be carefully discarded, particularly if they could become unstable.

Glassware

- Do not heat hard glass test tubes from the bottom. They should be tipped slightly, but not in the direction of another student.
- Ask students to report sharp edges on mirrors or glassware.
- Have a whisk broom and dustpan available for sweeping up pieces of broken glass.
- Warn students not to drink from glassware used for science experiments.
- Ensure that thermometers used in the elementary classroom are filled with alcohol (the usual red liquid in many thermometers), not mercury.

Electricity

- Teach students safety precautions for using electricity in everyday situations.
- At the start of any unit on electricity, ask students not to experiment with the electric current of home circuits.
- Check your school building code about temporary wiring for devices to be used continuously in one location. Breaks in insulation of extension cords could easily cause a short circuit.
- Ensure that all connecting cords are short, in good condition, and plugged in at the nearest outlet.
- Because water is a conductor of electricity, remind students that their hands should be dry when touching electrical cords, switches, or appliances.

The safety of children and teachers should be considered first, last, and always.

Ensuring safety is the first step in designing an effective learning environment. Once you feel confident that your classroom is hazard-free, you can think about more creative endeavors: designing work stations that stimulate young imaginations, arranging furniture and equipment in ways that encourage independent, active learning, and adding the personal touches—plants, animals, illustrations, demonstrations, or whatever—that give you the satisfaction of designing an environment to reflect your unique instructional approach.

_____ *LOOKING BACK* _____

1. What types of classroom facilities contribute to an effective science program? What should be considered when arranging facilities?
2. What are some effective means of managing equipment, resources, and materials in the classroom?
3. What must be done to prepare the learning environment prior to teaching a lesson? Upon what should that planning be based?
4. What is the teacher's role in protecting children from accidents and injury in the classroom?

ACTIVITIES

1. Review the unit you wrote for Chapter 7. Select one or two activities from the unit. Note the equipment and facilities (placement of furniture, equipment, and any other materials) needed for the activities.

   Look at the facilities, equipment, and activities you selected. Where should they be placed in the classroom? Where should equipment be kept? How will it get into the classroom? Who will take responsibility for obtaining or returning it?

   Now think about movement of children in the classroom. What traffic patterns might be used when children get and return equipment? When they conduct activities? What traffic patterns will the teacher follow?

   In answering these various questions, revise your floor plan as necessary to accommodate any new concerns.
2. If possible, request the permission of the principal and a teacher to conduct a safety survey of a classroom using the safety checklist. Discuss the results of the survey with the teacher; perhaps the teacher is using plans that are not evident.
3. Draw a science safety poster appropriate for use in the elementary school classroom.
4. Obtain a copy of school science safety guidelines and standards from your state's education agency. Are specific science standards for safety listed for the elementary classroom? Are these guidelines consistent with those recommended by the National Science Teacher's Association?

Resources for Teaching Science

9

Objectives

1. To identify resources for teaching children science.
2. To describe ways to use resources as an integral part of an activity-oriented science program.
3. To identify sources of topics to integrate into a science program.
4. To identify local resources for a science program.

_____ LOOKING FORWARD _____

Lack of resources frequently presents an obstacle to teaching children science. Some teachers are not sure which resources are most appropriate, while others are not sure how to make the best use of resources at hand. And for still others, the primary difficulty may simply be obtaining the resources in the first place.

We recognize that while some preservice teachers may be unaware of any resource problem, others feel overwhelmed by it. Though we may not have all the answers for everyone, we've tried to make this chapter highly informational, a kind of resource catalog as it were for those who teach elementary school science. The chapter deals with four primary types of resources: organisms, chemicals, equipment, and printed materials.

The section on living organisms identifies their purpose in the classroom and offers suggestions on their maintenance. The chapter covers the variety of organisms available and various ways in which they may enrich a science program. Additional information is provided about safety.

Teachers' concerns with chemical resources seem to be concentrated in three areas: (1) sources of chemical reagents; (2) uses for the chemical reagents; and (3) safety. We'll cover all three concerns.

Many science textbooks suggest activities that require the use of equipment; however, some teachers may have little or no experience with the specified equipment. This chapter offers some suggestions for constructing and using equipment, or finding alternatives when a specified piece of equipment is unavailable. Particular attention is given to such commercial sources of equipment as individual items or kits. Since activities requiring equipment are listed in teacher's editions of elementary science textbooks, additional activities are not suggested here.

The chapter concludes with a list of printed resources.

Many teachers may feel reasonably secure about teaching children science from a textbook. However, that security seems to dissipate as they prepare for science activities. Their knowledge about finding and using resources may be limited. However, with a little work and ingenuity these insecurities can be overcome.

Obviously, listing all available resources is far beyond the scope of this chapter. But instead, we can list representative examples of various resources. Creative teachers constantly are discovering, altering, and adapting resources for their science lessons. It's a career long task.

Four general types of resources are used in teaching elementary school science: equipment, living organisms, chemicals, and printed materials. Let's discuss these one at a time.

EQUIPMENT

Scientific equipment is obtained in two ways: you can construct it or you can buy it. Buying equipment generally saves time. But given the limited budget of most schools, the resourceful teacher learns to build things. It isn't as difficult or time-consuming as you might think.

Constructed Equipment

Many items of equipment that are used in the classroom are easily constructed. In this chapter, we'll describe just a few examples.

Two-dimensional Paper Shapes (2-d). The most common shapes used for science lessons are circle, square, rectangle, triangle, and ellipse. These may be made of different colors of construction paper or used manila folders. Shapes with straight sides can be cut on a paper cutter. To speed up the process, shapes can be cut from several sheets of paper at the same time. Draw the shapes to be cut on a sheet of paper; place two sheets of paper under the pattern sheet, then cut with the paper cutter. Shapes with curved sides need to be cut with scissors.

Two-dimensional Wooden Shapes (2-d shapes). Scraps of lumber may be used to make the same shapes as those made from paper. Frequently these scraps can be obtained free from local lumber yards, or from parents whose hobbies include woodworking. If possible, the shapes should be cut with a coping saw rather than a hand saw. After the shapes are cut, smooth the edges and corners with a fine sandpaper. The wood shapes may be painted, colored with several coats of water colors, or colored by cloth dye. If the latter two methods are used, wash the shapes in water after colors have dried to remove excess coloring. Use the shapes to teach shape identification or to construct larger shapes.

Black Box. Obtain a sturdy box that is a convenient size for children to handle. Place an assortment of objects in the box. These may include items of different shapes (spherical, cylindrical, boxlike), items with large flat surfaces, metal objects, and objects with varying weights. A sample of objects in a box could include a pencil, chalkboard eraser, thumbtack, paper clip, ball, piece of chalk, and a pebble. Place the items in the box and tape the lid securely in place. The box may be decorated if you wish. When given the box, children are asked to describe what is in the box, using the senses of touch and hearing. Older children may be asked to name the objects (inferring) in the box and state observations that support the inference.

Pulleys. These may be constructed from spools and a wire coat hanger (see Figure 9.1). For a single fixed pulley, cut a piece of wire from a coat hanger approximately 24 cm long. Center the spool in the wire. Bend the wire ½ cm from each end of the spool. Make another bend in the wire 3 cm from the first bend, as shown in the drawing. Make a hood at the ends of the wire. Pliers may be used to make the bends. The spool should turn freely on the wire. Moveable pulleys can be constructed in the same manner but left free to slide on the wire.

Aquarium. Aquaria may be made from glass or plastic gallon jars or plastic gallon milk jugs. Rinse the jar with water after the contents have been used. If soap or detergent is used to clean the container, great care must be taken to ensure that the jar is adequately rinsed. Even very small quantities of soap kill fish and other aquarium organisms. When clean, the aquarium is ready for stocking. To use a plastic milk jug, draw a line around the jug approximately 13 cm from the bottom. Cut along this line with a sharp knife or scissors. Smaller aquaria can be made by using plastic shoeboxes, which are available in most department and variety stores.

Rock Collection. Collect and identify small samples of rocks. Glue each specimen in one compartment of an egg carton. Write a number near each rock specimen and make a key on a separate sheet of paper. Place a drop of white paint on each rock and write the number on it when the paint dries. This rock collection can serve as a study guide for the children and as a model for their own collections.

Balance. Several different kinds of balances can be made at home. One is a hanging equal arm balance. To build it, start with three large paper clips, two paper or styrofoam cups or small aluminum pie pans, some string, and narrow piece of wood about 0.5 to 1 meter long. Bend the paper clips to form hoods as shown in the sketch. Cut six pieces of

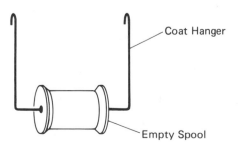

Coat Hanger

Empty Spool

Figure 9.1. Pulley

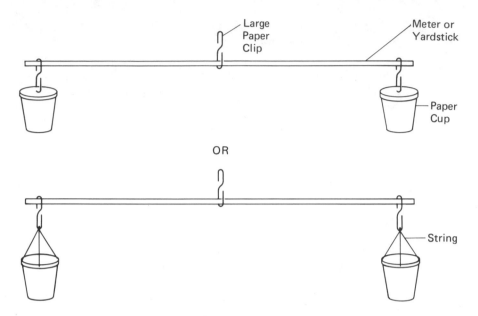

Figure 9.2. Balances

string 25 cm long. Make three holes in each cup or pie pan so that each hole is equal distance from the other two. Tie a piece of string onto the cup or pan at each hole. Tie the free ends of the three strings together and hook them onto a paper clip. Bore a hole in the middle of the stick. Through this hole tie a string so that the balance can hang from a support. Place the other paper clips with the cups or pans attached on the ends of the stick. When hung, the balance should be parallel with the floor. If it is not, place a small piece of clay on the high side to make it parallel. You may need to move the clay back and forth to make the balance exact. You are now ready to weigh objects. It is helpful to hold the pans as objects and weights are placed in them. The object to be weighed is placed in one pan and objects of known weight are placed in the other. Try using paper clips, pennies, buttons, or other small objects as weights.

Tripod. Obtain a metal can, such as a large juice can, and some shears designed to cut metal. Remove one end from the can. Leaving the bottom ring attached for strength, cut a door-shaped opening in the bottom of the can. Make the opening wide enough to insert a food-warming candle. Punch two or three holes along the top of the can for ventilation. Using pliers, bend any sharp edges inside the can. Place a heat source such as a warmer candle or can of sterno under the tripod. Place the object to be heated on top. (See Figure 9.3.)

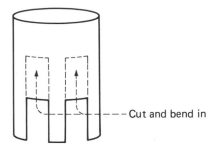

— — — Cut and bend in

Figure 9.3. Tripod

Metric Ruler. Manila folders may be used to make these rulers. Trace a 15-cm ruler on white paper, using a fine ballpoint pen. Mark the centimeter and half centimeter units. Use a very fine pen to draw in the millimeter units. Several of these may be drawn on a sheet of paper. Cut the manila folder into 8½ × 11 sheets, the size of a sheet of paper. Duplicate the rulers on a copying machine using sheets of manila folders instead of paper. If the copying machine will not permit the manila folder to pass through it, drawings of rulers may be made on regular paper, and photocopied. These copies may be cut out and pasted to the manila folder; the individual rulers may then be cut from the folders with a paper cutter. Each ruler will need to be cut separately.

Electric Switch. Obtain a strip of metal 2 cm wide and 7–8 cm long, four small nails, and a block of wood. The metal can be cut from a soup can or other small can. Drive one nail into the wood. Bend the metal strip as shown, and nail it to the wood so it touches the single nail. Use two nails to attach the strip leaving one of the nails protruding from the wood. This nail serves as a terminal for attaching a wire from the energy source. When the circuit is closed, energy will flow through it as the metal strip touches the single nail. (See Figure 9.4.)

Rain Gauge. A very simple rain gauge may be made from an empty olive jar. Place a piece of masking tape on the side of the jar from top to bottom. Use a ballpoint or permanent ink felt-tipped marking pen to make a scale on the tape. Use units of 1 cm and ½ cm. A stand can be made for the rain gauge using a margarine tub. Cut a hole the size of the olive jar in the lid of the margarine container. Place sand in the container for weight and stability. The rain gauge is now ready to measure the amount of rainfall.

Barometer. A barometer can be made from a glass tumbler, balloon, rubber band, soda straw, shoe box, and a scale made of masking tape. Cut a balloon lengthwise and stretch it over the top of the tumbler.

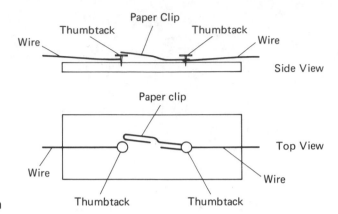

Figure 9.4. Switch

Place a rubber band around the balloon to keep it in place. Do not stretch the balloon too tight; if it can be easily moved with a light touch of the finger, it is not too tight. Glue a soda straw to the balloon as shown in the sketch. Place the tumbler in a shoe box with one side and the top removed. Mark a scale on a strip of masking tape using metric units of 1 and ½ centimeters. Place the scale on the back of the box. Position the tumbler so the end of the straw is covering the scale. As pressure changes, the straw will move up and down. This barometer is quite sensitive to temperature changes and these changes affect the readings of the instrument. As the pressure goes up and pushes on the balloon covering, the balloon is forced into the tumbler and the pointer goes up, indicating increasing pressure. When the air pressure falls, the reverse occurs. (See Figure 9.5.)

Funnel. Funnels may be made from the top half of a plastic gallon milk jug, the top half of a plastic detergent bottle, or a cone made of paper, aluminum foil, or waxed paper.

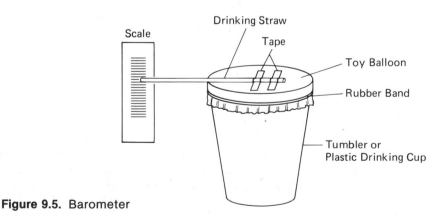

Figure 9.5. Barometer

Electromagnet. Obtain a large steel spike, 1 meter of insulated copper wire (#22 or 24), and a dry cell. Remove insulation from 3 cm of each end of the wire. Begin wrapping the wire around the nail 15 cm from one end and continue wrapping to 15 cm of the other end. Attach the system to a dry cell using the scraped ends of the wire. Test the magnetic properties of the object with paper clips. With paper clips attached to the magnet, remove one wire from the dry cell. Note that the nail retains some magnetism after the wire is disconnected. This magnet may be used in the same manner as any other magnet.

Wind Vane. A wind vane may be made using paper, a plastic soda straw, modeling clay, a straight pin, and a pencil. Cut two heads and two tails for the wind vane from heavy paper (tag or construction paper). Heads should be like the head of an arrow, tails like the feathers of an arrow. The tail should be larger than the head. Place a small amount of modeling clay (about the size of a pea) in one end of the straw. This will be the head of the wind vane. Put a straight pin through the straw about one-third of the way down its length. Rotate the straw on the pin so it turns freely. Cut a small slit in the ends of the straw with a razorblade and glue the head and tail onto the straw. Mount the wind vane on the eraser of a pencil or thin dowel, which can be placed in a soft drink bottle.

These are only examples of the kinds of equipment you can construct quickly and inexpensively. As you can see, many objects can be made from common household items that cost little or nothing to obtain; you may be able to build up a supply through parent donations. Another advantage to the do-it-yourself approach is that you can involve students in constructing the models. Often, they learn as much from building the equipment as from using it.

Commercial Equipment

Scientific equipment may be purchased from several science supply houses; however, all items are not available from all companies. Comparison shopping takes more time than ordering everything from one source, but it saves money. Some of the companies which supply science equipment are listed in Appendix A.

Many publishers also sell equipment kits or packages to accompany science programs. Some of these publishers are listed in Appendix I. Although some kits are intended for a specific program, the equipment frequently can be used with other programs. For instance, thermometers and balances are general kinds of equipment which can be used with virtually any textbook series or program.

Equipment for science programs can be expensive. Provided they are used and cared for properly, however, many items will last for years.

A list of equipment commonly used in elementary school science programs appears in Appendixes A, B, and C. Sources of individual items and intended grade levels are included on the list. Much of this equipment is available commercially.

LIVING ORGANISMS

The study of plants and animals is an integral part of elementary school science. Bringing live things into a classroom takes planning, however. Animals, in particular, can suffer from two kinds of difficulties: (1) too *much* care—including overfeeding and constant handling; or (2) too *little* care—lack of water or an inappropriate container. In addition, some animals require unique habitats. Before inviting any animal guests into your classroom, be sure you can provide proper food, water, and adequate shelter.

It's also vital to consider how living organisms will be observed or used. Two organizations offer information about the use of animals in the classroom: the National Science Teachers Association and the National Association for the Advancement of Humane Education (NAAHE). NAAHE publishes two brochures you may find helpful. One is entitled "Does the Idea of Dissecting or Experimenting on Animals in Biology Class Disturb You?" It is written for young people who care about animals and do not want to participate in classroom dissection activities or lessons that involve causing pain or stress to animals. The brochure provides support for the student's position.

The second brochure, "The Living Science: A Humane Approach to the Study of Animals in Elementary and Secondary School Biology," is written for teachers. It defines the objective of elementary and secondary school biology as developing "an appreciation for the uniqueness of each individual organism, the connections between living things, and the relationship of each individual to its environment." The brochure discusses ethical concerns associated with dissection, invasive experiments, and their potential negative impact on students. Copies of both brochures may be obtained from the NAAHE, Box 362, East Haddon, CT 06423.

The National Science Teachers Association has published a position statement on the use of animals in the schools. A copy of that statement is included in Appendix D.

Animals and Plants for Study in the Classroom

How do you decide what plants or animals can be successfully brought into the classroom? As a start, be sure you can answer *yes* to these three questions:

- Is the organism able to survive in the classroom environment?
- Can the children safely handle the organism?
- Will the organism contribute to the learning of the children?

Living organisms should be placed in as natural a setting as possible. Displays of several organisms which inhabit the same environment can help children understand the concepts of *niche, competition,* and *interaction.* For instance, a classroom display might focus on a local pond or stream and include drawings or models of:

- Plants which live near or in a pond or stream, such as algae, water lilies, moss, pitcher plants, sundews, sedges, rushes, cattails, and grasses.
- Animals which live near or in a pond or stream, such as insect larvae, snakes, crayfish, turtles, insects, and fish.

DO NOT collect live organisms for such a display. Generally speaking, animals—living or dead—should be left where they are found naturally. If children do bring animals such as insects into the classroom for observation, the animals should be released immediately following the lesson.

Sources of Animals and Plants for Study

Organisms for classroom observation are available from a variety of sources. Some can be brought into the classroom. In other cases, it may be simpler to take the classroom into the community. Sources include the following:

- Animals and plants on the school campus such as birds, insects, grass, and trees
- Pets such as dogs, cats, snakes, rabbits, fish, spiders, and turtles
- Animals and plants borrowed from libraries and museums
- Aquaria in the school or the community
- Cuttings from house plants and other plants
- Plants grown from seeds
- Outdated flowers from florists
- Plants given or loaned by florists
- Plants donated by nurseries
- Animals and plants on display in food markets, museums, botanical gardens, zoos, nature centers, parks, hatcheries, etc.
- Animals and plants observed in ponds, streams, and rivers
- Plants such as moss, mistletoe, and lichens that grow on other plants

- Plants growing on rocks
- Private collections of plants and animals
- Donations from pet stores
- Donations from science departments of local high schools, colleges or universities
- Animals observed at local farms
- Outdated fruits and vegetables from food markets
- Yeast from a packet of dry yeast

These sources are available at little or no cost. Specimens of living organisms may be offered to teachers, but usually they must be requested. In most cases, you'll get the best results through personal visits to homes or phone calls and letters. If you send letters, using school letterhead stationery frequently expedites the request. Be careful not to request too much from any one source.

Frequently, a study may require bringing an animal to school. Be sure to prepare a "home" for your guest *prior* to its arrival. If the animal is small, a glass gallon jar with a lid (don't forget to make air holes) can serve as a temporary home. Glass gallon jars are fine for such animals as insects, spiders, snakes or lizards. Animals can be observed easily in jars, but because glass is highly breakable, extra caution is necessary. At the end of the day, wild animals or those too large for such a small environment should be released or sent home.

Care of Animals in the Classroom

Maintaining living things in the classroom requires planning and loving care. Involving the children in caring for living organisms gives them a better understanding of the life requirements of various organisms and also relieves the teacher of some responsibilities. Careful supervision is a must, however, to ensure that plants and animals receive proper care and are well treated.

Animals can be a source of odor and can attract flies if cages or other containers are not cleaned regularly. Dirty environments also can spread disease. Half the water in unfiltered aquaria should be changed every two to three days if fish are to survive; an aquarium with a filter does not need fresh water quite so often.

Children often have a tendency to overfeed animals. Uneaten food attracts insects. Overeating leads to excess weight gain—which can prove very unhealthful. Some animals, including some fish, may eat until the stomach ruptures. Feeding animals is a favorite task for children—and that's fine. Just be sure to stress the importance of good nutrition and moderation.

Using Plants and Animals in Elementary Science Lessons

Children may study plants and animals to learn about the organisms themselves, or to develop their inquiry skills. Frequently both goals are combined in a single lesson. For example, children may classify fish in an aquarium or observe gerbils on an exercise wheel. They may experiment with the effects of low temperature on the activity of house flies or graph the active and resting periods of gerbils.

Two general kinds of studies can be conducted using plants and animals. One focuses on the characteristics of the organism. The second focuses on the interaction between the organism and its environment. Children can observe what and how animals eat, as well as differences in their body structures. Studies of plants could focus on the effects of various colors of light on leaf coloration or on flower structures.

Examples of different lessons involving living organisms are suggested on the pages that follow. In each lesson, living organisms are used to help children learn science concepts and practice inquiry skills.

LESSON 1: CONSTRUCTING A BIRD FEEDER

A bird feeder may be constructed in the following manner. Obtain an 8" or 9" (20 cm or 27 cm) pie pan and a piece of wood sheeting (30 cm × 30 cm). Attach the pie pan to the wood, then attach the piece of wood to a post, fence top or some other place where children can see it and get to it.

Depending on their maturity, children may construct their own bird feeders. If this is impractical, however, a commercial feeder may be used. The major attention should be observing the behavior of birds rather than on constructing the feeder.

Investigative Questions

- Do the same number of birds visit the feeder if it is placed at various heights from the ground?
- Does placing the feeder at various distances from buildings affect the same number of birds that visit it?
- If the feeder is placed among trees or in open areas or attached to buildings do the same number of birds visit it?
- If the feeder is placed close to where people walk or in isolated places, do the same number of birds visit it?
- Are more birds observed at one kind of feeder than at others?
- Does the material from which the feeder is made seem to have any effect upon the number of birds that visit it?

- Does the color of the bird feeder seem to have any effect upon the number of birds using it?
- Does the time of day have any effect upon the number of birds visiting the feeder?
- Do the same number of birds visit the feeder at the same time for several days?
- Does the type of food placed in the feeder seem to have an effect upon the number of birds visiting the feeder?
- How long does one bird typically stay at the feeder?
- How many different kinds of birds visit the feeder?
- What kinds of birds visit the feeder?
- Do you see more of one kind of bird than of others?
- Where do birds stand when they eat?
- How do the feathers of various birds differ in structure?
- What different colors of feathers can you observe?
- What behaviors of birds (in addition to eating) are observed at the feeder?
- How do the body structures of birds visiting the feeder differ (bill/beak, head, legs, feet)?

LESSON 2: PLANTING SEEDS

Other than the usual plants that may be grown from seeds or obtained commercially, several unusual plants can be grown from seed. Avocado plants can be grown from seeds, as can oranges, lemons, and grapefruit plants.

Herbs are excellent plants for observation and can be grown from seeds easily. Some easily grown herbs are dill, sage, parsley, thyme, and oregano.

Investigative Questions

- Can plants be identified by their odor?
- Do dry plants have the same odor as fresh plants?
- Does the amount of light (direct sunlight, indirect sunlight, artificial light) affect the growth of plants? (An operational definition for *growth* is needed to answer this question.)
- Do all plants require the same amount of water?
- How much light (in measured hours) do various plants require?
- Can plants be classified on the basis of their leaf size, leaf shape, leaf texture, leaf margin?
- Do plants have similar root structures?
- Do plants have similar stem structures, leaf structures?
- Do all plants have stems, leaves, and/or roots?
- Do plants respond to colored light in the same manner as they respond to white light?

- How do plants respond to differing amounts of fertilizers?
- Do plants respond to pollutants in waste water?
- Do plants respond to different pollutants in the air?
- How can a product of photosynthesis be observed?
- What is a plant's response to gravity?
- What is a root's response to various chemical reagents or other objects?
- Is it possible for a plant to exert a force on any object—such as a rock, asphalt, pavement, or wood?
- Which part of a plant stem grows the fastest?
- Which part of a plant root grows the fastest?

LESSON 3: GROWING PLANTS FROM CUTTINGS

Begin with a coleus, philodendron, African violet, or begonia. Cut a section of the stem and remove most of the leaves three inches from the cut. Place the cutting in water for several weeks. Rooting may be hastened by dipping the cut end in a rooting hormone available at a florist shop, variety store, or supermarket. Growth of roots can be measured and variables such as amount of light or water tested.

Sweet potato plants grown directly from the sweet potato root produce a beautiful plant.

Investigative Questions

- How rapidly does the sweet potato leaf increase in length?
- How rapidly does the sweet potato leaf increase in width?
- Do the same number of leaves grow on each stem?
- How rapidly does the sweet potato stem increase in length?
- What amount of time is required for the plant to form roots?
- Do sweet potato plants produce flowers?
- What is the smallest part of a sweet potato needed to produce a new plant?
- How many new plants may be produced from one root?
- Do all rooting hormones produce new plants in the same length of time?

LESSON 4: PINEAPPLE PLANTS GROWN FROM A PINEAPPLE TOP

The first step is to twist the top off the fruit and cut away all of the clinging flesh, then let the top dry for about a week. Next, plant the top in potting soil, water or sand. Keep the soil moist. Roots appear in a few weeks. Keep the plant in direct sunlight and fertilize it every two to three months. The plant is cactuslike and provides a contrast with more familiar plants. If you keep the plant for two years, it may produce a pineapple; it may also add atmosphere to the decor of your classroom. Many of the same questions suggested for investigating other plants may be asked about the pineapple.

LESSON 5: CARING FOR RATS, MICE, OR GERBILS

These animals require a minimum of care and are hardy enough to withstand quite a lot of handling. Their reproduction rate is both a blessing and a problem. Because these animals breed often and have a short gestation period, children can watch animals care for their young, and observe how the young change as they mature. Disposing of excess baby rats or mice can be a real nuisance, however. Children may be eager to take them home, but mothers tend to resist the idea. If all else fails, local pet shops will frequently accept these animals.

Investigative Questions

- How often are young animals born?
- How many young are in a litter?
- How do the young and adult animals differ in appearance?
- How does the mother care for the young?
- How does the father care for the young?
- How often do the young eat?
- How much of the mother's milk (by weight) do the young drink at one time?
- What behaviors do newly born animals display?
- Do the animals have definite periods of activity and rest (sleep)?
- If so, how long, relatively, are periods of activity and rest?
- What diet do the animals prefer?
- What foods constitute a balanced diet for the animals?
- How often do the animals eat?
- What quantity (by weight) of food does each adult animal eat at one time?
- Does the fur on each animal feel the same?
- Do male and female animals differ in weight?
- Do male and female animals differ in the size of body parts (feet, legs, ears, tail)?
- How quickly can an animal be taught to go through a maze?

LESSON 6: RAISING TADPOLES FROM EGGS

Collect the eggs in a jar and be sure to put water from the pond or stream in the jar with the eggs. If eggs are gotten from a commercial source, inquire about obtaining water for them. Place the jar in an undisturbed part of the room for a few weeks. Eggs in masses are frog eggs; eggs in ribbons are toad eggs. Return the animals to the water where the eggs were found after the study is complete.

Investigative Questions

- Are there the same number of eggs in each 10-gram mass of eggs?
- What length of time is required for the eggs to hatch?
- What is the size (length) of newly hatched tadpoles?
- What amount of time is required for the first appendages to appear on tadpoles?
- Where does the first appendage appear?
- What activities of tadpoles can be observed?
- How rapidly do tadpoles increase in length?
- Where do the second appendages appear on tadpoles?
- How rapidly do tadpoles increase in weight?
- What other changes in the tadpoles' body can be observed as they mature?
- How many of the tadpoles become frogs?
- How often do tadpoles eat?
- In what configurations do tadpoles swim?
- Do tadpoles seem to respond to color?
- Do tadpoles seem to respond to temperature?
- What food do frogs/toads eat?

LESSON 7: SEASONAL CHANGES IN PLANTS

Such changes as color change, bud formation, seed production, flower production, and maturation of plants may be observed. Set up a nature walk, around the block or through the schoolyard, to make observations. Walk the route once or twice each season and note any changes.

Another method for observing changes in plants during the seasons is to adopt a tree. Children may observe changes in the tree during fall, winter, and spring.

Observation of seasonal activities of animals such as birth of young and migration can be facilitated by the construction of bird feeders or nesting boxes. Schedule observations at regular intervals so changes can be noted.

Investigative Questions

- What plants and animals were observed?
- How many plants and animals were observed?
- What evidence of animals' presence was observed?
- What color changes were observed in plants?
- What activities of animals were observed?
- What plants seemed to remain unchanged?
- What plants and animals were most numerous?
- What interactions were observed among animals and plants?
- Where were the observed plants and animals usually found?
- What changes were noted in plants, animals, or the area itself?

LESSON 8: VISITING A POND OR STREAM

Observations may be made of plant and animal life found at various depths in the water as well as on the shore. The clarity and temperature of the water may also be noted. Similar activities may be conducted along a stream. Seasonal changes can also be noted. Taking hand lenses to the stream to observe characteristics of small organisms and other objects adds interest. After looking at animals through a lens, ask students to sketch them so they can identify body parts once you return to the classroom. Replace the animal where it was found.

Investigative Questions

- What animals are observed in the water?
- How many animals of each kind are observed at one place in a pond or stream?
- Do animals seem to be interacting with others of the same kind or with different kinds?
- What animals are observed at the shore of the water?
- How many animals of one kind are observed in a measured area (e.g., 1 square foot) along the shore?
- What plants are observed in the water?
- What plants are observed on the shore?
- What parts (roots, stem, leaf, flower) are missing from the plants observed?
- Do plants in the water or on the shore change during fall and winter?
- If the water in a stream or pond is frozen at the surface, are there plants and animals under the ice?

LESSON 9: SEED-OBSERVING WALK

Observe the techniques for scattering seeds and the numbers of seeds scattered.

Investigative Questions

- How many seeds are found in a seed pod of a particular plant?
- How many different kinds of plants with seeds were observed?
- Upon what structures of the plant were seeds found?
- What methods of seed dispersal were evident?
- Out of 100 seeds collected, how many germinate?

LESSON 10: SPRING BUD WALK

Observe the opening of buds. They may open naturally or you can force them by cutting one budding stem from a tree or shrub and placing it in water in a warm place. When the buds begin to open, place the stem under some light source for at least ten to twelve hours per day.

Investigative Questions

- Where are buds found on a plant?
- Do all buds on a plant look alike?
- As buds open, what do they contain?
- How much time is required for a bud to open?
- Can the time required for a bud to open be changed?
- Do all the buds on a plant open? If not, how many open?
- What conditions are necessary for buds to open?
- If the outer covering of a bud is removed, will the bud develop?

LESSON 11: GERMINATING SEEDS

Seeds can be germinated in several ways: Place seeds on damp cellulose sponges and cover them with a damp paper towel. Or, place seeds between two sheets of damp paper towel in a pan or pie plate. Or, using a drinking glass with straight sides, roll two paper towels in a cylinder and place them inside the glass so the paper towels are touching the glass. Place the seeds between the glass and paper towels, and add about 2 ml of water to the glass. This moistens the towels enough to soak the seeds and encourage germination.

Investigative Questions

- Do all seeds germinate?
- How many seeds found in a seed pod germinate?
- How much time is required for seeds to germinate?
- Can the time for seed germination be changed?
- What conditions (temperature, light, water) are necessary for seeds to germinate?
- Will seeds germinate equally well if planted at different depths in soil?
- Will seeds taken from fresh fruit germinate?
- How many seeds in a packet of seeds gotten commercially germinate?
- Which part—root or stem—emerges from a seed first?
- Will a seed germinate if the seed coat is removed?
- Will a seed germinate if the cotyledon is removed?

LESSON 12: HOW ROOTS AND STEMS GROW

Using the third method listed for germinating seeds in Lesson 11, watch which direction the roots and stems grow. Place another glass with paper towels and seeds on its side and observe any changes in the direction of stem and root growth.

Investigative Questions

- In which direction does a root grow?
- In which direction does a stem grow?
- Will the direction of root growth be the same in different containers?
- How does contact with the sides of a container influence the direction of root growth?
- Can the direction of root growth be changed by adding an object to the soil in which the plant is growing?
- Will colored light affect the direction in which a stem grows?
- Can the direction of stem growth be changed by submerging the plant in water?

LESSON 13: TRACKING

On nature walks, observe animal tracks. Use them to identify the kind of animal, and its activity. You can also make casts of observed animal tracks in the following way: Cut the top and bottom from a half-pint milk carton or the bottom from a styrofoam or paper drinking cup. Place the carton over an animal track. (Coating the inside of the carton or cup with oil or petroleum jelly will make it easier to remove the cast later.) Mix plaster of paris with water so it is thin enough to pour. Pour it in the container over the track. (Note the heat generated as water is mixed with plaster of paris.) Allow the plaster of paris to harden and remove it from the track. Brush debris from the cast. A raised track should appear on the bottom of the cast. This is a *negative* of the track. To make a *positive* of the cast, place some oil or petroleum jelly on the negative of the cast. Place a second container, similar to that used to make the negative, over the negative cast. Mix plaster of paris and pour it into the prepared container and let the plaster harden. The positive of the cast will be similar to the original track.

Investigative Questions

- What kind of animal made the tracks?
- In what ways do tracks of several kinds of dogs differ?
- How do the tracks of dogs and cats differ?
- What can you tell about the size of an animal by observing its track?
- Can you tell from looking at a track what the animal that made the track might have been doing?
- If tracks of two or more animals are observed in the same area, were the animals interacting?
- If the animals were interacting, what were they likely doing?
- In what direction was an animal that made a track moving?
- What similarities can be noted in the tracks of different animals?

LESSON 14: OBSERVING PLANT CELLS

Cut a thick slice of onion and separate the rings. A thin tissue is found on the inside of each ring. You will need a microscope to observe the cells. (Microscopes can frequently be borrowed from high school science teachers.)

Some information on preparing slides and focusing a microscope may be helpful. When a slide of fresh materials or other specimens is made and observed under the microscope, the most prominent item one can see is a circular object; the sides of this object appear to be thick and somewhat grey or black. The object being observed is an air bubble. To reduce the number of air bubbles, place a small drop of water on the slide. Place the onion tissue in the water and gently straighten it with a pin or pencil; there should be no wrinkles in the skin. Place one edge of a coverglass in the water containing the onion tissue. Gently drop the coverslip over the water and onion tissue. Put a small drop of tincture of iodine at the edge of the coverslip. (Tincture of iodine may be purchased at drug stores.) The iodine stains the onion cells. (Iodine will stain you and your clothing also.) Although air bubbles may be seen under the coverglass, it is likely that some area of the onion tissue will be in the water and will be visible through the microscope.

Focusing a microscope requires practice. Use the lower lens, frequently 10X.

Never focus a microscope toward the stage. This may break the lens, the coverglass, the slide, or all three. Looking at the side of the stage, lower the tube toward the stage with the coarse focus. Stop lowering the tube a short distance above the stage. After the tube has been lowered, look through the eyepiece, turn on the light below the stage, or adjust the mirror so light goes through the opening in the stage. Begin to focus by turning the coarse focus slowly upward. Although it may seem difficult at first, keeping both eyes open while using a microscope is more restful than closing one eye. When some object comes into sight, begin to focus very slowly. As the object becomes clearer, use the fine focus to see the object clearly. Remember that you may see some air bubbles. You will be able to recognize them easily. As you continue to focus the microscope, one surface of the onion cells may be seen. With further focusing, parts of the cells at various depths will become visible. Because you are looking at a three-dimensional object, different parts become clearly visible as you adjust the focus. If you have not focused a microscope previously, try it. You will become proficient very quickly.

The onion cells should look something like those in Figure 9.6.

Investigative Questions

- Are all onion cells the same shape?
- Are all onion cells the same size?
- Can you see a cell wall?
- Can you find the nucleus of the onion cell?
- Are all nuclei the same size?
- What part of the cell is between the cell wall and the nucleus?
- How many different kinds of cells can you find in the cross section of the leaf?
- Are all cells of the same kind the same size?
- Are all cells of the same kind the same shape?
- Can you find the nucleus of the different cells in the cross section of the leaf?
- Can you find the cell walls in the cross section of the leaf?
- Can you identify the green structures observed in some cells?

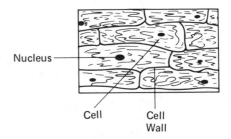

Nucleus

Cell   Cell
                Wall

Figure 9.6. Onion Skin Cells

- Do the cells in both outer layers of the cross section appear to be the same?
- Carefully break a leaf and attempt to get sections of the leaf covering (epidermis) from the upper surface and the lower surface of the leaf. Make a slide of the two epidermal sections and observe them under the microscope. Do the cells in the upper and lower epidermis look the same? (You may wish to consult a textbook for an explanation of what you observed.)

LESSON 15: CULTURING AND OBSERVING PROTOZOA

Use a quart jar filled about three-fourths full with pond water. Place 10 grains of rice in the jar and let it stand four to five days. Nontreated pond water frequently has many small plants and animals in it. Within a few days, the protozoa will multiply in the jar. Some of the protozoa can be seen in the jar through a hand lens, others only under a microscope. Population studies can be done with these pond water samples. Various populations will increase and decrease as the culture ages.

Investigative Questions

- How many different kinds of organisms can be found?
- How do the different organisms move?
- How many of the organisms can you identify?
- Observe one organism for five minutes. What behaviors did you observe?
- How many of the same kinds of organisms were observed?
- What colors are organisms?
- What internal structures of organisms are visible?
- Make a slide of organisms every three days for a period of three weeks. Stir the water in the culture before placing any of it on the slide. How do the numbers of various organisms change with each observation?

LESSON 16: MAKING COLLECTIONS

Two very interesting insects to collect are butterflies and moths. A quick way to distinguish between the two kinds of animals is by observing the antennae. The antennae of moths look like feathers, while those of butterflies are rather plain with a knob at the end. Butterflies and larger moths should be stretched to be displayed more effectively. To stretch a butterfly, make a stretching board from two pieces of corrugated cardboard. Cut an opening in the cardboard. Mount the animals with strips of paper and pins. Use a pencil or pin to spread the wings. Leave the animal on the stretching board for approximately a week. Be sure to place a pin in the thorax while the animal is fresh (pliable). Avoid touching the wings; they are covered with colored scales which easily fall off.

Collections need not be limited to plants and animals. They may include feathers, sands, rocks, egg shells, sea shells, samples of liquids or soils—virtually anything found in nature.

Collections may be used to illustrate the variety of specimens within a large group of objects or living organisms. They are useful in encouraging children to observe, compare, and classify. Collecting should be viewed as a means of encouraging inquiry, rather than as an end in itself.

Investigative Questions

- What differences do you observe among the specimens in the collection?
- What are some common features among members of the collection?
- What patterns, colors, or shapes can be observed in the specimens?
- Observe the specimens in a collection under a hand lens and/or microscope. What features can be seen which were not visible without magnification?
- What differences do you note between the observations with and without magnification?
- Do specimens within the collection differ in weight, color, structure, shape, and size?
- How can the dimensions of specimens in the collection best be measured?
- How might the specimens within the collection be classified?

LESSON 17: STUDYING AND OBSERVING NONGREEN PLANTS

Mold colonies can be grown on bread, cheeses or fruits, and observed with a hand lens. To observe a spore pattern, invert a mushroom cap on a piece of white paper and let it stand for a day or so. You may observe a pattern of spores as they fall from the gills. (NEVER pick a mushroom from the ground for observation; it may be poisonous. If you wish to observe a wild mushroom, do so without touching it.)

Investigative Questions

- How many kinds of nongreen plants can be found on the school campus, along a nature trail, or in a forest?
- What nongreen plants are found in nature?
- What colors are molds?
- What body parts of molds can be observed?

- What conditions are necessary for mold to grow on an object?
- What conditions are necessary for mushrooms to grow?
- What kinds of nongreen plants can be found in a decaying log?
- How does the growth of nongreen plants affect a log?
- Are the same kinds of nongreen plants found in different environments?
- What is the source of mold spores that get onto food?
- Can both green plants and nongreen plants grow in the same environment?

LESSON 18: THE MOVEMENT OF LIQUIDS IN PLANT STEMS

Place a stem of a plant such as a celery stem or the stem of a flower in a container of water. Color the water with red food coloring. Observe the movement of the colored water in the stem (it will eventually appear in petals or leaves). Celery conducts water more quickly if the bottom part of the stalk is removed *while the stalk is submerged* in the water. This prevents air from getting into the ducts and blocking the flow of the liquid.

Investigative Questions

- How fast does water move in the stem?
- Does water move in two different directions in a plant stem?
- Which moves faster in a stem—hot or cold water?
- What liquids, other than water, will move through a stem?
- Will substances dissolved in water move through a variety of stems at the same rate?

LESSON 19: THE LIFE CYCLE OF AN INSECT

Careful searching may reveal tiny mealworm eggs on pieces of apple. A lens or microscope is needed to see the eggs. The larva (what we know as the mealworm), pupa, and adult beetle are easily observed.

Investigative Questions

- How long is the life cycle of a selected insect?
- Does high temperature have any effect upon the length of an insect's life cycle?
- Does low temperature have any effect upon the life cycle of an insect?
- Insects have two basic kinds of life cycles: complete metamorpho-

sis and incomplete metamorphosis. What are the stages within each life cycle?

- How many eggs can a female insect lay in one year? (Specify the kind of insect.)
- Of the insect eggs laid in one year, how many will develop into adult insects?
- What are some means of controlling insect populations by preventing maturation during some stage of the life cycle?
- What is the appearance of insects at various stages of the life cycle?
- Do insect larvae of the same species differ in weight?
- Do the larvae and adult insects of the same species weigh the same?
- Does the weight of a larva change as it develops?
- Does the weight of a pupa change as it develops?

LESSON 20: SNAILS

The feeding of snails makes for an interesting study with either the land or water variety. Land snails can be used to show one type of hibernation when dry conditions are in effect. The actions of water snails may be observed in the aquarium.

Investigative Questions

- How rapidly can snails move?
- What activities of snails can be observed in an aquarium?
- Where can snails be found in an aquarium?
- In what kind of a habitat can land snails be found?
- What is the food of land snails?
- What is the food of water snails?
- Based on observations, why are snails put in an aquarium?
- How much do the *same kinds* of snails differ in weight and body dimensions?
- How much do *different kinds* of snails vary in body dimensions and weight?
- Where can land snails be found in winter?

LESSON 21: OBSERVING THE EFFECTS OF TEMPERATURE ON COLD-BLOODED ANIMALS

Observe the action of goldfish in an aquarium. Place them in water that has several ice cubes in it and place a thermometer in the jar. Note the action of the goldfish as the temperature drops. (Do not lower the temper-

ature below 10 degrees Celsius (°C) as this may harm the fish. Also, do not increase temperature above 27°C.)

Investigative Questions

- What changes in the activities of cold-blooded animals are noted when their body temperature is 30°C, 25°C, 20°C, 15°C, 10°C, and 5°C?
- Will cold-blooded animals eat when their body temperature is 10°, 15°, or 20° lower than atmospheric temperature?
- Will insects fly when their body temperature is 20° below atmospheric temperature?
- When the body temperature of a fish is lowered 20°, to what part of the aquarium does the fish go?

The preceding lessons and related questions should encourage development of strong inquiry skills. They also point children toward interesting and important information about the topic under study. Listen carefully, and note children's questions; investigating to find answers to their questions can add interest to science lessons.

CHEMICALS FOR ELEMENTARY SCHOOL SCIENCE

Many activities suggested for elementary school science require chemicals. Most are common chemicals found in the school or at supermarkets or variety stores. Some of the more commonly used chemicals are listed in Appendix B. Following are sample lessons and inquiries based on the use of chemicals.

Lessons Related to Using Chemicals in the Classroom

LESSON 1: GROWING CRYSTALS

Use a pint glass jar or a junior-size baby food jar. Fill the jar with hot water and add salt to the water until no more dissolves. Tie a piece of string with a small weight (noniron if possible) at one end to a pencil. Measure the length of the string; it should nearly reach but not touch the bottom of the jar. Place the string in the hot salt solution. Place the jar in a warm place where it will be undisturbed. Observe the jar for several days. If some of the liquid is placed in a saucer and observed, comparisons can be made.

For sugar crystals, heat about 100 ml (½ cup) of water in a pan. When the water boils, add sugar until no more dissolves. Pour the hot solution into a jar. (*Note:* Placing a piece of metal in the jar—spoon, knife blade, fork, letter opener—will help absorb some heat and prevent the jar from breaking.) Prepare a weighted string as directed in the salt crystal activity. Place the string in the jar and put the jar in a warm place where it will remain undisturbed. Observe as the crystals form on the string. You may wish to compare the salt and sugar crystals.

Investigative Questions

- Will crystals form when substances other than sugar and salt are dissolved in water?
- What are some characteristics of crystals formed from various substances?
- Would crystals form on paper if it were put in the solution instead of the weighted string?
- Will crystals form on copper wires or a plastic spoon placed in the solution?
- How rapidly do crystals form in a solution?
- Do all the crystals from a given substance have the same size and appearance?
- Will crystals form if a substance is dissolved in a liquid other than water?

LESSON 2: EFFECTS OF WATER POLLUTION ON PLANT GROWTH

Plant some bean seeds in soil using five milk cartons or styrofoam drinking cups and soil. Seedlings will grow in a few days. Label the cups 0, 5, 10, 20, and 40. Prepare stock solutions of different strengths of laundry detergent dissolved in water. To make these solutions you need to use a balance to measure out quantities of the detergent. Be sure to label the jars clearly to avoid any errors.

The 0 solution should be pure water. To prepare the other four solutions, measure out 5, 10, 20, and 40 grams of detergent. Place each given amount in a jar and add 250 ml of water.

Using a medicine dropper, water each plant daily with the same quantity of its prescribed solution. Place the plants in a warm place in indirect sunlight. Observe and compare the plants every two days. Children may record and graph changes in heights of the plants, or their colors, numbers of leaves, sizes of leaves, and any other changes in the plants that are observed. A similar procedure may be followed by substituting other types of possible pollutants: e.g., household ammonia, shampoo, alcohol, or oil. Measure liquids in milliliters instead of grams.

Investigative Questions

- How do various amounts of pollutants affect the color of the plants?
- What is the maximum ratio of water pollutant that a plant can tolerate?

- Can a plant that has been adversely affected by pollutants return to a healthy state?
- Do various plants react in the same manner to pollutants?

LESSON 3: BLOWING BUBBLES

Make a concentrated solution of dish detergent and water (2 to 3 parts detergent to 1 part water). Dip a soda straw in the solution and blow gently through the straw. Observe the bubbles which form.

Investigative Questions

- If food coloring is added to the detergent-water solution, are the bubbles the same color?
- Can more bubbles be blown from a warm solution than from a cold solution?
- In what shapes can bubbles be blown?
- Do bubbles float in air, and if so, for how long?
- Do large bubbles or small bubbles break first?
- Can a bubble be held in the hand?
- Can a bubble be frozen?
- Can one bubble be blown inside another bubble?
- Do bubbles unite to form larger bubbles?
- If soap is added to the detergent-water solution, can bubbles be blown?
- What interactions are observable in the bubble system?

LESSON 4: SURFACE TENSION

Float a needle on the surface of a glass of water. (This takes a little practice but it *is possible.* Don't drop the needle onto the surface; place it gently.) Place one drop of detergent on a plastic or waxed surface. Touch a toothpick to the detergent; then touch the water near the needle. The interaction of needle and water surface changes and students can investigate to find some reasons for the change.

Investigative Questions

- Do liquids other than water have surface tension?
- If the toothpick is dipped into liquid soap, will the results be the same as with the detergent?
- Is there tension over the entire surface of water in the container?
- If you sprinkle pepper on the surface of water in a glass and dip your

finger into some detergent and then place your finger in the water, what happens? Why?
- Does water heated to 99°C have surface tension?
- Does water cooled to 5°C have surface tension?
- Does water with salt or sugar dissolved in it have surface tension?
- Does water with rubbing alcohol dissolved in it have surface tension?

LESSON 5: COAL GARDENS

Obtain an 8″ or 9″ (about 20 cm) aluminum pie pan and a lump of coal. Mix a solution of water (1 part), salt (1 part), household ammonia (¼ part). For example, the solution may be made of ½ cup water, ½ cup salt, and 2 tablespoons ammonia. Pour the solution over the coal in the pie pan. Place the pan in a place where it will be undisturbed, but clearly observable. Watch what occurs over the next few days.

Investigative Questions

- From which ingredients do crystals develop?
- Could charcoal, stone, or brick be substituted for the coal?
- Must the solution be poured over an object or can it be placed in the pan and crystals developed from it?
- If food coloring is placed upon the coal, do colored crystals develop?
- Are the crystals the same shape as other crystals (such as those formed from salt or sugar)?
- In what directions do crystals grow?
- Does temperature seem to affect the development of crystals?
- Does light seem to affect the development of crystals?

LESSON 6: MAKING CARBON DIOXIDE

Pour a mixture of ¼ cup vinegar and 1 cup water into a 1-liter soft drink bottle. Wrap 2 teaspoons of baking soda in a paper tissue or paper towel and drop it into the vinegar solution. Quickly place the stopper on the bottle. This gas can be trapped and the quantity measured. The gas can also be bubbled from the soft drink bottle into other containers. If the proper size cork with a hole for rubber tubing is available, run the tubing to a water-filled container (an aquarium works fine). Place a jar in the aquarium, and let it fill with water. When the tubing from the gas generator is placed into this container, the gas coming through the tubing will displace the water and be trapped. If only a small amount of carbon dioxide is needed, it may be obtained using a seltzer tablet or powder. Place the tablet in water and quickly replace the stopper. Another method for generating carbon dioxide with a seltzer tablet is to place about 100 ml (about ½ cup) water in a balloon. Add a tablet and place a soda straw in the opening of the balloon. Hold it tightly. A stream of carbon dioxide comes out of the balloon.

Carbon dioxide may be used to extinguish a candle flame or to enrich the atmosphere of green plants. The effect of carbon dioxide upon fruit—particularly bananas, apples, pears, and tomatoes—may be observed by placing one piece of unripe fruit in a container with the gas and a similar one outside the jar as a control.

Investigative Questions

- Is CO_2 heavier or lighter than air?
- How much CO_2 is produced by a seltzer tablet?
- Will an excess of CO_2 cause a change in a plant or a piece of fruit?
- Will CO_2 pass through a membrane or wet paper towel?
- What are the characteristics of solid CO_2 (dry ice)? (Be sure to use very thick gloves or tongs to touch dry ice.)
- Does CO_2 have any odor?
- Will all fruit react in the same manner when placed in CO_2?

LESSON 7: SEPARATING COLORS

Fill a small jar one-third full of water. If no filter paper is available, cut strips of paper towel and attach them to a pencil. Paint a strip of food coloring approximately 2 cm from the end of the toweling. Hang the towel so the lower end of it is touching the water. The food coloring band should not be in the water. Water travels up the tissue; as it reaches the food coloring, observe what happens. The various pigments of the color separate. Those that are more dense remain at the bottom of the column, as others are carried up. This procedure may be used with several pigments such as those from tempera paint, ink, and cloth dye. This process is called paper chromatography.

An interesting activity with chromatography involves studying some pigments of plants. This should be demonstrated by the teacher. Put some green leaves in a container of water and boil them until they're wilted. Then place the leaves in a container of alcohol. Place the container of alcohol and leaves in a larger container of water. Heat the container of water (which in turn heats the alcohol). Do not heat the alcohol directly; there is too much danger of fire. As the alcohol boils, pigments in the leaves dissolve. After the pigments have been removed from the leaves, take the container off the heat. Follow a procedure similar to that described above. Place a paper tissue or other absorbent paper in the colored alcohol solution.

(*CAUTION:* Alcohol burns at a very low temperature. If the alcohol in the container of water should start to burn, suffocate the fire with a piece of glass or some nonflammable cover.)

Investigative Questions

- Do several kinds of plants have the same colors of pigments?
- Does the red in cabbage come from one pigment or a combination?
- Can rubbing alcohol rather than water be used in the chromatography activity?
- Will pigments in latex house paint separate?
- Does white latex paint contain other pigments?
- Do several brands of latex house paint of one color contain equal amounts of pigments?

LESSON 8: SEPARATING A MIXTURE (SALT AND SAND)

Measure out ¼ cup of salt and ¼ cup of sand. Mix the two substances together thoroughly. If the sand is white, it should be very difficult to tell the two materials apart. Put the salt-sand mixture in a jar and add about ½ cup of water. After shaking, let the contents of the jar settle. Pour off the water and observe what is left.

Investigative Questions

- Can sand be seen?
- Can salt be seen? Let the contents dry and let the liquid poured from the container evaporate.
- Can something be seen after all the liquid evaporates?
- Mix iron filings (2 tablespoons) and sand (¼ cup) together. Does the substance dissolve in water?
- Can the two substances be separated with a magnet?
  (*CAUTION:* Wrap the magnet in plastic wrap before putting it in the iron filings. The plastic wrap prevents the iron filings from getting on the magnet.)
- Mix together dried grass seed and flour. How can these be separated?
- How can the CO_2 be separated from a soft drink?
- Mix together paper clips and glass marbles. How can they be separated without picking either the clips or the marbles out with your hand?

LESSON 9: ACIDS AND BASES

Obtain several strips of red and blue litmus paper. (This paper is used to indicate acids and bases.) Place a few drops of ammonia on a strip of red and on a strip of blue litmus paper. A base turns red litmus paper blue, but does not change the blue paper. Acids turn blue paper red. Extend this lesson by testing some liquids (fruit juices, milk, household cleaners, etc.) to determine which are acids and which are bases.

Investigative Questions

- What common fruits contain acid?
- Does saliva contain acid?
- Does milk contain acid?
- Does acid rain exist in your area?
- Does the exhaust of an automobile contain an acid or a base?
- Does wood smoke contain an acid or a base?
- Does drinking water contain an acid or a base?
- What cleaning substances used around the home contain acids and bases?

LESSON 10: TESTING FOR STARCH

Mix a small amount of laundry starch with water. (If none is available, use water in which potatoes have been boiled.) Dilute a bottle of tincture of iodine with ½ bottle of alcohol. (This will provide a great deal more iodine solution for testing.) Place a few drops of the diluted iodine solution in the starch-water mixture. Note the color change. This color change indicates the presence of starch. Once you have done the test, other materials can be tested.

Investigative Questions

- Which of the following substances contain starch?
  Bread
  Milk
  Salt
  Sugar
  Carrots
  Paper
  Crackers
  Cereals
- Do artificial substances contain starch?

- Does overripe fruit contain starch?
- Does unripened fruit contain starch?

LESSON 11: TESTING FOR CARBON DIOXIDE

If lime water is available, use it. If not, dissolve 2 tablespoons of slaked lime in 1 liter of water to make lime water. Shake the mixture well and let it stand until the liquid clears. Pour off the clear liquid and store it in a tightly covered jar. Later, put about 20 ml of the lime water into a jar. Blow into the jar through a soda straw. Note the color change. The color is an indication of the presence of carbon dioxide.

Investigative Questions

- Place some lime water in an open container in a classroom. Is carbon dioxide in the air in the classroom?
- Place a small potted plant in a small container of lime water in a large plastic bag. Is there carbon dioxide in the air in the plastic bag? If so, can you tell if it comes from the air in the bag or from the plant?
- Is there carbon dioxide in automobile exhaust?
- Use your gas generator (made in Lesson 6) and bubble the gas through lime water. Does it contain CO_2?

LESSON 12: DISSOLVING SUBSTANCES

Dissolve 5 gm of salt or sugar in 100 ml of water. Pour the solution into a large container and let it stand until the liquid evaporates. Repeat the activity using undiluted tincture of iodine. Is anything left in the container?

Investigative Questions

- Put some iodine solution in an open container and let the liquid evaporate. (Iodine solution consists of iodine dissolved in alcohol.) Is anything left in the container?
- Could you make tincture of iodine from the substance in the container?
- Does a gas dissolve in a liquid?
- Does temperature affect the rate at which substances dissolve in water?
- What substances will dissolve oil?

- What substances will dissolve oil-based paint?
- Will water dissolve latex-based paint after it has dried?

LESSON 13: ODORS OF SUBSTANCES

Select several extracts such as almond, peppermint, and lemon. Use a styrofoam cup for each extract. Cut off the top half of the cup and discard. Place a few drops of each extract in each cup. Cover each cup with aluminum foil and make holes in the foil with a pencil. Ask children to identify the odor. (This activity may be extended using other substances: peanut butter, onion, garlic, after-shave lotion, etc.)

Investigative Questions

- Can the odor of a liquid be removed by filtering?
- Can the odor of a liquid be removed by boiling or freezing the liquid?
- How rapidly does the odor of a substance disperse through a room?
- Is the flavor of foods generally due to odor or taste?

LESSON 14: BUOYANCY OF WATER

Fill each of two pint jars two-thirds full of water. Dissolve 1 cup salt in one jar. Place two thumbtacks into the eraser of a pencil. Place the pencil, tack end down, into the water and observe how deep the pencil goes. Next, place the pencil in the salt solution. Note how deep the pencil goes.

Putting salt in water changes the density of the water. The more dense the water, the greater the buoyancy. Each liquid has its own density, and density exerts a different buoyant force. (For a related activity, use equal amounts of rubbing alcohol and water. Place ice cubes of the same size in each liquid. Observe what happens to the ice cubes.)

Investigative Questions

- How can you tell if a liquid is more dense or less dense than water?
- How can you tell if a solid is more dense or less dense than water?
- How can the density of a gas, such as carbon dioxide, be determined?
- Does a relationship exist between the size of an object and its density?

The preceding lessons, like those relating to investigations of live organisms, should be extremely valuable in helping children develop strong inquiry skills.

USING COMMERCIALLY AVAILABLE RESOURCES

Selecting from among the vast array of commercially available resources presents a challenge. The following sections should help simplify the selection by indicating some important things to consider.

Contemporary Elementary Science Textbook Series

Textbooks are widely used, trusted resources for teaching children science. They represent the thinking of knowledgeable authors and they are readily available for most teachers. Although there is little agreement in content among different textbook series, each offers a sequence of topics likely to integrate well with a particular kind of curriculum.

In many ways, the diversity among textbooks is a strength. With so many topics available, there is likely to be something for everyone.

Content, the primary focus of science lessons in the past, continues to be an important consideration in textbook selection. Contemporary textbooks, however, tend to place great emphasis on inquiry skills. Understanding science content is still considered critical, but the means by which children acquire knowledge is changing. Increasingly, children are encouraged to investigate science topics to new depths, to explore, and to question. Most contemporary texts no longer view children as passive absorbers of information, but rather as active developers and users of information.

Elementary School Science Curriculum Studies

Curriculum studies, unique science programs especially designed for the elementary school in the late 1960s and early 1970s may serve as excellent resources for teachers who wonder which topics to teach and what learning activities will be appropriate for students with varying abilities and needs. These studies are being used currently as the science program rather than a textbook or as a supplement to the textbook. Three curriculum studies are compared in Table 9.1.

Although the topics within these curriculum studies may seem similar, they are apt to be treated quite differently in each study. Different subtopics may be stressed and the learning activities associated with various topics may also differ. Some learning activities may encourage a learner to plan individual investigations once a question is

TABLE 9.1. SCIENCE TOPICS SUGGESTED BY THREE CURRICULUM STUDIES

Curriculum Study	Science Content
1. Science—A Process Approach II (S-APA)	Colors, shapes, temperature, movement, measurements, sets, sound, animals, order, changes, sails, weather, graphing, forces, life cycles, symmetry, mixtures, plants, scale drawings, static and moving objects, circuit boards, conductors and nonconductors, solutions, and biotic communities
2. Science Curriculum Improvement Study (SCIS)	Properties of objects, seeds, plants, habitats, food webs, pulley systems, electrical interactions, life cycles, solutions, populations, food relationships in a terrarium and aquarium, position and motion, environments, plant responses, energy transfer, communities, and ecosystems
3. Elementary Science Study (ESS)	Growing seeds, small things, kitchen physics, gases and airs, tracks, mapping, crayfish, butterflies, rocks and minerals, solutions, microorganisms, electric circuits

asked or a problem defined, while others may take a more structured approach.

Methods and Resource Books

Methods and resource books give teachers a philosophical background for teaching modern elementary science as well as information on methodology and content. Many list topics and subtopics as well as learning activities which are appropriate for elementary science programs. Several also identify topics and learning activities suited to specific grade levels. Several of these methods and resource books are listed in Appendix C.

Science Programs for Early Childhood

Most science experiences for young children consist of series of activities. A few programs are available such as the one from the Department of Science Education at The University of Georgia, Athens, Georgia. This is a complete science program for children ages three to five. The program consists of ten units that stress scientific process as well as content. Topics treated in the program include the following:

- Shapes (two- and three-dimensional)
- Textures
- Hardness

- Sounds
- Temperature
- Size
- Phases of matter
- Directions
- Colors

Science Topics in Periodicals

Many professional and popular periodicals suggest science topics and activities for young children. Some of these are *Young Children, Science and Children, Science Activities, Instructor, Teacher, Childhood Education, Early Years,* and *Learning.* Each covers a wide range of topics; many also suggest relevant learning activities.

Becoming familiar with the available resources for teaching children science starts with the first book you read and the first item you collect.

A list of resources can acquaint you with the thinking of your colleagues. But remember: Each idea and sequence represents one person's belief about how best to develop scientific attitudes, investigative behaviors, and understanding in students. You know the needs of your own students best. Therefore, your task is to take these ideas, refine and combine them, using your own knowledge and experience, to fit the unique set of circumstances represented in your own classroom.

Creating a total science curriculum, or even a portion of it for a particular grade level, is a difficult and time-consuming task. Few teachers have the necessary time to manage it. But for most, particularly as they begin their planning, a good textbook series offers a sound basic program that can be expanded as teachers become more confident of their knowledge and begin to move beyond the confines of other's ideas to develop their own.

Consult Appendix G for material on use of the metric system and measuring equipment.

Appendix H covers ecological topics and issues.

_____ *LOOKING BACK* _____

1. What types of resources are available for teaching elementary school science?
2. Where may resources for teaching elementary school science be obtained locally?
3. Where might you obtain some common resources (equipment and printed materials) for teaching elementary school science)?

ACTIVITIES

1. Review the tables of contents from at least three series of elementary school science textbooks. Note the topics presented for each grade level. What commonalities and variations do you notice?
2. Select one curriculum study. Review the teacher editions for the selected study. What kinds of science topics are suggested? How are the topics organized? How would you teach the curriculum study if it were your science program? What is your opinion of the study?
3. Review an elementary school science curriculum guide from a local school district. Notice the content, sequence of lessons, instructional plans, and resources. Would you enjoy teaching science using this guide?
4. Become familiar with your state's mandatory guidelines and standards for teaching elementary school science. Are you comfortable with your state's expectations for science at the elementary level? Would you add to, delete, or change any of the standards or guidelines? Are the mandates consistent with your philosophy for teaching science to children?

10

A New Horizon

Objectives

1. To describe the characteristics of a scientifically literate person.
2. To describe the role of science and technology in the elementary science curriculum.
3. To identify the goals of computer literacy.
4. To classify the uses of microcomputers in education.
5. To describe criteria used to select appropriate software.
6. To describe some ways to use microcomputers with children.

_____ LOOKING FORWARD _____

You have learned about appropriate classroom methods and procedures for integrating science concepts, principles, and information with inquiry skills. You have explored the nature of learners and ways to engage them effectively in the study of science content and skills. You have been provided with some background for assisting children in developing scientific attitudes, and have explored ways of planning and implementing scientifically and educationally sound lessons. Finally, you have realized the impact of Sputnik in inaugurating the "space age" and awakening Americans to the need for scientific literacy.

Today we are living in an information-driven society, driven by changes in technology, technology that gave birth to the integrated circuit microprocessor—the computer on a chip.

This chapter focuses on a new horizon in education, the use of microcomputers in the elementary school classroom. The chapter is written for individuals with limited experience using microcomputers. The introduction presents a brief overview of various national reports concerned with the place of science and technology in education. A rationale for the inclusion of a strong science and technology component in school curricula is provided, with emphasis on computer literacy as the major focal point of educational technology.

The first part of the chapter covers the use of microcomputers in school. You will have opportunities to familiarize yourself with criteria used to evaluate appropriate science software packages and with suggestions to assist you in using microcomputers with children. The chapter also offers appropriate information to help formulate your philosophy about the appropriate use of microcomputers in elementary school science.

The computer revolution has arrived. And it brings with it profound social changes that raise new questions for educators. Most educators recognize the need to improve schooling in the United States, especially in the area of science. What role can—or should—computers play in helping us realize that goal? Answering that question is the focus of this chapter.

NATIONAL CONCERNS ABOUT TECHNOLOGY

The National Science Board (NSB) Commission on Precollege Mathematics, Science and Technology report, _Educating Americans for the 21st Century_ (1983), provides guidance on the direction that science education improvement efforts should take. The report emphasizes two key points: First, science education must be modified to include a substantial technological component; and second, "scientific and technological literacy" should be established as one of the primary academic goals of K-12 education for *all* students.

The philosophy embodied in these two points is in keeping with that expressed by the National Science Teachers Association (1982), which defines a scientifically literate person as one who

- understands how society influences science and technology as well as how science and technology influence society;
- understands that society controls science and technology through the allocation of resources;
- appreciates science and technology for the intellectual stimulus they provide;
- understands the application of technology and the decisions entailed in the use of technology;
- has sufficient knowledge and experience to appreciate the worthiness of research and technology development;
- knows reliable sources of scientific and technology information and uses these sources in the process of decision making.

All citizens need a solid information base and the know-how to access it in order to expand their understanding of the world. The NSB suggests two reasons for a more extensive reformulated K-12 science program: First, scientific and technological understanding are keys in adjusting to and participating in a world that continues to change rapidly through expanding technology. And second, because these changes affect all realms of life—work, civic affairs, and personal life—such education is relevant to virtually all Americans.

Technological literacy demands a special curriculum, one that provides children with basic concepts and intellectual tools relevant to their everyday lives. This means, among other things, some attention to computer literacy. Computer literacy means different things to different people; not even science educators agree precisely on how this term should be defined. For purposes of this discussion, computer literacy may be defined as a basic understanding of how a computer works and of its capabilities and limitations.

The following is a list of selected computer literacy goals. The student will acquire:

- knowledge of the history of computers;
- knowledge of the components of a computer and how they interact;
- knowledge of the issues surrounding computer technology (such as privacy and the appropriate applications of artificial intelligence);

- skill in using the computer;
- skill in flowcharting;
- skill in programming the computer to do simple tasks;
- recognition of the computer as a valuable tool.

USE OF MICROCOMPUTERS IN SCHOOLS

Microcomputers are used in a number of ways in school, depending on the knowledge and interest of the teacher and on the kinds of hardware and software available. Here are a few of the most common ways in which teachers offer students experiences using computers.

Drill and Practice. This provides children with opportunities to improve and reinforce skills previously introduced or learned. Good drill and practice programs address the individual needs of children and concerns of teachers, and provide immediate and appropriate feedback and positive reinforcement. Most programs written for young children emphasize drill and practice.

Simulations and Educational Games. Games encourage children to participate as role players in realistic problem-solving situations. Simulations provide opportunities for children to use higher-level thinking skills.

Problem Solving. Children can use basic programming skills and knowledge in solving problems. Giving the computer instructions—which is programming at its most basic—presents opportunities to develop reasoning and critical thinking skills.

Through drill and practice, simulations and games, and problem solving, the computer serves as a kind of tutor, providing instruction in basic skills. Many educators also value the computer as a tool for computer-managed instruction, computer-based testing, records management, word processing, graphics production, data retrieval, and data analysis. As an educational tool, the computer has virtually limitless uses—some involving direct interactions with students and some relating to materials production, record keeping, or educational management.

Software

Software is frequently defined as anything that can be loaded into the computer by disk or cassette. In effect, the software is what enables us to interact with the computer, through words, numbers, images, or graphics. While elementary software programs abound, many believe these programs tend to neglect hands-on experience. Children do manipulate graphic substitutes (simulations) of real objects. The question is: How understandable are these graphic representations to children? Research has yet to tell us.

The supply of science software continues to grow at a rapid pace. How does one select good software? Well, the first step is deciding on a purpose. What do you want to achieve? What skills do you want to teach? Math? Problem solving? Once you've answered these basic questions, some information on the criteria of quality software should be helpful.

The following criteria are taken from the publication *Science Computer Software: A Handbook on Selection and Classroom Use* (1986).

A. Instructional Content/Applications
1. *Is the content accurate?*
Incorrect content, whether in textbooks or computer programs, is unacceptable. It is true that our knowledge about nature is subject to change, but we should use the most accurate facts and ideas available in our instructional materials.
2. *Is the content relevant?*
This question can be answered well only by the science teacher who intends to use the software.
3. *Is the content of interest to students?*
The best way to learn of students' interest in and involvement with the software is to use it in the classroom. Short of this, experience with students and computer software is necessary.
4. *Does the content provide for different ability levels?*
Except for rote learning of terms, etc., this is an important factor. For programs that provide problem-solving practice, various levels of difficulty should be provided.
5. *Is the student actively engaged or passive?*
A high degree of interaction takes advantage of the computer as a patient and (hopefully) intelligent tutor. If the student is expected to input numeric values for an upcoming dynamic simulation or to solve sample problems, active involvement and learning are much more likely to result.
6. *Is self-testing built in?*
A student should be able to monitor her/his progress. Questions and problems with feedback can provide the necessary feedback. Of course, with some software, especially simulations and games, progress is evident to the user. Some software packages offer feedback to the teacher as well as the student.
7. *Are inquiry processes integrated into the software?*
Since the nature of science as inquiry/process is well established, this should be reflected in most software.
8. *Is important lab work replaced?*
The computer should not be used as an excuse to reduce lab

work that provides students with a concerted sense of exploration, measurement, and the excitement of discovery. As [an] extraordinary number cruncher, a computer can extend and supplement regular lab work. Lab interface devices can be very helpful tools, as can other specialized programs (tools) designed for data analysis and representation.

9. *Is the content free from stereotyping?*

It is important that all students be encouraged to develop free, inquiring minds.

B. Technical Quality

1. *Are the graphics of high quality?*

Where graphics are used, they should be of high quality. After viewing a dozen or so software packages, the meaning of quality will likely become clearer. In simulations and games, dynamic graphics are of utmost importance.

2. *Are the graphics used intelligently?*

Having a nice replica of a dinosaur on the viewing screen does not mean the graphics are used intelligently. Instructional software should take advantage of the unique capabilities of the computer. If the viewing screen simply replicates a page of a textbook, why use the computer? Dynamic graphics do what the textbook cannot and usually offer the user a high degree of control over the system being simulated on the screen. Representing and rotating chemical molecules as three-dimensional figures cannot be done with textbooks.

3. *Is the program "user-friendly"?*

Can the student easily learn how to use the software or must many commands be mastered first? Once into the instructional sequence (e.g., level of a game or step in a problem) can the user easily move to another part of the program?

4. *Are documentation and other guidance materials comprehensive and well-designed?*

With some software, documentation is not particularly important. A good tutorial, for example, might need little accompanying documentation. A simulated harmonic motion system, however, should have background information and, if the program is not list protected (a *very* desirable feature), some information should be included on the internal operation of the program. Vernier, publisher of physics software, does an excellent job of providing documentation that allows students to learn physics *and* computer programming.

5. *Are there long delays?*

Especially for tutorials and drill and practice software, the pace of the program is important.

6. *Can sound be controlled?*

Where sound is an important part of the instruction, there should be a way to control the volume. In tutorials, students should have control over sounds indicating correct/incorrect answers. In games, the teacher should be able to reduce or eliminate unwanted sounds.

The selection of software can be a time-consuming task. In addition to the many concerns we've already noted, cost must also be considered. The best way to choose any software program is to try it out firsthand. It doesn't hurt, however, to get some information and advice from the experts. Following is a brief list of publishers and evaluators of software programs for elementary school science:

- Minnesota Educational Computing Consortium (MECC)
  2520 Broadway Dr.
  St. Paul, MN   55113
- Micro-Ed, Inc.
  P.O. Box 24156
  Minneapolis, MN   55424
- Right On Programs
  27 Bowdon Rd.
  Greenlawn, NY   11740
- *Classroom Computer Learning*
  19 Davis Dr.
  Belmont, CA   94002
- *The Computing Teacher*
  The University of Oregon
  1787 Agate St.
  Eugene, OR   97403
- *Electronic Education*
  1311 Executive Center Dr., Suite 220
  Tallahassee, FL   32301
- *Electronic Learning*
  730 Broadway
  New York, NY   10003
- *Educational Technology*
  140 Sylvan Avenue
  Englewood Cliffs, NJ   07632
- *The Journal of Computers in Mathematics and Science Teaching*
  P.O. Box 4455
  Austin, TX   78765

Additional publishers and suppliers are listed in Appendix A.
Marge Kosel, an educational software developer, suggests considering the following criteria when purchasing software:

- Good software must use the computer well.
- Software should change the way we think about ideas in the curriculum.
- Programs should help you use the computer to structure what's happening in the classroom.

- A good program should enable you to accomplish a task quickly.
- A good program should have lasting value (Shalvoy, 1987).

Microcomputers: Selection and Use

The microcomputer came into existence in the late 1970s and quickly gained recognition as a very adaptable tool for the classroom. Today, many elementary students have microcomputers in their homes. Some may have experience in working with word processing, graphics, or telecommunications software—or may have observed a parent doing so.

New software programs and computers on which to run them are being developed and released constantly. Computer-oriented magazines have inundated the marketplace. Probably the school district and county or state departments of education have the best current publications that list and review new hardware and software. Another good source of information is the local computer software or hardware retailer, whose representatives would be pleased to demonstrate their products to you. Do not rely solely on demonstrations, however. You should sit down at the computer yourself and try out any piece of hardware or software you're considering buying.

Many factors must be considered in selecting a microcomputer. Here are just a few of the most important questions to ask yourself:

- How much money do you wish to spend?
- How do you intend to use the microcomputer?
- How much power does your software require?
- Do you want a machine for each student?
- Do you want many machines with limited capabilities or few machines with extended capabilities?
- Do you need a single or dual disk drive? (*Note:* Some software requires two disk drives.)
- Will the software you've chosen (if any) run on the computer you are considering?
- Does your software (if any) require graphics capability? That is, does it require the computer to display charts, graphs, or images on screen?
- Are color capabilities really worth the extra costs? Color graphics enhance elementary science software programs, yet they require a more expensive monitor and more memory space.
- Do you need a printer? A printer supplies hard copy (printed material) of the information stored on the disk. A printer with every microcomputer is convenient, but not necessary. Rarely do students need to print out all the information they enter. Most students work with the information displayed on the mon-

itor screen. Nevertheless, at least one printer should be available in the building.

- If you have a printer, is the computer you're considering compatible with that printer?
- Is elementary science software available for your computer?
- Is service for your computer easily available?

Even though you may be an infrequent user of microcomputers, you should possess the necessary skills, understanding, and attitudes to use them effectively. That means, in part, understanding the capabilities and limitations of the computer in today's classroom. The following suggestions may assist you in using microcomputers with children:

- Remember that a computer is a learning tool. It does not solve all instructional problems.
- Think positively. Computers are neither as intimidating nor as complicated to operate as they're sometimes made out to be.
- Attend workshops and inservice programs on the computer. Hands-on experiences are absolutely necessary.
- Learn correct computer terminology so that your students can learn it too.
- Organize a computer-learning center where teachers and students can share information.
- Practice evaluating software. It isn't all of equal quality, as you'll soon discover. Colleagues will appreciate your efforts.
- Become familiar with the care of the microcomputer and software programs.
- Provide time for children to share their experiences with the computer.

The following activities for introducing young children to the microcomputer have been taken from Betty Baker's (1986) article in the journal *Dimensions*. Although the activities are recommended for young children, they may be adapted and modified for use with older children:

- Interview children about their experiences with a computer, asking what they think a computer is.
- Arrange a computer center in the room where children can investigate and learn about computers.
- Place computer catalogs in the art center for children to use in constructing collages or mobiles.
- Make a step-by-step chart showing how to operate a computer through pictures and words. Place this in the computer center.
- Play "Simon Says" with the children using the cursor. Example:

Simon says move the cursor two lines up and three spaces to the left.

- Provide students the opportunity to write a program on a chart. Then try it out on the computer. (This can be a class or independent project.)
- Select programs for children to use independently for drill and practice.
- Write songs using numerals from a program like *Hodge Podge* (Meredith, 1981).
- Ask children to discuss their (possibly changing) ideas about the computer.
- Let children work with partners or in small groups at the computer. This may stimulate language development and problem-solving skills.
- Individualize instruction by selecting programs based on children's identified needs and interests.
- Read about the history of computers in an encyclopedia. Compare the early computers with those of today.
- Allow children to observe the teacher (or another experienced adult) programming the microcomputer.
- Arrange demonstrations that allow young children to see computers at work. Include a demonstration of a printer or plotter in action.
- Make a scrapbook for the library center identifying the many uses of the computer, including those observed or described by the children.
- Write stories about computers observed on field trips, uses of computers, care of the computer, or fantasies about supercomputers of the future.
- Visit businesses, computer science departments, computer centers, or other places where computers are used.
- Construct keyboards on posterboard for each child to use in practice and in writing simple programs.
- Place a typewriter in the language center for keyboard practice.
- Introduce vocabulary words including *computer, cursor, data, diskette, input, microcomputer, output, program, programmer, software, keyboard, terminal.* (A helpful source is *Computer Picture Dictionary* by Rice and Hagley.)

EMERGING NEW HORIZONS

Innovations in technology such as interactive video, sophisticated simulations, software programs with high resolution graphics, laboratory probes interfacing with computers, massive networking of educational programs via communication satellites, and videodisc technology are shaping new horizons in elementary school science. Many educators predict that the impact of these innovations may actually revolutionize the teaching of science in ways few of us may now imagine.

You will be teaching the next generation of decision makers who will be expected to function in a scientific and technologic way. You will therefore not only need to acknowledge the impact of these innovations, but to become knowledgeable about how to use them successfully to enhance learning in the classroom. This challenging task awaits you as you embark upon a career in elementary school education.

_____ *LOOKING BACK* _____

1. What are some characteristics of a scientifically literate person?
2. What role does technology play in the science curriculum?
3. What are some goals related to achieving computer literacy?
4. What criteria are helpful in selecting microcomputer or software programs?

ACTIVITIES

1. If you're a beginner in computer technology, you'll find this activity helpful. It does require that you do some outside research.

   Define the following terms as they apply to computers. You may use software catalogs and computer advertisements to complete the task.

   - *microcomputer*
   - *input*
   - *output*
   - *hard copy*
   - *soft copy*
   - *keyboard*
   - *load*
   - *dump*
   - *memory*
   - *bug*
   - *debug*
   - *execute*
   - *CAI*
   - *MBL*
   - *software*
   - *hardware*
   - *bit*
   - *byte*
   - *chip*
   - *microprocessor*
   - *command*
   - *BASIC*
   - *LOGO*

2. If you have not used a microcomputer before, complete this independent activity:

   Go to a microcomputer and do the following:
   - Power up (Turn on the computer).
   - Print your name (Usually a command PRINT "your name" will appear on the monitor).
   - Load and run a program (Put the disk into the disk drive).
   - Dump your program (Remove the disk).
   - Power down (Turn everything off).
   - Share your experiences and attitude toward the computer with your peers.

3. Select an elementary science software package and evaluate it according to your perceptions of its usefulness in your classroom.

4. Interview an elementary school teacher and a few students about their experiences using a computer in elementary science.

REFERENCES

Baker, Betty Ruth (1986, July). "Let's Use Microcomputers with Young Children." *Dimensions, 14* (4), 8–11.

The National Science Board Commission on Precollege Education in Mathematics, Science, and Technology (1983). *Educating Americans for the 21st Century.* Washington, DC: The National Science Board and the National Science Foundation.

National Science Teachers Association (1982). *Science-Technology-Society: Science Education for the 1980's.* Washington, DC.

Science Computer Software: A Handbook on Selection and Classroom Use. Prepared by the Science and Mathematics Software Lab at Florida State University, July, 1986, pp. 1–4.

Shalvoy, MaryLee (1987, January). "Sunburst's Marge Kosel: Striving to Set the Software Standard." *Electronic Learning, 6* (4), 25.

Science Education Supplies

COMPUTERS/SOFTWARE

A² Educational Support Software
P.O. Box 1828
Riverton, WY 82501
(307) 856–1958

Accent Science
P.O. Box 1444
Saginaw, MI 48605
(517) 799–8103

Acorn Computer
400 Unicorn Park Dr.
Woburn, MA 01801
(617) 935–1190

Addison-Wesley Publishing Co.
2725 Sand Hill Rd.
Menlo Park, CA 94025
(415) 854–0300

Apple Computer, Inc.
20525 Mariani Ave.
Cupertino, CA 95014
(408) 996–1010

Applied Computer Systems, Inc.
3060 Johnstown-Utica Rd.
Johnstown, OH 43031
(800) 237–LINK

Astronomical Society of the Pacific
1290 24th Ave.
San Francisco, CA 94122
(415) 661–8660

Austin Computer Workshop
1005 W. 22nd St.
Austin, TX 78705
(512) 480–8743

Bare Bones Software
5817 Franklin Ave.
LaGrange, IL 60525
(312) 246–7457

Bergwall Educational Software, Inc.
106 Charles Lindbergh Blvd.
Uniondale, NY 11553-3695
(516) 222–1111, (800) 645-1737

Berkshire Scientific Software
   Concepts Assoc.
Astor Square—19 US Rt. 9
Rhinebeck, NY 12572
(914) 876–7097

BioLearning Systems
Rt. 106
Jericho, NY 11753
(516) 433–2992

Broderbund Software
17 Paul Dr.
San Rafael, CA 94903-2101
(415) 479–1700

Cambridge Development Lab
1696 Massachusetts Ave.
Cambridge, MA 02138
(800) 637–0047, (617) 491-0377

Career Aids, Inc.
20417 Nordhoff St.
Chatsworth, CA 93021
(818) 341-8200

Carolina Biological Supply Co.
2700 York Rd.
Burlington, NC 27215
(919) 584-0381

C.C. Publications, Inc.
P.O. Box 23699
Tigard, OR 97005
(800) 547-4800, (503) 692-6880

Central Scientific Co. (CENCO)
11222 Melrose Ave.
Franklin Park, IL 60131
(312) 451-0150

COMPress
P.O. Box 102
Wentworth, NH 03282
(603) 764-5831/5225

Compuware
15 Center Rd.
Randolph, NJ 07869
(201) 366-8540

CONDUIT
The University of Iowa
Oakdale Campus
Iowa City, IA 52242
(319) 335-4100

Connecticut Valley
  Biological Supply Co.
82 Valley Rd., Box 326
Southampton, MA 01073
(800) 628-7748
(800) 282-7757 in MA

Create a Test
80 Tilley Dr.
Scarborough, Ontario
Canada M1C 2G4
(416) 284-4119

Creative Technology, Inc.
P.O. Box 1009
Carlisle, PA 17013
(717) 245-2988, (717) 245-1242

Cross Educational Software
1802 N. Trenton St.
P.O. Box 1536
Ruston, LA 71270
(318) 255-8921

Curriculum Research
  & Development Group
University of Hawaii
Honolulu, HI 96822
(808) 948-7863/7842

Datatech Software Systems, Inc.
19312 E. Eldorado Dr.
Aurora, CO 80013
(303) 693-8982

Delta Education, Inc.
P.O. Box M
Nashua, NH 03061-6012
(800) 258-1302

Discovery Corner
Lawrence Hall of Science
University of California
Berkeley, CA 94720
(415) 642-1016

Diversified Educational Enterprises
725 Main St.
Lafayette, IN 47901
(317) 742-2690

E & L Instruments An Interplex
  Electronics Co.
70 Fulton Terr.
New Haven, CT 06509
(800) 225-0125, (203) 624-3103

Educational Activities, Inc.
P.O. Box 392
Freeport, NY 11520
(800) 645-3739, (516) 223-4666

Educational Computing
10661 John Ayres Dr.
Fairfax, VA 22032
(703) 250-2408

Educational Field Expeditions Div.
  of International Expeditions, Inc.
Suite 101, 1776 Independence Ct.
Birmingham, AL 35216
(205) 870-5550
(800) 633-4734

Educational Materials
  and Equipment Co.
P.O. Box 2805
Danbury, CT 06813
(203) 798-2050

Encyclopaedia Britannica
Educational Corp.
425 N. Michigan Ave.
Chicago, IL 60611
(800) 554-9862, (404) 257-1690

Fisher Scientific
4901 W. LeMoyne St.
Chicago, IL 60651
(800) 621-4769, (312) 378-7770

Focus Media, Inc.
839 Stewart Ave.
P.O. Box 865
Garden City, NY 11530
(516) 794-8900

Frey Scientific Company
905 Hickory Ln.
Mansfield, OH 44905
(419) 589-9905

Gamco Industries
P.O. Box 1911
Big Spring, TX 79721
(915) 267-6327

Glow Software Systems
P.O. Box 362
Little Rock, AR 72203-0362
(501) 664-9469, (501) 664-2214

Harcourt Brace Jovanovich
Orlando, FL 32887
(305) 345-2000

D.C. Heath and Co. Secondary Division
125 Spring St.
Lexington, MA 02173
(617) 860-1348, (800) 235-3565

Holt, Rinehart and Winston
383 Madison Ave.
New York, NY 10017
(212) 872-2000

Houghton Mifflin Co.
One Beacon St.
Boston, MA 01208
(617) 725-5000

HRM Software
175 Tompkins Ave.
Pleasantville, NY 10570
(800) 431-2050, (914) 769-7496

Hubbard Scientific Co.
P.O. Box 104, 1946 Raymond Dr.
Northbrook, IL
(312) 272-7810, (800) 323-8368

IBM/DRM
Department DB
101 Paragon Dr.
Montvale, NJ 07645

J & S Software
14 Vanderventer Ave.
Port Washington, NY 11050
(516) 944-9304

Kemtec Educational Corp.
P.O. Box 57
Kensington, MD 20895
(301) 585-0930

Kons Scientific Co., Inc.
P.O. Box 3
Germantown, WI 53022-0003
(800) 242-5667, (414) 242-3636

Krell Software
Flowerfield Bldg., #7 Suite 1D
St. James, NY 11780
(516) 584-7900

Laidlaw Educational Publishers
Thatcher and Madison
River Forest, IL 60305
(312) 366-5320

LEGO Educational/LEGO
Systems, Inc.
555 Taylor Rd.
Enfield, CT 06082
(800) 243-4870, (203) 749-2291

J.M. Lebel Enterprises, Ltd.
6027-103 A St.
Edmonton, Alberta
Canada T6H 2J7

MECC/Minnesota Educational
Computing Corp.
3490 Lexington Ave. North
St. Paul, MN 55126
(612) 481-3500

Media Learning Systems
1532 Rose Villa St.
Pasadena, CA 91106
(818) 449-0006

Merlan Scientific
247 Armstrong Ave.
Georgetown, Ontario
Canada L7G 4X6
(416) 877-0171

Metrologic Instruments, Inc.
143 Harding Ave.
Bellmawr, NJ 08031
(609) 933-0100

Micro Learningware
Route #1, Box 162
Amboy, MN 56010-9762
(507) 674-3705

Microphys
1737 W. Second St.
Brooklyn, NY 11223
(718) 375-5151

Micro Power and Light Co.
12820 Hillcrest Rd., #219
Dallas, TX 75230
(214) 239-6620

Milliken Publishing Co.
1100 Research Blvd.
P.O. Box 21579
St. Louis, MO 63132-0579
(314) 991-4220

MMI Corp.
2950 Wyman Pkwy.
P.O. Box 19907
Baltimore, MD 21211
(301) 366-1222

The Mole Co.
1012 Fair Oaks Ave., #356
S. Pasadena, CA 91030

The C. V. Mosby Co.
11830 Westline Industrial Dr.
St. Louis, MO 63146
(314) 872-8370

NARCO Bio-Systems
7651 Airport Blvd.
Houston, TX 77061
(713) 644-7521

NASCO
901 Janesville Ave.
Fort Atkinson, WI 53538
(414) 563-2446

Nasco West Inc.
P.O. Box 3837
Modesto, CA 95352
(209) 529-6957

National Dairy Council
6300 N. River Rd.
Rosemont, IL 60018-4233
(312) 696-1020

National Geographic Society
17th & M Sts., N.W.
Washington, DC 20036
(202) 857-7378

Ohaus Scale Corporation
29 Hanover Rd.
Florham Park, NJ 07932
(201) 377-9000

Optical Data Corp.
66 Hanover Rd.
Florham Park, NJ 07932
(800) 524-2481

PASCO Scientific
1876 Sabre St.
Hayward, CA 94545
(800) 772-8700

Prentice Hall Allyn & Bacon
Sylvan Ave.
Englewood Cliffs, NJ 07632
(201) 592-2540

Programs for Learning, Inc.
P.O. Box 1199
New Milford, CT 06776
(203) 355-3452

Quantum Technology Inc.
P.O. Box 1396
Englewood, CO 80150
(303) 789-9994

Radio Shack Education Division
1400 One Tandy Center
Ft. Worth, TX 76102
(817) 390-3832

Sargent-Welch Scientific Co.
7300 N. Linder Ave.
Skokie, IL 60077
(312) 677-0600

Scholastic Software
730 Broadway
New York, NY 10003
(314) 636-8890

Schoolmasters
745 State Circle
P.O. Box 1941
Ann Arbor, MI 48106
(313) 761-5072

Science Kit and Boreal Laboratories
777 East Park Dr.
Tonawanda, NY 14150
(716) 874-6020

Scott, Foresman and Co.
1900 E. Lake Ave.
Glenview, IL 60025
(312) 729-3000

Scott Resources, Inc. ESNR Division
P.O. Box 2121
401 Hickory St.
Fort Collins, CO 80522

Silver Burdett Co.
250 James St., CM 1918
Morristown, NJ 07960-1918
(201) 285-7740

Society For Visual Education, Inc.
1345 Diversey Pkwy.
Chicago, IL 60614
(312) 525-1500

Software Library Services Co.
9404 Genesee Ave. #284
La Jolla, CA 92037
(619) 453-3081/3080

Sunburst Communications
39 Washington Ave.
Pleasantville, NY 10570-9971
(800) 431-1934
(914) 769-5030

Tandy/Radio Shack
1500 One Tandy Center
Fort Worth, TX 76103
(817) 390-2195

Thornton Associates, Inc.
1432 Main St.
Waltham, MA 02154
(617) 890-3399

Trillium Press, Inc.
P.O. Box 209
Monroe, NY 10950
(914) 783-2999

Vernier Software
2920 S.W. 89th St.
Portland, OR 97225
(503) 297-5317

Videodiscovery, Inc.
1515 Dexter Ave., #200
Seattle, WA 98109
(206) 285-5400

Wadsworth Publishing Co.
10 Davis Dr.
Belmont, CA 94002
(415) 595-2350

Ward's Natural Science Est., Inc.
5100 W. Henrietta Rd.
P.O. Box 92912
Rochester, NY 14692-9012
(800) 962-2660, (716) 359-2502

J. Weston Walch, Publisher
P.O. Box 658
321 Valley St.
Portland, ME 04104-0658
(800) 341-6094, (207) 772-2846

Yaker Environmental Systems, Inc.
P.O. Box 18
Stanton, NJ 08885
(201) 735-7056

MEDIA PRODUCERS

Accent Science
P.O. Box 1444
Saginaw, MI 48605
(517) 799-8103

American Association of
  Physics Teachers
5110 Roanoke Pl.
College Park, MD 20740
(301) 345-4200

Addison-Wesley Publishing Co.
2725 Sand Hill Rd.
Menlo Park, CA 94025
(415) 854-0300

American Gas Assn., Ed. Prog.
1515 Wilson Blvd.
Arlington, VA 22209
(703) 841-8676

American Geophysical Union
2000 Florida Ave., N.W.
Washington, DC 20009
(202) 462-6903

American Iron & Steel Institute
1000 16th St. N.W.
Washington, DC 20036
(202) 452-7112

American Nuclear Society
555 N. Kensington Ave.
LaGrange Park, IL 60525
(312) 352-6611

The American Radio Relay League
225 Main St.
Newington, CT 06111
(203) 666-1541

Ampersand Press
691 26th St.
Oakland, CA 94612
(415) 832-6669

Apple Computer, Inc.
20525 Mariani Ave.
Cupertino, CA 95014
(408) 996-1010

Astro Media
Div. of Kalmbach Pub. Co.
1027 N. Seventh St.
Milwaukee, WI 53233
(414) 272-2060

Astronomical Society of the Pacific
1290 24th Ave.
San Francisco, CA 94122
(415) 661-8660

Bare Bones Software
5817 Franklin Ave.
LaGrange, IL 60525
(312) 246-7457

Bausch & Lomb
1400 N. Goodman Street
Rochester, NY 14692
(716) 338-6000

Beacon Films
P.O. Box 575
Norwood, MA 02062
(617) 762-0811

Bergwall Inc.
106 Charles Lindbergh Blvd.
Uniondale, NY 11553-3695
(516) 222-1111

Berkshire Scientific
Astor Square, 19 U.S. Rt. 9
Rhinebeck, NY 12572
(914) 876-7097

Bio Learning Systems
Route 106
Jericho, NY 11753
(516) 433-2992

Cambridge Development Lab
1696 Massachusetts Ave.
Cambridge, MA 02138
(800) 637-0047, (617) 491-0377

Career Aids
20417 Nordhoff
Chatsworth, CA 91311
(818) 341-8200

Carolina Biological Supply Co.
2700 York Rd.
Burlington, NC 27215
(919) 584-0381

C.C. Publications, Inc.
P.O. Box 23699
Tigard, OR 97223
(800) 547-4800, (503) 692-6880

Celestial Products, Inc.
P.O. Box 801
10 W. Washington St.
Middleburg, VA 22117
(703) 687-6881

Celestron International
2835 Columbia St.
Torrance, CA 90503
1 (800) 421-1526

The Center for Humanities
Communications Park
Box 3000
Mount Kisco, NY 10549
(800) 431-1242, (914) 666-4100

Central Scientific Co. (CENCO)
11222 Melrose Ave.
Franklin Park, IL 60131
(312) 451-0150

CIBA-GEIGY Corp.
444 Saw Mill River Rd.
Ardsley, NY 10502
(914) 478-3131
x2945/2946

College Biological Supply Co.
8857 Mount Israel Rd.
Escondido, CA 92025
(619) 745-1445

COMPress
P.O. Box 102
Wentworth, NH 03282
(603) 764-5831

CONDUIT
The University of Iowa
Oakdale Campus
Iowa City, IA 52242
(319) 335-4100

Coronet/MTI Film & Video
  Distributors of LCA
108 Wilmot Rd.
Deerfield, IL 60015
(800) 621-2131, (312) 940-1260

Create A Test
80 Tilley Dr.
Scarborough, Ontario
Canada M1C 2G4
(206) 733-5024
(416) 284-4119

Creative Dimensions
P.O. Box 1393
Bellingham, WA 98227
(206) 733-5024

Creative Technology, Inc.
P.O. Box 1009
Carlisle, PA 17013
(717) 245-2988
(717) 245-1242

Cross Educational Software
P.O. Box 1536
1802 N. Trenton
Ruston, LA 71270
(318) 255-8921

Crystal Prod.
P.O. Box 12317
Aspen, CO 81612
(303) 925-8160

Dale Seymour Publications
P.O. Box 10888
Palo Alto, CA 94303
(415) 324-2800

Damon/Instructional Systems
80 Wilson Way
Westwood, MA 02090
(617) 329-4300

Data Processing Educational
  Corp. (DPEC)
4588 Kenny Rd.
Columbus, OH 43220
(614) 457-0577

Datatech Software Systems
19312 E. Eldorado Dr.
Aurora, CO 80013
(303) 693-8982

Delta Education, Inc.
P.O. Box M
Nashua, NH 03061-6012
(800) 258-1302

Denoyer-Geppert Co.
5711 N. Milwaukee Ave.
Chicago, IL 60646
(312) 775-0150

Walt Disney Educational Media Co.
500 S. Buena Vista
Burbank, CA 91521
(800) 423-2555

Diversified Educational
  Enterprises, Inc.
725 Main St.,
Lafayette, IN 47901
(317) 742-2690

Eagle River Media Productions
9420 Westlake Dr.
Eagle River, AK 99577
(907) 694-4684

Educational Activities, Inc.
P.O. Box 392
Freeport, NY 11520
(800) 645-3739

Educational Computing
10661 John Ayres Dr.
Fairfax, VA 22032

Educational Dimensions Group
P.O. Box 126
Stamford, CT 06904
(800) 243-9020, (203) 327-4612

Educational Field Expeditions,
  Div. of International Expeditions, Inc.
Suite 101, 1776 Independence Ct.
Birmingham, AL 35216
(205) 870-5550; 1 (800) 633-4734

Educational Materials and
  Equipment Co.
P.O. Box 2805
Danbury, CT 06813-2805
(203) 798-2050

Educational Media International
175 Margaret Pl.
P.O. Box 1288
Elmhurst, IL 60126
(312) 832-3363

EduTech, Inc.
303 Lamartine St.
Jamaica Plain, MA 02130
(617) 524-1774

Encyclopaedia Britannica
  Educational Corp.
425 N. Michigan Ave.
Chicago, IL 60611
(800) 554-9862
(800) 558-6968

Entomological Society of America
4603 Calvert Rd.
College Park, MD 20740
(301) 864-1334

Films Inc.
5547 N. Ravenswood
Chicago, IL 60640
(800) 323-4222 x43
(312) 878-2600 x43

FlipTrack Learning Systems
999 Main, Suite 200
Glen Ellyn, IL 60137
(312) 790-1117

Fluortography
9 Chassyl Rd.
Commack, NY 11725
(516) 543-4512, (516) 543-6289

Focus Media, Inc.
839 Stewart Ave.
Garden City, NY 11530
(516) 794-8900, (800) 645-8989

W. H. Freeman and Co.
41 Madison Ave.
New York, NY 10010
(212) 532-7660

Frey Scientific Co.
905 Hickory Ln.
Mansfield, OH 44905
(419) 589-9905

Gamco Industries
Box 1911
Big Spring, TX 79720
(915) 267-6327

Guidance Associates
Communications Park
Box 3000
Mount Kisco, NY 10549
(800) 431-1242, (914) 666-4100

Hansen Publications
1098 South 200 West
Salt Lake City, UT 84101
(801) 538-2242
(800) 321-2369

Harcourt Brace Jovanovich
Orlando, FL 32887
(305) 345-2000

D.C. Heath and Co.
125 Spring St.
Lexington, MA 02173
(617) 862-6650

Holt, Rinehart and Winston
383 Madison Ave.
New York, NY 10017
(212) 872-2000

How the Weatherworks
1522 Baylor Ave.
Rockville, MD 20850
(301) 762-SNOW

H.S. Center for Educational Resources
T-281 HSB SB-56
University of Washington
Seattle, WA 98195
(206) 545-1186

Hubbard Scientific Co.
P.O. Box 104
1946 Raymond Dr.
Northbrook, IL 60062
(312) 272-7810, (800) 323-8368

Human Relations Media
175 Tompkins Ave.
Pleasantville, NY 10570
(800) 431-2050;
(914) 769-7496

Ideal School Supply Co.
11000 S. Lavergne Ave.
Oak Lawn, IL 60453
(312) 425-0800

Insights Visual Productions
P.O. Box 644
Encinitas, CA 92024
(619) 942-0528

International Film Bureau, Inc.
332 S. Michigan Ave.
Chicago, IL 60604
(312) 427-4545

ITL Vufoils Ltd.
10-18 Clifton St.
London EC2A 4BT
England
01-247-7305

J&S Software
14 Vanderventer Ave.
Port Washington, NY 11050
(516) 944-9304

Jeppesen Sanderson
55 Inverness Dr. E
Englewood, CO 80112
(303) 799-9090

Jewel Industries, Inc.
P.O. Box 104, 1946 Raymond Dr.
Northbrook, IL 60062
(312) 272-7810, (800) 323-8368

The JN Company
Video Outreach Division
610 Broadhollow Road
Melville, NY 11747
(516) 752-8800

Junior Engineering Technical Society
   (JETS), Inc.
1420 King St., Suite 405
Alexandria, VA 22314-2715
(703) 548-JETS

Kemtech Edu. Corp.
P.O. Box 57
Kensington, MD 20895
(301) 585-0930

Kons Scientific Co., Inc.
P.O. Box 3
Germantown, WI 53022-0003
(414) 242-3636

Krell Software
Flowerfield Bldg., #7 Suite 1D
St. James, NY 11780
(516) 584-7900

Lab-Aids, Inc.
249 Trade Zone Dr.
Ronkonkoma, NY 11779
(516) 737-1133

Lab Safety Co.
3430 Palmer Dr., P.O. Box 1368
Janesville, WI 53547
(800) 356-0783, (608) 754-2345

LaMotte Chemical Products Co.
P.O. Box 329
Chestertown, MD 21620
(301) 778-3100
(800) 344-3100

Lawrence Hall of Science
Discovery Corner
University of California
Berkeley, CA 94720
(415) 642-1016

Learning Spectrum
1390 Westridge
Portola Valley, CA 94025
(415) 851-7871

Library Filmstrip Center
205 E. Locust St.
Bloomington, IL 61701
(309) 827-5455

Martinells Enterprises
P.O. Box 10369
Costa Mesa, CA 92627
(714) 645-1700

McGraw-Hill Webster Division
1221 Avenue of the Americas
New York, NY 10020
(212) 997-4978

McKilligan Supply Corp.
435 Main St.
Johnson City, NY 13790
(607) 729-6511

Minnesota Educational Computing
   Corp. MECC
3490 Lexington Ave. North
St. Paul, MN 55126
(612) 481-3500

Media Associates, Inc.
7322 Ohms Ln.
Minneapolis, MN 55435

Media Design Associates
855 Broadway
P.O. Box 3189
Boulder, CO 80307
(303) 443-2800

Media Learning Systems
1532 Rose Villa St.
Pasadena, CA 91106
(818) 449-0006

Medical Plastics Laboratory, Inc.
P.O. Box 38
Gatesville, TX 76528
(800) 433-5539, (817) 865-7221

Merlan Scientific Ltd.
247 Armstrong Ave.
Georgetown, Ontario,
Canada L7G 4X6
(416) 877-0171

Metrologic Instruments, Inc.
143 Harding Ave.
Bellmawr, NJ 08030
(609) 933-0100

Micro Learningware
Route No. 1, Box 162
Amboy, MN 56010-9762
(507) 674-3705

Milliken Publishing Co.
P.O. Box 21579
St. Louis, MO 63132-0579
(314) 991-4220

Ministry of Environment and Parks
810 Blanshard St.
Victoria, B.C., Canada V8W 3E1
(604) 387-9422

MMI Corp.
2950 Wyman Pkwy./P.O. Box 19907
Baltimore, MD 21211
(301) 366-1222

Moody Institute of Science
12000 E. Washington Blvd.
Whittier, CA 90606
(213) 698-8256 & 8257

Moonlight Productions
2243 Old Middlefield Way
Mountain View, CA 94043
(415) 948-0199

NARCO Bio-Systems
7651 Airport Blvd.
Houston, TX 77061
(713) 644-7521

NASCO
901 Janesville Ave.
Fort Atkinson, WI 53538
(414) 563-2446

Nasco West, Inc.
P.O. Box 3837,
Modesto, CA 95352
(209) 529-6957

National Dairy Council
6300 North River Rd.
Rosemont, IL 60018-4233
(312) 696-1020

National 4-H Council Educational Aids
7100 Connecticut Ave.
Chevy Chase, MD 20815
(301) 656-9000

National Geographic Society
17th & M Streets, N.W.
Washington, DC 20036
(202) 857-7378

National Science Programs, Inc.
P.O. Box 41
W. Wilson St.
Batavia, IL 60510
(312) 879-6901

National Teaching Aids, Inc.
1845 Highland Ave.
New Hyde Park, NY 11040
(516) 326-2555

National Wildlife Federation
1412 16th St., NW
Washington, DC 20036
(202) 790-4233

The New Film Co., Inc.
7 Mystic St., Suite S-200
Arlington, MA 02174
(617) 641-2580

New York Zoological Society
  Education Department
Bronx, NY 10460
(212) 220-5131

Norris Science Labs and Kits
4561 Sacks Dr.
Las Vegas, NV 89122
(702) 458-6427

Nystrom
3333 Elston Ave.
Chicago, IL 60618
1 (800) 621-8086

Ohaus Scale Corp.
29 Hanover Road
Florham Park, NJ 07932
(201) 377-9000

Optical Data Corp.
66 Hanover Rd.
Florham Park, NJ 07932
(800) 524-2481

Owl/TV
% Bullfrog Films
Oley, PA 19547
(215) 779-8226

PARCO Scientific Co.
P.O. Box 189
316 Youngstown Kingsville Rd. SE
Vienna, OH 44473
(216) 394-1100

Phoenix/BFA Films and Video, Inc.
468 Park Ave. South
New York, NY 10016
(212) 684-5910
(800) 221-1274

Play-Jour Inc.
200 Fifth Ave., Suite 1024
New York, NY 10010
(212) 243-5200

Programs for Learning, Inc.
P.O. Box 1199
New Milford, CT 06776
(203) 355-3452

Radio Shack/Tandy Corp.
1400 One Tandy Center
Ft. Worth, TX 76102-3832
(817) 390-3832

Rockefeller University Press
1230 York Ave.
New York, NY 10021
(212) 570-8572

Sargent-Welch Scientific Co.
7300 N. Linder Ave.
Skokie, IL 60077
(312) 677-0600

Scavenger Scientific Supply Co.
P.O. Box 211328
Auke Bay, AK 99821

Scholastic Software
730 Broadway
New York, NY 10003
(314) 636-8890

Schoolmasters Science
745 State Circle
P.O. Box 1941
Ann Arbor, MI 48106
(313) 761-5072

Science and Mankind, Inc.
Communications Park
Box 2000
Mount Kisco, NY 10549
(914) 666-4100
(800) 431-1242

Science Kit and Boreal Laboratories
777 E. Park Dr.
Tonawanda, NY 14150
(716) 874-6020

The Science Man Co.
A Div of TSM Marketing, Inc.
4738 N. Harlem Ave.
Harwood Hts., IL 60656
(312) 867-4441

Science Screen Report, Inc.
2875 South Congress Ave.
Delray Beach, FL 33444
(305) 265-1700

Science Videos
P.O. Box 25047
Houston, TX 77265-5047
(713) 522-1827

Scott, Foresman and Company
1900 E. Lake Ave.
Glenview, IL 60025
(312) 729-3000

Scott Resources/ESNR Division
P.O. Box 2121
401 Hickory St.
Fort Collins, CO 80522
(303) 484-7445

Sea Otter Press
P.O. Box 2845
Seattle, WA 98111
(206) 842-1102

Silver Burdett & Ginn
250 James St. CN 1918
Morristown, NJ 07960-1918
(201) 285-7740

Sky Publishing Corp.
49 Bay State Rd.
Cambridge, MA 02238-1290
(617) 864-7360

Society for Visual Education, Inc.
1345 Diversey Pkwy.
Chicago, IL 60614
(312) 525-1500

Space and Rocket Center Gift Shop
One Tranquility Base
Huntsville, AL 35807
(205) 837-3400

S & S Publishing Co.
3550 Durock Rd.
Shingle Springs, CA 95682
(916) 677-1545

Stasiuk Enterprises
3150 NE 30th Ave.
P.O. Box 12484
Portland, OR 97212
(503) 284-6887

Sunburst Communications
39 Washington Ave.
Pleasantville, NY 10570
(914) 769-5030
(800) 431-1934

PUBLISHERS

Accent Science
P.O. Box 1444
Saginaw, MI 48605
(517) 799-8103

Addison-Wesley Publishing Co.
2724 Sand Hill Rd.
Menlo Park, CA 94025
(415) 854-0300

American Association of Physics
  Teachers
5110 Roanoke Pl., Suite 101
College Park, MD 20740
(301) 345-4200

Bi-Lab Educational Service
536 W. Valley View Drive
Fullerton, CA 92635
(714) 879-5585

Biological Sciences Curriculum
  Study (BSCS)
The Colorado College
Colorado Springs, CO 80903
(303) 473-2233 (ext. 732)

Wm. C. Brown Company Publishers
2460 Kerper Blvd.
Dubuque, IA 52001

Burgess Publishing
7110 Ohms Ln.
Edina, MN 55435
(612) 831-1344

CABISCO Press
(a div. of Carolina Biological)
1308 Rainey Street
Burlington, NC 27215
(919) 226-6000

C.C. Publications, Inc.
P.O. Box 23699
Tigard, OR 97005
(800) 547-4800

Coronado Publishers, Inc.
1250 Sixth Ave.
San Diego, CA 92101
(619) 699-6280

Curriculum Research & Development
  Group
University of Hawaii
Honolulu, HI 96822
(808) 948-7863/7842

Delta Education, Inc.
P.O. Box M
Nashua, NH 03061-6012
(800) 258-1302

Digital Press/Digital Equipment Corp.
12 Crosby Dr.
Bedford, MA 01730
(617) 276-4007 (editorial)
12A Esquire Rd.
Billerica, MA 01862
(617) 663-4123 (orders)

Diversified Educational Enterprises
725 Main St.
Lafayette, IN 47901
(317) 742-2690

Doubleday Canada Ltd.
105 Bond St.
Toronto, Ontario
Canada M5B 1Y3
(416) 977-7891

Eagle River Media Productions
9420 Westlake Dr.
Eagle River, AK 99577
(907) 694-4684

E & L Instruments
An Interplex Electronics Co.
70 Fulton Ter.
New Haven, CT 06509
(800) 225-0125
(203) 624-3103

W.H. Freeman and Co.
41 Madison Ave.
New York, NY 10010
(212) 532-7660

Globe Book Co., Inc.
50 W. 23rd St.
New York, NY 10010
(212) 741-0505
(800) 221-7994

Graphic Learning Publishing
1123 Spruce St.
Boulder, CO 80302
(303) 440-7620, (800) 874-0029

Harcourt Brace Jovanovich
Orlando, FL 32887
(305) 345-2000

Harcourt Brace Jovanovich
College Department
1250 Sixth Ave.
San Diego, CA 92101
(619) 231-6616

Harper & Row, Publishers, Inc.
10 East 53rd St.
New York, NY 10022-5299
(212) 207-7513

Hayden Book Co., Inc.
10 Mulholland Dr.
Hasbrook Heights, NJ 07604
(800) 631-0856, (201) 393-6315

D.C. Heath and Co.
125 Spring St.
Lexington, MA 02173
(800) 235-3565
(800) 334-3284

Heinemann Educational Books, Inc.
70 Court St.
Portsmouth, NH 03801
(603) 431-7894

Holt, Rinehart & Winston
383 Madison Ave.
New York, NY 10017
(212) 872-2000

Houghton Mifflin Co.
One Beacon St.
Boston, MA 02108
(617) 725-5000
(Send catalog requests to
Dept J.)

Hubbard Scientific Co.
P.O. Box 104
Northbrook, IL 60065
(312) 272-7810, (800) 323-8360

Janus Book Publishers
2501 Industrial Pkwy., West
Hayward, CA 94545
(415) 887-7070

Jeppesen Sanderson
55 Inverness Dr. E.
Englewood, CO 80112
(303) 799-9090

Jewel Industries, Inc.
P.O. Box 104, 1946 Raymond Dr.
Northbrook, IL 60062
(312) 272-7810, (800) 323-8368

The Johns Hopkins University Press
701 West 40th St., Suite 275
Baltimore, MD 21211
(301) 338-6956

Kendall/Hunt Publishing Co.
2460 Kerper Blvd.
Dubuque, IA 52001
(319) 588-1451

Robert E. Krieger Publ. Co., Inc.
P.O. Box 9542
Melbourne, FL 32902
(305) 724-9542

Laidlaw Educational Publishers
Thatcher & Madison
River Forest, IL 60305
(312) 366-5320

LaMotte Chemical Products Co.
P.O. Box 329
Chestertown, MD 21620
(301) 778-3100
(800) 344-3100

Lawrenceville Press, Inc.
P.O. Box 6490
Lawrenceville, NJ 08648
(609) 771–6831

J.M. LeBel Enterprises Ltd.
6027-103 'A' St.
Edmonton, Alberta, Canada
T6H 1G9
(403) 436–8205

Macmillan Publishing Co.
866 Third Ave.
New York, NY 10022
(212) 702–5544

McGraw-Hill Book Co.
College Division
1221 Avenue of the Americas
New York, NY 10020
(212) 997–2220

McGraw-Hill Webster Division
1221 Avenue of the Americas
New York, NY 10020
(212) 997–4585

Media Associates
5230 W. 73rd Street
Edina, MN 55435

Merrill Publishing Co.
P.O. Box 508
1300 Alum Creek Dr.
Columbus, OH 43216
(614) 890–1111
(800) 848–1567

Metrologic Instruments, Inc.
143 Harding Ave.
Bellmawr, NJ 08031
(609) 933–0100

Modern Curriculum Press, Inc.
13900 Prospect Rd.
Cleveland, OH 44136
(216) 238–2222

The C.V. Mosby Co.
11830 Westline Industrial Dr.
St. Louis, MO 63146
(314) 872–8370

NASCO West Inc.
P.O. Box 3837
Modesto, CA 95352
(209) 529–6957

Observe, Inc.
P.O. Box 62078
Virginia Beach, VA 23462-0078
(804) 424–2798

Prentice-Hall Allyn & Bacon
Secondary Division
Sylvan Ave.
Englewood Cliffs, NJ 07632
(201) 592–2439
(800) 524–2349

Sargent-Welch Scientific Co.
7300 N. Linder Ave.
Skokie, IL 60077
(312) 677–0600

Saunders College Publishing
383 Madison Ave.
New York, NY 10017
(212) 872–2244

Scott, Foresman and Co.
1900 E. Lake Ave.
Glenview, IL 60025
(312) 729–3000

Scribner Educational Publishers
866 Third Ave.
New York, NY 10022
(212) 702–5544

Silver Burdett & Ginn
250 James St. CN 1918
Morristown, NJ 07960-1918
(201) 285–7400

Chemicals Used in Elementary Science Lessons

CHEMICAL	SOURCE
Acid, acetic (white or brown vinegar	School cafeteria, home, high school laboratory
Acid, citric	Drugstore, high school laboratory
Acid, hydrochloric	High school laboratory, drugstore, building supply store
Alcohol, isopropyl (rubbing), ethyl, methyl	Supermarket, home, high school laboratory, school nurse
Baking soda (sodium bicarbonate)	School cafeteria, home, supermarket, high school laboratory
Base, liquid ammonia used for cleaning	Supermarket, home, school cafeteria
Bluing	Supermarket, home
Carbon dioxide	From seltzer tablets or baking soda and vinegar
Charcoal	Supermarket, home
Corn starch	Supermarket, home, school cafeteria
Detergent, dish and laundry	Supermarket, school cafeteria, home
Extracts (maple, peppermint, lemon, orange, chocolate, wintergreen, etc.)	Supermarket
Food coloring	Supermarket, home
Gelatin	Supermarket, home, school cafeteria
Ink (for fountain pen)	Drugstore, variety store
Lemon juice	Supermarket, school cafeteria
Oil, cooking or vegetable	Home, high school industrial shop, auto repair shop, service station
Paraffin	Supermarket, home
Plaster of paris	Drugstore, high school laboratory, art supply store

(cont.)

CHEMICAL	SOURCE
Salt, table and rock	(Same as above)
Sand	Building supply store, pet shop, home, beach
Slaked lime	Drugstore, high school laboratory
Soap	School supply, home, supermarket
Starch	Supermarket, home
Sugar	School cafeteria, home, supermarket
Sulfur (powdered)	High school laboratory
Talc (talcum powder)	Supermarket, drugstore, home
Tincture of iodine	Supermarket, drugstore, school nurse

The chemicals listed are those most commonly used in elementary science programs. This is not intended to be a complete list, however; others may be required from time to time. Textbooks frequently list sources required for various activities. High school teachers can be of great help in obtaining resources also.

Sources of Materials

It is not necessary that all of the following items of equipment be available for you to teach science effectively. However, it is not too early for you to begin collecting items of equipment and to become familiar with sources of equipment.

	Source				Grades Where It Is Likely to Be Used						
	Publisher or Science Supply House	Teacher Made	Local Store	Discarded Items	K	1	2	3	4	5	6
Air pump			X		X				X	X	X
Alcohol burner	X	X				X	X	X	X	X	X
Aluminum foil			X		X	X	X	X	X	X	X
Aluminum pans			X	X	X	X	X	X	X	X	X
Aquarium	X	X	X	X	X	X	X	X	X	X	X
Assorted rubber stoppers	X				X	X	X	X	X	X	X
Baby food jars				X	X	X	X	X	X	X	X
Balances	X	X			X	X	X	X	X	X	X
Balloons			X		X	X	X	X	X	X	X
Balls			X		X	X	X	X	X	X	X
Barometer	X	X	X		X	X	X	X	X	X	X
BB shot			X		X				X	X	X
Birthday candles			X		X	X	X	X	X		
Black box		X		X	X	X	X	X	X		
Buttons			X	X	X	X	X	X	X	X	X
Clock			X	X	X	X	X	X	X	X	X
Clock face		X			X	X	X				
Cloth of different textures				X	X	X	X				
Coal		X		X	X						
Coat hangers				X	X	X	X	X	X	X	X
Compass	X		X		X	X	X	X	X	X	X
Construction paper			X		X	X	X	X	X	X	X
Copper wire (#22 or #24)	X		X	X	X	X	X	X	X	X	X
Corks	X		X		X	X	X	X	X	X	X
Dowels			X		X	X	X	X	X		
Dry cells			X		X	X	X	X	X	X	X

Materials checklist (continued)

Item	1	2	3	4	5	6	7	8	9	10	11
Egg cartons	X	X	X	X	X	X	X				
Electric bell	X	X	X	X	X	X	X			X	X
Electric buzzer	X	X	X	X	X	X	X		X		X
Electric motor	X	X	X	X	X	X	X		X		X
Electric sockets	X	X	X	X	X	X	X		X	X	X
Electric switches	X	X	X	X	X	X	X		X		
Electromagnets	X	X	X	X	X	X	X	X			X
Flashlight	X	X	X	X	X	X	X				
Flashlight bulb	X	X	X	X	X	X	X				X
Food-warming candles			X	X	X	X	X				X
Forceps or tweezers	X	X	X	X	X	X	X		X		X
Funnels	X	X	X	X	X	X	X				X
Gallon glass jars		X	X	X	X	X	X	X	X		
Gallon jars or cans		X	X	X	X	X	X	X			X
Gallon metal cans with lid (ditto fluid)		X	X	X			X	X			
Glass slides for microscope		X	X	X	X	X	X		X	X	
Globe	X	X	X	X	X	X	X		X		
Gravel	X	X	X	X	X	X	X				X
Heating tripod	X	X	X	X	X	X	X			X	X
Hot plate		X	X	X			X	X	X		
Iron filings	X	X	X	X	X	X	X				X
Lenses (concave and convex)	X	X	X	X	X	X	X	X	X		X
Magnets	X	X	X	X	X	X	X		X	X	X
Magnifying glasses	X	X	X	X	X	X	X		X		X
Marbles		X	X	X	X	X	X		X		X
Matches		X	X	X	X	X	X		X		X
Measuring cups	X	X	X	X	X	X	X		X		X
Mechanical toys	X	X	X	X	X	X	X	X	X		X

(cont.)

	Source				Grades Where It Is Likely to Be Used						
	Publisher or Science Supply House	Teacher Made	Local Store	Discarded Items	K	1	2	3	4	5	6
Medicine droppers		X	X		X	X	X	X	X	X	X
Metal soup cans				X	X	X	X	X	X	X	X
Metal washers			X		X	X	X	X	X	X	X
Meterstick		X					X	X	X	X	X
Metric weights	X							X	X	X	X
Microscope	X		X			X	X	X	X	X	X
Milk cartons: 1/2, 1 quart				X	X	X	X	X	X	X	X
Mirrors	X		X	X	X	X	X	X	X	X	X
Modeling clay			X		X	X	X	X	X	X	X
Nails			X		X	X	X	X	X	X	X
Needles			X			X	X	X	X	X	X
Nylon hose				X	X	X	X	X	X	X	X
Paper bags			X	X	X	X	X	X	X	X	X
Paper cups			X	X	X	X	X	X	X	X	X
Paper napkins			X		X	X	X	X	X	X	X
Paper towels			X		X	X	X	X	X	X	X
Paper trays			X		X	X	X	X	X	X	X
Paper tubes from toilet paper				X	X	X	X	X	X	X	X
Pill bottles				X	X	X	X	X	X	X	X
Pinch-type clothespins			X		X	X	X	X	X	X	X
Pipe cleaners			X		X	X	X	X	X	X	X
Plastic bags, large and small			X		X	X	X	X	X	X	X
Plastic gallon milk jugs				X	X	X	X	X	X	X	X
Plastic margarine tubs with lids				X	X	X	X	X	X	X	X

Plastic tubing	X				X	X	X	X	X	X	X
Plastic wrap			X		X	X	X	X	X	X	X
Puffed rice			X		X	X	X				
Pulleys	X	X	X		X	X	X	X	X	X	
Rain gauge	X	X			X	X	X	X	X	X	X
Ringstand support	X	X			X	X	X	X	X	X	X
Rock collections	X	X	X		X	X	X	X	X	X	X
Rope			X		X	X	X	X	X	X	X
Rubber bands			X		X	X	X	X	X	X	X
Rubber tubing	X				X	X	X	X	X	X	X
Rulers, metric		X	X		X	X	X	X	X	X	X
Rulers, unmarked	X	X			X	X	X	X	X	X	X
Sand		X		X	X	X	X	X	X	X	X
Scissors			X		X	X	X	X	X	X	X
Screening			X	X	X	X	X	X	X	X	X
Screwdriver			X		X	X	X	X	X	X	X
Shells	X	X	X	X	X	X	X	X	X	X	X
Shoe boxes				X	X	X	X	X	X	X	X
Single-edge razor blades			X					X	X	X	X
Soft drink bottles				X	X	X	X	X	X	X	X
Soda straws			X	X	X	X	X	X	X	X	X
Squares of different colors		X			X	X	X	X	X	X	X
Steel wool			X		X	X	X	X	X	X	X
Sterno			X		X	X	X	X	X	X	X
String			X	X	X	X	X	X	X	X	X
Styrofoam cups			X	X	X	X	X	X	X	X	X
Styrofoam ice bucket			X		X	X	X	X	X	X	X
Tacks			X		X	X	X	X	X	X	X
Test tubes	X		X			X	X	X	X	X	X
Three-dimensional shapes			X	X	X	X	X				

(cont.)

Item	Source				Grades Where It Is Likely to Be Used						
	Publisher or Science Supply House	Teacher Made	Local Store	Discarded Items	K	1	2	3	4	5	6
Thermometers, Celsius and Fahrenheit	X				X	X	X	X	X	X	X
Tinker toys			X		X	X	X	X	X	X	X
Tongs			X		X	X	X	X	X	X	X
Tongue depressor			X		X	X	X	X	X	X	X
Toothpicks			X		X	X	X	X	X	X	X
Tuning fork	X				X	X	X	X	X	X	X
Two-dimensional paper shapes		X			X	X	X				
Two-dimensional wood shapes		X	X		X	X	X				
Waxpaper			X	X	X	X	X	X	X	X	X
Wind vane		X			X	X	X	X	X	X	X
Wood building blocks			X		X	X	X				
Wood or plastic spools				X	X	X	X	X	X	X	X
Wood samples		X		X	X	X	X				

Code of Practice on Animals in Schools

POSITION STATEMENT OF THE NATIONAL SCIENCE TEACHERS ASSOCIATION, WASHINGTON, D.C.

This code of practice is recommended by the National Science Teachers Association for use throughout the United States by elementary, middle/junior high, and secondary-school teachers and students. It applies to educational projects involving live organisms conducted in schools, or in school-related activities, such as science clubs, fairs, competitions, and junior academies.

The purpose of these guidelines is to enrich education by encouraging students to observe living organisms and to learn proper respect for life. Study of living organisms is essential for an understanding of living processes. This study, however, must go hand-in-hand with observation of humane principles of animal care and treatment which are described below. These principles apply to vertebrates.

A. A teacher must have a sure understanding of and *strong commitment to responsible care of living creatures* before making any decision to use live organisms for educational purposes. Preparation should include acquisition of knowledge on care appropriate for that species, as well as housing and other equipment needs and food, and planning for care of the living creatures after completion of study.

B. Teachers should try to assure that live organisms entering a classroom are *healthy and free from transmissible diseases* or other problems that may endanger human health. Not all species are suitable. Wild animals, for instance, are frequent carriers of parasites and disease and generally are not appropriate.

C. Of primary importance is *maintenance of good animal health and provision of optimal care* based on an understanding of the life habits of each species. Animal quarters shall be spacious and avoid overcrowding, and be sanitary. Handling shall be gentle. Food shall be palatable to the species and of sufficient quantity and balance to maintain a good standard of nutrition at all times. No animal shall be allowed less than the optimum maintenance level of nutrition. Clean drinking water shall always be available. Adequate provision shall be made for the animal's care at all times, including weekends and vacation periods.

D. *Experimental procedures conducted on vertebrate animals shall include only those which do not involve pain* or discomfort to the animal (see details below under "Experimental Studies").

E. All aspects of animal care and treatment shall be *supervised by a qualified individual* who will ensure that proper standards are maintained.

F. Supervisors and students should be familiar with appropriate *literature on care and handling* of living organisms. Practical training in learning these techniques is encouraged.

G. Adequate plans should be made to *control possible unwanted breeding* of the species during the project period.

H. Appropriate plans should be laid for *what will happen to the living creatures at the conclusion of the study.* Sometimes it may be possible to find a comfortable home for an animal with a responsible person.

I. As a general rule, *laboratory-bred or non-native species should not be released into the wild.* For instance, in some climates, *Xenopus* frogs, or gerbils, if released, can disturb the normal ecosystem or become pests.

J. On rare occasion it may be appropriate to sacrifice an animal for educational purposes. This shall be done in an approved humane (rapid and painless) manner by a person experienced in these techniques and it should *not* be done in the presence of immature or young students who may be upset by witnessing such a procedure. Maximum efforts should be made to study many biological principles and *utilize as many body tissues as possible from a single animal.*

K. The procurement, care, and use of animals must comply with existing local, state and federal regulations.

Experimental Studies

1. In biological procedures involving living organisms, *species of plants, bacteria, fungi, protozoa, worms, snails, insects and other invertebrate animals should be used wherever possible.* Their wide variety, ready availability, and simplicity of maintenance and subsequent disposal make them especially suitable for student work.

2. *Some sample plant, protozoan, and/or invertebrate projects* include: field studies and natural history (life cycle, incidence in nature,

social structure, etc.); germination; genetics; reproduction; effect of light, temperature, other environmental factors, and hormones on growth and development; feeding behavior; nutritional requirements; circulation of nutrients to tissues; metabolism; water balance; excretion; movement; activity cycles and biological clocks; responses to gravity and light; perception to touch, humidity and vibration; learning and maze running; habituation; communication; pheromones; observations of food chains and interdependence of one species on another.

3. *No experimental procedures shall be attempted on mammals, birds, reptiles, amphibians, or fish that cause the animal pain* or distinct discomfort or that interfere with its health. As a rule of thumb, a student shall only undertake those procedures on vertebrate animals that could be done on humans without pain or hazard to health.

4. Students shall *not perform surgery* on vertebrate animals.

5. *Examples of non-painful, non-hazardous projects on some vertebrate species* (including in some instances, human beings) include some already mentioned under item (2) and also: group behavior; normal growth and development; properties of hair; pulse rate and blood pressure; various normal animal behaviors such as grooming, and wall-seeking; reaction to novelty or alarm; nervous reflexes and conditioned responses; special senses (touch, hearing, taste, smell, and proprioceptive responses); and respiration. None of these projects requires infliction of pain or interference with normal health.

6. *Experimental procedures shall not involve* use of microorganisms which can cause diseases in man or animals, ionizing radiation, cancer-producing agents, or administration of alcohol or other harmful drugs or chemicals known to produce toxic or painful reactions or capable of producing birth defects.

7. *Behavioral studies should use only reward* (such as providing food) and not punishment (such as electric shock) in training programs. Food, when used as reward, shall not be withdrawn for periods longer than 12 hours.

8. *Diets deficient in essential nutrients are prohibited.*

9. If *bird embryos* are subjected to invasive or potentially damaging experimental manipulations, the embryo must be destroyed humanely two days prior to hatching. If normal embryos are to be hatched, satisfactory humane provisions must be made for the care of the young birds.

10. On rare occasion it may be appropriate to *pith a live frog* for an educational demonstration. Correct procedure is rapid and virtually painless, and the animal should never recover consciousness. However, if done incorrectly, this procedure can cause pain. The technique should be learned initially using dead animals. Pithing live animals should only be undertaken by a person knowledgeable in the technique.

For conservation reasons, efforts should be made to protect depleted animal species such as *Rana pipiens.* Similar educational objectives can frequently be achieved using alternative species, or pursuing alternative methods of study.

11. *Protocols* of extracurricular projects involving animals *should be reviewed in advance* of the start of work by a qualified adult supervisor. Preferably, extracurricular projects should be conducted in a suitable area in the school.

12. High school students may wish to take assistant positions with professional scientists working in established, USDA-registered research institutions.

Care of Animals in the Classroom

Animal	Food
Birds	
Tame	Prepared food (consult a pet store) or small seeds, cereal, suet, nuts, raisins
Chickens	Commercial food
Chameleons and Salamanders	Live insects (Provide water by sprinkling water on small plants and place them in the container with the animal.)
Crayfish	Meat, insects, water plants
Earthworms	Their food is obtained from the soil in which they live.
Fish, guppies, and goldfish	Commercial food
Frogs and Toads	Living insects and worms, caterpillars, and mealworms (For some the food must be alive to be eaten.)
Guinea pigs, hamsters, gerbils	Dry cereal, fresh vegetables such as carrots, lettuce, and celery, leaves, nuts, rabbit pellets
Insects	
Bees	Sugar water
Praying mantis	Live insects, mealworms
Ants	Food scraps, water, dead insects
Butterflies	Thick sugar water
Grasshoppers	Celery leaves and other kinds of leaves and grasses
Crickets	Crushed seeds, soft fruit
Moths	Thick sugar water
Fruit flies	Over-ripe fruit
Mealworms	Cereal, nonsweetened (bran, wheat, oats)
Caterpillars	Leaves upon which the animal was found (Leaves may be frozen for later use.)

(cont.)

Animal	Food
Lizards	Live insects and mealworms
Newts	Dead insects, ant eggs (from pet store) and uncooked ground beef
Rabbits	Grains, grass, clover, lettuce leaves, commercial food
Rats and Mice	Small grains, vegetables, bread, commercial food
Snails (land, water)	Lettuce, celery leaves, and soft fruit, commercial fish food, lettuce, dried shrimp, ant eggs
Snakes	Live insects and earthworms, live mice and eggs. (Consult a pet store for specific food requirements of a snake.)
Spiders	Live insects
Tadpoles	Small algae, cooked cereal, and uncooked ground beef
Turtles	Insects, worms, commercial food, and mealworms

Many animals do not require special shelter or containers. However, some suggestions are provided to care for animal guests in the classroom. Suggestions on constructing homes are also given.

Animal	Shelter
Ants	Use a glass jar, either a gallon, quart or pint size. Fill the jar with soil to about 2 cm from the top. Obtain ants from an anthill; perhaps the soil can be gotten from the anthill also. Get as large a number of ants as possible and also eggs. Place them on the soil in the jar. Cut black construction paper 2 cm shorter than the height of the jar. Wrap the paper around the jar and tape in place. Place the jar in a container with about 2½ cm of water in it. This prevents ants from escaping from the jar. The ants will quickly begin to construct tunnels in the jar as they tend to avoid light, and the construction paper prevents light from entering the side of the jar; the tunnels will be constructed there. Remove the paper when you wish to observe the ants in their tunnels.
Bees (It is not advisable to have a bee hive in primary classrooms.)	Buy or build a demonstration bee hive; get the advice of a local beekeeper before beginning this. Keeping a bee hive is extremely fascinating for adults and children. Because establishing and maintaining a bee hive requires a great deal of work and expertise, you may wish to view bees on a field trip if hives are available in the

Animal	*Shelter*
	community. Care must be exercised due to the inhospitality of bees.
Birds from pet stores or a pet of a child or adult in the community	Purchase or borrow a bird cage. Be sure the cage is large enough to allow the bird to move about freely and exercise.
Earthworms	Use a clear container such as a pint or quart jar of glass or transparent plastic. Fill with soil rich in organic matter. Decaying leaves or peat moss may be added to the soil. Earthworms may be obtained from freshly spaded ground or under rocks, damp pieces of wood, or from a bait shop. Place the earthworms on the soil. They will dig in very quickly. Do not put a large number of worms in any one container and be careful not to overwater; keep the soil moist, not wet. Cover the jar with construction paper as with the ant jar.
Fish, crayfish, watersnails	An aquarium provides an excellent home. If no aquarium is available, use the bottom half of a gallon plastic jar or milk jug. Wash and rinse the container thoroughly. Obtain sand from a river bank or other source. Let water run through the sand to wash it; the sand is clean when the water running throught it is clear. If sterile sand is desired, it may be put in the oven at 350° F for fifteen minutes. Sterile sand is seldom necessary. Crayfish may also be kept in a child's plastic wading pool. Place rocks in the pool for them to crawl under.
Frogs, turtles, tadpoles	An aquarium with a top is ideal for keeping tadpoles and frogs. For adult frogs and turtles place a rock in the water. Part of the rock must be above the water level. This provides a place for animals to crawl out of the water.
Fruit flies	Place some well-ripened fruit in a pint jar and leave the lid off. Fruit flies will soon collect on the fruit. Place the lid on the jar after the flies are inside. Don't worry if not too many adults are present; eggs will have been laid and larvae will soon hatch.
Insects and spiders, grasshoppers, butterfiles, moths, beetles, caterpillars	Insect cages. These may be large glass jars with holes in the lids. Other cages may be made from frames covered with wire screening.
Mealworms	Use a plastic container such as the bottom half of a gallon milk jug or a plastic shoe box. Place about 5 cm of cereal such as bran flakes, in the container. Place mealworms in the container. Mealworms can be obtained at a local bait store under the name "golden grubs or larvae." Place

(cont.)

Animal	Shelter
	an apple core or 1/8″ slice of apple in the container occasionally for moisture and food. Cover the cereal with a paper towel. The worms will take care of themselves with a minimum of care thereafter.
Rats, mice, gerbils, rabbits, hamsters, guinea pigs, chickens	Although animal cages can be built, it may be less difficult to buy them. Exercise wheels add a great deal of interest to cages for mice and gerbils. If no cages are available, large aquaria can be used as temporary homes for small animals.
Salamanders, chameleons, newts, lizards, snakes, land snails	Woodland terraria provide habitats for these animals. A glass gallon jar or aquarium can function as a home. Place coarse gravel and several pieces of charcoal on the bottom of the container. Charcoal prevents the soil in the terrarium from becoming sour. Add rich soil from a forest area on top of the sand and any plants desired. Place animals in the terrarium. Sprinkle water over the plants and soil to moisten but not soak. Be sure to place a lid on the terrarium.

(NOTE: All water used in an aquarium should be aged in an open container for 24–48 hours to allow chlorine to disperse from the water.)

Questions for Investigation

1. ELECTRICITY AND MAGNETISM

- Can a flashlight bulb be lighted with one piece of wire and one flashlight battery?
- What kinds of substances conduct electricity?
- How can an electroscope be made with dry cereal and thread?
- How is an electric buzzer made?
- What kinds of objects do magnets attract?
- Through what thickness of paper will magnetism penetrate?
- Will magnetism go through a piece of aluminum foil? A quarter?
- Where on a magnet is magnetic attraction the strongest?
- How can a compass be made?
- How can the magnetic strength of an electromagnet be increased?
- Can two flashlight bulbs be lighted with one piece of wire and one flashlight battery?
- Can a needle be magnetized?
- Do electromagnets have north and south poles?
- How can static electricity be produced?
- What kinds of substances does magnetism penetrate?

2. THE UNIVERSE AND THE EARTH

- What parts of the universe can be seen?
- What does the surface of the moon look like?
- How can the location of the moon be described to another person?

- What constellations are near each other?
- What kinds of energy does the Earth get from the sun?
- What causes an eclipse of the moon? Of the sun?
- How can the history of the Earth be read from rock layers? From fossils?
- How can a working model of a volcano be constructed?
- How can erosion of the Earth be illustrated?
- How can the position of the sun at different times of the day be illustrated?
- How can the phases of the moon be illustrated?
- How can gravity be illustrated?
- Do green plants use energy from the sun?
- Can the surface of Mars be illustrated?
- How can the cause of seasons be illustrated?

3. WEATHER

- What other liquid is most like rain?
- What is the temperature of air on the Celsius thermometer?
- Does cool air weigh the same as an equal amount of warm air?
- What kinds of clouds can be seen?
- How does water from lakes, streams, and oceans get into the air?
- How can a weather chart be constructed?
- How can air pressure be illustrated?
- Where is the air the warmest in the classroom? The coolest?
- Does the temperature of the air out-of-doors change during the day?
- How much water would there be if a gallon of snow were melted?
- From which direction do most thunderstorms seem to come?
- In what direction do clouds move in the atmosphere?
- How are rain, wind, high pressure areas, low pressure areas, storms, and cloudiness represented on a weather map?
- How can the process of cloud formation be illustrated?
- How can the presence of water vapor in the atmosphere be illustrated?

4. HEAT

- Will the temperature of an ice cube increase when it is heated?
- At what temperature does popcorn pop?
- Does food coloring spread faster through warm water or cold water?
- Is heat transmitted more rapidly through wood or metal?

- How can the sun's heat be used for cooking?
- What happens to the volume of liquid when it is heated?
- What happens to the length of a piece of wire when it is heated?
- In which direction do heated air currents move?
- How rapidly does a container of water cook if it is wrapped in home insulation?
- Does thick home insulation prevent loss of heat better than thin insulation?
- Do certain colors absorb heat equally?
- How can heat from the sun be concentrated to start a fire?
- Does the color of a car have any effect on the amount of heat that is absorbed into it?

5. SOUND

- Can a telephone be constructed with two metal cans or paper cups and a piece of string and two buttons?
- How does the human voice produce sound?
- Does sound travel better through air or wood?
- Does sound travel better through water or air?
- If a soft drink can is half full of water, how much water can be added before the pitch of the sound changes as the bottle is crunched?
- Can a musical instrument be made by stretching rubber bands across an empty cigar box or shoe box?
- How many animal sounds can be heard on the school campus?
- How many human-made sounds can be heard on the school campus?
- How can the pitch of the sound made by plucking a rubber band be changed?
- In what directions do sound waves move out from the source?
- How can sound waves be directed in one direction?
- Do certain colors of walls reflect sound waves better than others?
- What is the maximum length of string through which sound waves travel?
- How do crickets produce sound?
- How can sound waves be produced?

6. SPACE TRAVEL (MODES OF FLIGHT AND FACTORS AFFECTING FLIGHT)

- Can jet propulsion be illustrated with a balloon?
- In which directions do jet-propelled balloons travel?

- How far does a paper airplane fly when it is thrown into the air?
- What designs of paper airplanes fly farthest?
- How can a paper clip be used to increase the distance a paper airplane flies?
- What shape of kite flies the highest?
- What exercises do astronauts in space do to keep muscle tone?
- Do dried foods and the amount of water needed to reconstitute them together weigh the same as an equal quantity of fresh food?
- Does freeze-dried food need to be refrigerated?
- How do astronauts determine direction in space?
- How far into space does the Earth's gravity extend?
- How can a hot-air balloon be constructed and operated?
- How many holes can a person make in a parachute made from a 30-centimeter square of cloth, string, and rock before it will not operate as intended?
- How can an airplane which weighs several thousand pounds be lifted into the atmosphere?
- How can air moving parallel to the Earth exert a lifting force on objects?

7. MACHINES AND ENERGY

- What are some simple machines in the classroom?
- Which one—water, oil or syrup—will best reduce friction in a machine?
- What parts of the human body may be used as a simple machine?
- How might a screwdriver be used as a wedge?
- How might a screwdriver be used as a lever?
- How can the directions wheels turn when connected with rubber bands be changed?
- How can motion from a fixed wheel be transferred to another wheel 2 meters from the first wheel?
- Which produces more heat energy when burned, a lump of coal or an equal volume of wood?
- Can magnetic force be felt?
- What happens to the arms of persons as they begin to turn around very fast?
- Is more force needed to start an object moving or to keep it in motion?
- How can the force needed to move a brick be reduced with soda straws?
- What simple machines can be made from a paper clip?

- What kind of energy can be felt in the exhaust of a car?
- How can electrical energy be produced from chemicals?

8. LIGHT

- What kinds of objects reflect light?
- How large an image of a person can be seen in a 10-cm mirror held 40 cm from the person?
- How are shadows produced?
- How large can children make their shadows?
- From how many mirrors at an angle to each other can a beam of light be reflected?
- What colors are seen when sunlight passes through a fine spray of water?
- What happens to the appearance of a pencil when it is put in a glass of water?
- What does the image of an object look like when seen through a convex lens held 1 meter from the eyes?
- How does light affect the direction in which the stem and leaves of a plant grow?
- If a coin is placed in a shallow container of water, how much does the placement of the coin seem to change?
- Does the placement of a coin in water seem to change more if additional water is placed in the container?
- Does light always travel in a straight path?
- How does black light seem to affect the appearance of rocks? Of butterfly wings?

9. HUMAN BODY

- Is there carbon dioxide in the air exhaled from the lungs?
- What organ is used for the sense of touch?
- Can a human skeleton be drawn using only information gained through the sense of touch?
- Is the flavor of food detected by the sense of taste or the sense of smell?
- How do the biceps and triceps in the upper arm work against each other to produce motion?
- Where can the pulse be felt in the human body?
- How much air can be expelled from the lungs at one time?
- How long, on average, does it take a child to grow an inch in height?
- Do human hands just get bigger as a person's body matures?

- Where are valves of the heart located?
- Can the skin detect the number of objects touching it at one place?
- How can the heart beat be increased while a person is resting?
- After a person stops running, how long does it take for the heart beat to slow down?
- How long can a person stand on one foot with the eyes closed?

10. GEOLOGY

- How can rocks be classified?
- Can soil be made from rocks?
- How many layers of substances are found in ½ pint of soil?
- How can rocks be classified according to hardness?
- How much sand can be put in a jar filled with pebbles?
- What rocks contain lime?
- What substances are found in soil?
- How could the layers of rocks in the Earth become tilted?
- How can rocks be classified according to streaks?
- Do all rocks have the same odor?
- Do rocks absorb water?
- How are stalactites and stalagmites made?
- Will rocks expand when heated?
- How can soil be transported from one place to another on the Earth?
- Do all rocks break in the same manner?

11. ENVIRONMENT

- How many different kinds of insects are seen in one day (within a specified area) and how many of each kind?
- What kinds of objects make up litter?
- Out of one hundred maple seeds, how many will germinate?
- How clean is air in the classroom? Outside the room?
- How can noise pollution be reduced in the classroom?
- How does the animal community in an aquarium change over a period of time?
- How many different kinds of plants and animals can be found in a 30-cm × 30-cm square plot on the school campus? On a lawn? In a forest? In a cultivated field?
- Are substances which cannot be seen polluting the air?
- What happens to solid wastes that are buried?

- What happens if too many plants are put in the same flower pot?
- What are three different kinds of animals in a food chain?
- How may sewage be purified?
- Can solid particles be found in the exhaust of automobiles?
- What kinds of substances are made from oil other than fuels and lubricants?
- How can atomic energy be used to generate electricity?

12. METRIC MEASUREMENT

- About how long is a centimeter?
- What objects in the classroom are approximately 1 cm long?
- What objects in the room are 2 cm long?
- About how long is a meter?
- What objects in the room are about 1 m long?
- If the speed limit is 55 miles per hour, what is the speed limit in kilometers?
- If a liter and quart of a soft drink sell for the same price, which is the better value?
- About how many drops of water weigh 1 gram?
- Can you cut a piece of paper that would weigh approximately 1 gm?
- Can you measure a baseball diamond in metric units?

13. DEATH AND DYING
(FROM A BIOLOGICAL VIEW)

- What are some differences between an animal that is alive and one that is dead?
- Do dead animals feel (have the same texture) the same as living animals?
- At what ages do various animals die?
- What happens to an animal's body after it dies?
- What happens to a plant after it dies?
- What happens to the parts of a dead tree in a forest?
- What evidence of dead animals is found in soil?
- Are some parts of an animal's body dead before the entire animal dies?
- What uses can be made of the bodies of dead animals?
- How many dead animals can be found in one day? Dead plants?

14. LIVING ORGANISMS

- Will any plants grow in the dark?
- What part of a stem grows the fastest?
- Will seeds sprout if they are completely submerged in water?
- How do plants respond to various colors of light?
- How many leaves can be removed from a plant before it dies?
- How do household chemicals such as salt, sugar, laundry detergent, dishwasher detergent, bath soap, drain cleaner, and scouring powder affect the growth of plants?
- Does the length of time a plant is exposed to light affect its growth?
- How many different shapes of leaves can be found? In what ways are leaves different?
- Do fish move in specific directions in an aquarium?
- How long does a gerbil or a mouse run on an exercise wheel?
- How do mealworms react to noise, temperature, color, acidity, food, and their position?
- How rapidly does a baby gerbil, hamster, or guinea pig gain weight and grow in length?
- Do crayfish grow another claw if one is lost?
- Do fish in an aquarium react to sound?
- Does temperature affect the growth of plants?
- Will plants grow regardless of the way seeds are placed in the ground?
- Do all eggs hatch? Do all seeds sprout?
- How many seeds come from one dandelion flower?
- How many insects can a praying mantis eat in one day?
- In how many ways are two animals alike? Different?

15. CHEMICALS

- Does adding salt to water change its boiling point? Its freezing point?
- Does adding sugar to water change its boiling point? Its freezing point?
- Does the amount of fertilizer a plant receives affect its growth?
- How can the rusting of iron be prevented?
- Does acid have any effect on aluminum?
- What happens when water of different colors is mixed together?
- Does salt dissolve faster in warm water or cold water?
- Do all liquids evaporate at the same rate?
- Do all liquids boil at the same temperature?
- Do all liquids freeze at the same temperature?

- Is the combined weight of water, bottle, seltzer, and cork the same after seltzer dissolves in the water as before?
- Can carbon dioxide be used to put out a fire?
- What happens when oil is mixed with food coloring?
- What happens to sulfur when it is heated? When it is heated and then placed in water?

Refresher Course on Measurement

Although you may have used equipment in some of the science courses you have taken, you may find it helpful to refresh your memory about its use.

Linear Measurements Using Meter Units

Get a meterstick. Observe the length of the stick. Look away from the stick and try to reproduce a meter length by holding your hands one meter apart. Try this several times. Check the distance between your hands to see how close to the meter distance you are. Look around you and try to find a distance that is approximately a meter long. Check your accuracy with the meterstick. Try this with several items or distances. Try to find distances that are two meters in length. This may require that you place the meterstick on the floor and measure a two-meter distance to get an idea of this distance.

Look again at the meterstick. Notice ten distances on it: These are decimeters. They are designated with numerals 10 through 90. Follow the same procedure as you did with the meterstick for measuring distances in decimeters. Estimate the decimeter distance, then check your estimate using the meterstick.

The next smaller unit of distance on the meterstick is the centimeter. Using your thumb and first finger, attempt to represent a distance of one centimeter between the fingers. Follow the same procedure as you followed in estimating the meter and decimeter distances. Check the estimated distances with the meterstick.

The shortest distance on the meterstick is the millimeter. Follow the same procedure with the millimeter as you did with the other metric units.

With these activities, it is important that you are cognizant of two factors: First, don't cheat—that is, estimate distances from memory rather than comparing them with familiar objects. (This is an example of conservation of length.) If you conserve metric distances, you are likely to develop a useful understanding of them rather than having to rely on comparisons with other objects. Second, estimate metric distances frequently. The more frequently you estimate metric distances, the more likely you will become secure in your ability to use the metric system.

Metric Weight

The basic unit of metric weight is the newton; however, the gram is the unit commonly used. The newton is a unit of weight, while the gram is really a unit of mass. In this exercise, you are asked to work with the gram.

Obtain an envelope of artificial sweetener. The sweetener and the packet weigh one gram. Hold the gram of sweetener in your hand. Place another object in your other hand that you estimate weighs one gram. Place both objects in a pan balance and compare the masses. Try this with a variety of objects. Try the activity using 2-, 5-, and 10-gram mass weights. Each time, attempt to estimate the mass before putting the object on the balance.

Metric Volume

The unit of volume is the liter. Several subunits of volume exist. One that is most familiar is the milliliter. The ring marks on most graduated cylinders represent a milliliter of liquid. The volume of 1000 milliliters is the same as 1 liter. Using a graduated cylinder, place 1 liter of water in a glass or plastic container which will hold that amount. Note the level of water. Using a different glass or plastic container, fill it with 1 liter of water by conserving the volume. Do not compare the water level in the second container until AFTER you have put the estimated liter of water in it. Check your measurements with a graduated cylinder. Repeat this several times until you become accurate. Fill the container with 1 half liter of water and check your accuracy using the graduated cylinder. Next, follow the same procedure with ¼ liter.

Using a Pan Balance

Using a pan balance that is calibrated (balanced as indicated by the pointer mounted near the place where the pans rotate or when both pans are the same distance above the surface over which the balance rests), weigh several objects. First hold the metric mass weights in your hand and attempt to estimate whether they weigh more or less than the object you are holding. Then weigh them on the balance. Try this with a variety of objects.

Using a Graduated Cylinder

Note that there are rings around the graduated cylinder. These rings are used to indicate the volume of liquid in the cylinder. Someplace on the cylinder, generally at the end where the pouring spout is, there is a designated volume of liquid the cylinder holds in milliliters. Place 5 milliliters of water in the cylinder. If you look carefully, the water surface is not level. The surface is higher at the sides of the cylinder and lower in the middle. You use the lowest water level as an indication of the quantity of water. Measure several different quantities of water such as 5 milliliters, 10 milliliters, 20 milliliters, and any volume you choose.

Metric Education

Metric education makes many adults feel insecure—especially if their initial experiences have been with mathematical conversions of metric units to Imperial units and vice versa. A more realistic approach to metric education is the conceptualization of metric lengths, weights, and volumes. Metric unit conversion becomes meaningful once this is done. Following are some suggested topics for metric education:

- Estimating metric units of length
- Estimating metric units of volume
- Estimating metric units of weight
- Using the Celsius thermometer to identify temperatures
- Making your own folding meterstick or tape measure
- Using glass jars, make two or more calibrated graduated cylinders
- Making a set of metric weights
- Translating a recipe from customary (Imperial) units to metric units
- Measuring heights of children in metric units

Many teachers have questions about using or teaching the metric system. Let's consider a few.

Will I be expected to teach metrics? Yes, probably. Children will need to use metric measurements as part of many science activities.

Is it necessary to learn all the metric units? Definitely not. It is not necessary to learn all the units in the customary system. For most people, the following eight units will be sufficient for effective communication: millimeter, centimeter, meter, kilometer, milliliter, liter, gram, and kilogram.

Is it necessary to teach both the customary and metric systems simultaneously? For now—yes. For the next few years, during the period of conversion, one will have to be "bilingual" in measurement communication. Greater emphasis should be given to the use of metrics in the classroom because it is the system that is used internationally and, increasingly, in the United States.

What is the best way to teach the metric system? The best way to teach the metric system is to "think metric" and use the system.

What kinds of activities should I design for children? Continue to do the same kinds of activities that are currently being done. Crash courses on metric education are seldom effective.

What kinds of materials will I need to teach the metric system? Few special materials are needed. A school needs to obtain centimeter rulers, metersticks, tape measures, Celsius thermometers, and metric bathroom scales.

How can I learn to estimate metric units when I have no concept of a particular unit? Develop the skill of estimating first, then making the actual measurement. With enough practice, your estimates will grow increasingly accurate.

Environmental/ Ecological Education

This area continues to receive attention in contemporary elementary school science programs. What once consisted mainly of plant and animal identification and nature walks has evolved into concern for the total man-made and natural environment. Some topics suggested for study in dealing with environmental-ecological education follow.

Pollution of the air, water, and soil

Sources of pollution

Noise pollution

Trade-offs

Conservation of natural resources

Economic implications of pollution

The study of a biotic community

Management of renewable resources

Utilization of wilderness areas

Effects of insecticides and herbicides

World population and overpopulation

Human nutrition

Protein starvation

Utilization of water resources

Product packaging

Psychological concerns

Rapid transportation

Future shock

Population and resources

Littering

The effects of better roads

Thermal pollution

Private homes or apartments

Traffic density

Eutrophication

Food production

Food sources

Hydroponics

Habitats and criminal populations

Solid waste management

Biological controls of insects

Natural habitats of animals

Decomposers

Ecology in the inner city

Constructing stream profiles

Particulate matter in the atmosphere

Food webs

Insect populations

Natural succession	Germ-free environments
Life cycles of animals	Communication among animals
Dynamics of population growth	Genetic variations
Utilization of recreational areas	Contour mapping
Seasonal changes in plants and animals	Life cycles of plants
Fresh water supplies	Vacant lot studies
Weather cycles	Phosphate and nitrate pollution of water
Economics of forest fires	Mapping

A word of caution: Topics should be carefully selected to ensure they are appropriate for the developmental levels of children. For example, young children may be able to identify animals in their environment, but a study of natural succession is too abstract for their thinking level.

ALTERNATE ENERGY SOURCES

The search for energy sources will continue for many, many years. The amount of fossil fuels is limited and other sources of energy are needed. The study of these possible sources may be of interest to older children. Some relevant topics include the following:

- The utilization of nuclear energy in generating electricity
- Waste products from nuclear reactors
- Radiation leakage from reactors
- Thermal pollution from reactors
- The tides as a source of energy
- Wind as a source of energy
- Mechanisms for capturing the sun's energy
    Green plants (biomass)
    Photoelectric cells
    Solar heating systems
- Geothermal energy
- Generation of electricity in space
- Oxidation of hydrogen as a source of energy
- Photosynthesis

BIO-ETHICS

Bio-ethics deals with the implications of biological research and its impact on society and our environment. Some bio-ethical topics include death education, value clarification, food distribution to the people of the world, utilization of the world's natural resources, and population control. While these topics have a science content base, they are also intimately linked to personal beliefs, values, and education related to these topics should not focus on fostering one belief over another, but rather on stressing the value of sufficient and accurate information in sound decision making.

Probably no subject is more fraught with emotionalism than dying. Adults express personal insecurity about it and children tend to mimic adults. It is extremely difficult to treat the subject from a biological standpoint only; the personal feelings associated with death are too powerful. Studying death may help students view dying as a natural part of the life cycle. Much is being written about helping children of all ages cope with death, particularly at the attitudinal level.

The sequence listed below may be functional. (Adopted from units on *Life Cycles* in Zeitler, 1980.)

Level I (grades K-3):

- Distinguishing between living and nonliving objects.
- Identifying living organisms.
- Characteristics of living organisms.
- Living organisms have varying life spans.
- Death is a characteristic shared by all organisms at some time.

Level II (grades 4-6):

- Death is universal among living organisms.
- An organism's body changes after death.
- Decay of organism's bodies in nature.
- Agents of decay.

REFERENCE

Zeitler, W. R. (1980). *A Study of Death and Dying.* Athens, GA: Department of Science Education, The University of Georgia.

Resources for Teachers: A Bibliography

ACTIVITIES AND MATERIALS

Abruscato, J., and Hassard, J. (1977). *The whole cosmos: Catalog of science activities for kids.* Santa Monica: Goodyear Publishing.
A listing of science activities, puzzles, games, and biographies for teaching science.

Blackwelder, S. (1980). *Science for all seasons: Science experiments for young children.* Englewood Cliffs, NJ: Prentice-Hall.
Suggested activities to assist in answering children's questions.

Davis, A. R., and Miller, D. C. (1974). *Science games.* Belmont, CA: Fearon-Pitman.
A listing of games which can be made by students and require a minimum of equipment.

Horn, R. E., and Cleaves, A. (Eds.). (1980). *The guide to simulations/games for education and training* (4th ed.). Beverly Hills: Sage Publications.
A guide to games for all levels.

Hounshell, P. B., and Trollinger, I. R. (1977). *Games for the science classroom: An annotated bibliography.* Washington, DC: National Science Teachers Association.
Information about choosing, purchasing, and preparing games for the classroom.

Keyser, T., and Souviney, R. (1983). *Measurement and the child's environment.* Glenview, IL: Goodyear Books.
Activities and games that make measuring fun.

McCormack, Alan J. (1979). *Outdoor areas as learning libraries: CESI sourcebook.* Washington, DC: Council for Elementary Science, International.
Suggests outdoor learning experiences for several grade levels.

Orlans, F. B. (1977). *Animal care from protozoa to small mammals.* Reading, MA: Addison-Wesley.
Suggestions for the proper use and care of animals in the classroom.

Wolton, R. W., with Richtmyer, J. (1975). *Science equipment in the elementary school* (Rev. ed.). Boulder, CO: Mountain View Center for Environmental Education.
A guide to equipment and materials for teaching elementary school science.

Woodbury, M. (1980). *Selecting materials for instruction: Subject areas and implementation.* Littleton, CO: Libraries Unlimited.

GENERAL REFERENCES

Bartholomew, R. B., and Cawley, F. E. (1980). *Science laboratory techniques: A handbook for teachers and students.* Reading, MA: Addison-Wesley Publishing Co.
Suggests laboratory activities and demonstrations in science for several grade levels.

Bergman, A. B., and Jacobson, W. (1980). *Science for children: A book for teachers.* Englewood Cliffs, NJ: Prentice-Hall.
Suggestions for adapting a science program to the differing learning styles of children.

Bloom, B. S. (Ed.). (1956). *Taxonomy of educational objectives: The classification of educational goals. Handbook I: The cognitive domain.* New York: McCay.
A taxonomy of objectives useful in developing instructional plans.

Blosser, P. E. (1975). *How to ask the right questions.* Washington, DC: National Science Teachers Association.
A guide to selecting and using inquiry activities in the classroom.

Divito, A., and Krockover, G. H. (1980). *Creative sciencing: Ideas and activities for teachers and children* (2nd ed.). Boston: Little, Brown.
A list of activities for teaching various topics and process skills.

Ellington, H. I. et al. (1980). *Games & simulations in science education.* New York: Nichols Publishing.
Suggestions for using games in the classroom.

Good, R. G. (1977). *How children learn science: Conceptual development and implications for teaching.* New York: Macmillan.
Discussions of concept development in children and how it relates to the teaching of science.

Gross, P. (1972). *Teaching science in an outdoor environment.* Berkeley: University of California Press.
Presents many suggestions about learning science in a natural setting.

Hofman, H., and Ricker, K. S. (1979). *Sourcebook: Science education for the physically handicapped.* Washington, DC: National Science Teachers Association.

Olson, R. W. (1980). *The art of creative thinking.* New York: Harper & Row.
Suggests methods for stimulating creativity in children.

Romey, W. D. (1980). *Teaching the gifted and talented in the science class-room.* Washington, DC: National Education Association.
A discussion of relationships between gifted learners and science.

Saterstrom, M. H., and Renner, J. W. (Eds.). (1980). *Educators' guide to free science materials* (21st ed.). 1980-81. Randolph: Educators Progress Service.
An extensive listing of resources for teaching science.

Schmidt, V. E., and Rockcastle, V. N. (1968). *Teaching science with everyday things.* New York: McGraw-Hill.
A list of everyday items that can be used to teach science and suggestions for using them.

Thelen, J. (1976). *Improving reading in science.* Newark, WI: International Reading Association.
Suggestions for improving reading skills in science.

Wadsworth, B. J. (1978). *Piaget for the classroom teacher.* White Plains, NY: Longman.

PERIODICALS

Instructor. Instructor Publications. Instructor Park, Dansville, NY 14437.

Journal of Environmental Education. Heldref Publications, 4000 Albemarle Street, N.W., Suite 500, Washington, DC 20016.

National Geographic World. National Geographic Society, Department 00481, 17th and M Streets, N.W., Washington, DC 20036.

Science Activities. Heldref for Institutions, 4000 Albemarle Street, N.W., Washington, DC 20016.

Science and Children. National Science Teachers Association, 1742 Connecticut Avenue, N.W., Washington, DC 20009.

Index